BLACK EARTH WISDOM

ALSO BY LEAH PENNIMAN

Farming While Black: Soul Fire Farm's Practical
Guide to Liberation on the Land

BLACK EARTH WISDOM

Soulful Conversations with
Black Environmentalists

EDITED BY
LEAH PENNIMAN

AMISTAD

An Imprint of HarperCollinsPublishers

Black Earth Wisdom is dedicated to

Naima and Allen Penniman
My beloved earthwise siblings

TABLE OF CONTENTS

Soil

Defense

Witness

Closing

Opening

FOREWORD

By Dr. Ross Gay

first visited Soul Fire Farm, the farm Leah Penniman cofounded with her partner, Jonah Vitale-Wolff, in the summer of 2015. I was participating in one of their BIPOC farmer-in-training programs, which I found out about from an article in *Yes* magazine sent to me by two different friends who knew I had been researching Black farming, and was doing so because in my ten years of serious gardening and classes and workshops and certifications and such, Black folks seemed to be, well, few and far between. Scarce. Put it like that. Most of the gardening and farming and eco-books I was reading were by white people (Wendell Berry, Rachel Carson, Aldo Leopold, Michael Pollan, etc.; Masanobu Fukuoka's wonderful *The One-Straw Revolution* was among the exceptions), as were most of the movies in that vein. The articles in magazines and such, the same. At some point it became very clear to me that something was off, and so I started searching. And, quickly, *finding.* The Black Farmers and Urban Gardeners Conference in New York. Will Allen up in Milwaukee. Black Oaks permaculture farm in Pembroke, Illinois. Gilliard Farms down in Brunswick, Georgia.

I rooted around and found the email for Soul Fire, then sent them a note expressing my interest. About a day later I got a note back from Leah, followed by a phone call during which, after we got to know each other a little bit, I convinced her I was serious about this stuff—I was by then on the board of the Bloomington Community Orchard and had worked with some other growing projects. She invited me to join them for the next session. A couple months later, I was with about twenty or twenty-five other farmers-in-training, in Muck Boots on the wet days, barefoot on the dry, harvesting raspberries and garlic, learning about companion planting and greenhouse growing and herbal medicine and George Washington Carver and Fannie Lou Hamer, sharing food and stories and dreams, and dancing hard to Kendrick Lamar, Whitney Houston, and D'Angelo.

Toward the end of the week, I remember leaning on my rake, taking a drink, sweating hard, looking down onto the fields as we were in the middle of a workday. The sky was clear, the sun was high, it was hot, and people were working hard—harvesting, weeding, transplanting—but no one seemed to be *toiling*. There was lots of laughter, and some singing, too. And no one seemed to be suffering. In fact, it seemed precisely the opposite—we seemed to be glad. We seemed to be joyful. We seemed, maybe, to be healing. As I looked down over those fields, it struck me like a bell—*I've never seen a truer thing*. In case you believed slavery and sharecropping and land theft and general misery was the entirety of Black peoples' relationship with the earth, here was a different story: all us Black people smiling with our hands (and feet) in the soil. Believe me, I wasn't the only one who said this as that week concluded, and maybe crying a little bit as we said, "It feels like I'm finally home." And, speaking for myself anyway, *home* didn't mean only that beautiful gathering with those beautiful people at this beautiful farm on this beautiful land in Upstate New York (though it for sure meant that, too): *home* meant being in the ongoing stream of Black and Brown people through time—that enormous, rhizomatic, mycelial, polyvocal, choral community—caring for and being cared for by the land. It meant returning, together, to the beloved earth.

That transformative gathering at Soul Fire, that *togethering*, is precisely the energy and spirit and power of Leah Penniman's beautiful book *Black Earth Wisdom*, which brings together a diversity of voices, all of whom are guides to us, deep in the long practice of listening to the earth (one of the beautiful verbs Leah uses to imply closeness, attention, and devotion is *listening*: those who practice are *earth-listeners*). She talks with other farmers, marine biologists, lawyers, filmmakers, writers, musicians, ornithologists, teachers, activists, healers, and more; all wondering together how we might better listen to, or care for, or *love* the earth. Which, it turns out, we sometimes have to be shown how to do. Maybe especially if there's pain or sorrow to move through: which, for me, maybe for you, too, there is. Though pain and sorrow do not foreclose joy. In fact, and maybe this is some Black earth wisdom: it's from the sorrow tended together that the joy grows.

Another wisdom of this book is the way Leah has crafted the interviews into conversations, because conversations, if they are good, are also collaborations. They require that we listen to one another, and they understand that the answers are yet to be discovered. They offer us the opportunity to move toward one another. They offer us the opportunity *to be moved*. Leah, of course, is one of our guides—and an astonishing one at that. Her reverence for the earth, her storytelling, her intimacy with the land, well, it's almost like if you shook the pages of this book, seeds would drop out. She is among the earth-listeners I rely on, one of the earth-lovers who has changed my life. But it's crucial to note that this book, Leah's book, comes of her reaching toward other earth-listeners. *What do you think?* she asks again and again. *What might we do?* She asks that of those who walk the earth now, and she asks it of earth-listeners who walked the earth hundreds or thousands of years ago. *What might we do?* That's to say, she adamantly does not do it alone. In fact, you might say this book is a model for how not to do it alone. For how to do it together. Which, if we're going to survive, we're going to have to practice doing.

Oh, I could go on! But let me just tell this last little story from that time at Soul Fire. After lunch and before getting back to work one day, someone rounded us all up to play a little game. I think they called it the mangrove game. It goes like this: Everyone gathers in a circle within arm's reach of their neighbors, twists into some swampy arboreal shape, something awkward and teetery that you'd never in a million years be able to hold on one foot. Then you grab hold of who's next to you, their forearm or shin or hand, and on the count of three, everyone picks up one foot, at which point, I was afraid, we would topple (I was the biggest person in that group and really didn't want to smoosh anyone). I don't quite know how to describe to you the pulse, the cinching or gripping up, the sudden rooting of fifteen or twenty people becoming one sturdy organism. But I can tell you we shouted and laughed and looked, some of us, baffled with delight. Baffled by how easy it was, how strong we were, in a grove, all our roots grown together like that. We could've done it forever, it seemed to me. Holding each other up. Like the Black earth's been saying all this time.

A WATATIC CHILDHOOD

An Introduction by Leah Penniman

s children, my siblings and I spent long hours in the forested wetland, hopping from one sun-dappled mossy mound to the next, never slipping into the soggy muck, and never stepping on any rare lady's slipper flowers or vibrant red-spotted newts. When we grew tired of this game, we wrapped our arms around the nearest sticky white pine or fragrant yellow birch and breathed deeply. Having recently read about photosynthesis and respiration in the heavy encyclopedias our father kept, we imagined that the tree was gratefully taking in our carbon dioxide and gifting us with oxygen to inhale. We siblings passed hours this way, in the delightful safety and supportive embrace of Watatic lands.

The swamp has long been a place of refuge for Black people in the Americas, a destination of escape, marronage, or the promise of passage to a better land. As three Black Kreyol children growing up in a conservative rural white town in the eighties, we also relied on this refuge. To say that the Ashburnham public schools were racially brutal would be an understatement. From elementary school, when we were informed by a classmate that "brownies are not allowed in this school"; to the interminable bullying of middle and high school, which included taunting, assaults, and one student attempting to blind me with her fingernails so that I would be "too ugly for white boys to look at"; to the school officials' complicity with and excuses for the assaults, public school was a place of terror.

Mount Watatic, Lake Watatic, and the forests in between became surrogate parents and protectors for us. These sacred lands of the Wabanaki, Pennacook, and Abenaki were rich in biodiversity, and each being offered an opportunity for relationship. We learned to make salads of wood sorrel, blueberries, and wintergreen, and to fish for rainbow trout. We became strong paddlers and navigated a dented aluminum canoe around the small islands in the lake. Our sense of home and wonder in the forest informed our invented religion called "mother nature." We decorated an old, abandoned woodshed with blue jay feathers and cedar, transforming it into our temple.

Senegalese poet Baba Dioum wrote, "In the end, we will conserve only what we love."[1] It must have been around third grade when we learned that nature was in trouble. A panicked alarm rose in our small hearts to hear for the first time about global warming, air pollution, and toxic waste. My sister, Naima, and I sprang into action and formed the Junior Ecologists Kids Club, which had exactly two members. When we could not convince our elementary school to start a recycling program, we put out our own bins and dragged home aluminum cans on the school bus to rinse in our backyard and redeem. We went on "pollution patrol" with our blue Huffy bicycles, picking up garbage, placing our bodies between loggers and trees, and guerilla planting the denuded medians in the road. We wrote original anthems and spoken word poems, and sang these praise lyrics to the forest. Perhaps most ambitiously, we researched long lists of actions people could take to protect the environment, and handwrote this advice on hundreds of postcards that we sent to people listed in the phone book. Naima and I made a solemn covenant with the wild animals and plants, pledging allegiance to the earth with these words, "We will never forget how to listen to you; we will always stand with you."

This intimate and fierce love affair with Earth remained intact as I matured. In the black soils of greater Boston, I found a passion for vegetable farming that eventually led me to study agriculture with Indigenous peasant farmers in Haiti and West Africa. While studying traditional farming and eco-spirituality in Ghana with the Queen Mothers of Kroboland, I was offered a teaching that has been seared into my soul ever since. Manye Nartike (in blessed memory) asked, "Is it true that in the United States, a farmer will put the seed into the ground and not pour any libations, offer any prayers, sing, or dance, and expect that seed to grow?" Met with my ashamed silence, she continued, "That is why you are all sick! Because you see the earth as a thing and not a being."

I majored in environmental science in university and launched a seventeen-year career as a high school science teacher, simultaneously lauded and infamous for my students' infrequent presence in the classroom; they were instead inventorying stream macroinvertebrates, conducting energy audits for local businesses, or testing community garden soils for lead. Concurrent with teaching, my family started Soul Fire Farm in 2010, an Afro-Indigenous-centered community farm dedicated to uprooting racism and seeding sovereignty in the food system through our emphasis on farmer training, feeding folks who lack access to life-giving food, and rabble-rousing for systems change. This learning journey revealed that the "mother nature" religion of our childhood was ancestrally remembered, rather than invented, and I subsequently spent many years training as a member of clergy in the earth-based traditional religions of Yoruba and Vodun.

As an introvert who is more at home "speaking flowers"[2] than any of the oral human languages, the written word has become a place for safe and joyous expression. *Farming While Black: Soul Fire Farm's Practical Guide to Liberation on the Land* (2018) was my first full-length book, and it helped to shift the dominant narrative about the role of Black genius in creating organic and regenerative farming technologies. From the time when our West African ancestors braided rice seeds into their hair before being forced into the bowels of Suriname-bound slave ships, Black folks have been contributing crop varieties, soil-building techniques, cooperative labor strategies, polyculture design, and more to the agricultural canon.

In a similar vein, my hope is for *Black Earth Wisdom* to unequivocally define the past, present, and future of environmental stewardship as inexorably connected to Black brilliance. The inspiration for the book came from a dream vision that visited me during my Ifa initiation ceremony in 2020. In this vision, all of the forest animals crowded into my home. The deer, hawk, snapping turtle, coyote, barred owl, black bear, and hummingbird moth surrounded me and asked me why I had forgotten the covenant of my childhood—why I was not listening to them anymore. They spoke the truth. In my focus on educating the rising generation of Black and Brown farmers, I was paying less and less attention to the voices and needs of wild creatures. They told me to write a book that centers the narratives of those who remember how to listen to the earth.

Contrary to mainstream mythology, the movement to listen to and defend the earth did not begin with Rachel Carson, Henry David Thoreau, John Muir, or any other European-heritage thinker. From the Sahel farmers who turned the desert green, to the enslaved herbalists who cured white and Black folks alike, to the Negro 4-H Wildlife Conservation Camps and Planetwalker's righteous quest, ecological thought and practice have run deep and wide in Black communities. The people whose skin is the color of earth have long advocated for the well-being of our beloved Mother.

Some historians argue that the system of white supremacy is a major catalyst for the destruction of Earth's life support systems. Embedded in the theory of the supremacy of white people over other races is the theory of human supremacy over nature. This is exemplified in the white supremacist philosophies of the Doctrine of Discovery, private property, and Manifest Destiny, which led directly to the exploitation of land and natural resources, and the displacement of Indigenous people globally.

In 1846, Senator Thomas Hart Benton asserted, "It would seem that the White race alone received the divine command, to subdue and replenish the earth: for it is the only race that has obeyed it—the only race that hunts out new and distant lands, and even a New World, to subdue and replenish . . ."[3] By way of example, as European settlers displaced Indigenous peoples across North America in the 1800s, they exposed vast expanses of land to the plow for the first time. It took only a few decades of intense tillage to drive over 50 percent of the original organic matter from the rich prairie loam soils. The productivity of the US Great Plains decreased by 71 percent during the twenty-eight years following that first European tillage. The initial anthropogenic rise in atmospheric carbon dioxide levels was due to that breakdown of soil organic matter. Land clearing and cultivation emitted more greenhouse gasses than the burning of fossil fuels until the late 1950s.[4] As expressed by Mary Annaïse Heglar, "The fossil fuel industry was born of the industrial revolution, which was born of slavery, which was born of colonialism."[5] The philosophies and practices of colonial conquest, subjugation, extraction, and commodification mutually reinforce each other, and simultaneously exploit racialized people and the earth. In his chilling and unapologetic indictment, Wendell Berry pronounced:

> The white man, preoccupied with the abstractions of the economic exploitation and ownership of the land, necessarily has lived on the country as a destructive force, an ecological catastrophe, because he assigned the hand labor, and in that the possibility of intimate knowledge of the land, to a people he considered racially inferior; in thus debasing labor, he destroyed the possibility of meaningful contact with the earth. He was literally blinded by his presuppositions and prejudices. Because he did not know the land, it was inevitable that he would squander its natural bounty, deplete its richness, corrupt and pollute it, or destroy it altogether. The history of the white man's use of the earth in America is a scandal.[6]

It stands to reason that any hope of solving the environmental crisis will require an examination and uprooting of the white supremacist ideologies that underpin the crisis. The voices and expertise of Black, Brown, and Indigenous environmentalists, amplified by all those who have eschewed white supremacy, must be heeded if we are to halt and reverse planetary calamity. Ecological humility is part of the cultural heritage of Black people. While our four-hundred-plus year immersion in racial capitalism has attempted to diminish that connection to the sacred earth, there are those who persist in believing that the land and waters are family members, and who understand the intrinsic value of nature. In this moment, we are acutely aware of the fractures in our system of runaway consumption and corporate insatiability. We feel the hot winds of wildfire, the disruptions of pandemic, and the choked breath of the victims of state violence. We know there is no going back to "normal." The path forward demands that we take our rightful places as the younger siblings in creation, deferring to the oceans, forests, and mountains as our teachers.

To begin the book's gestation, I called up a few of the earth-listening Black elders in my life, Mama Claudia J. Ford, Mama Savi Horne, and Mama Ira Wallace, and asked them what the earth is telling us right now. Then I asked who else was listening, and I called up those folks for interviews. In no time, there were thirty-eight interviews to delight in, hundreds of ancestors to research, and thousands more people, organizations, books, and connections to explore. The salient challenge in the process, aside from the fact that we need a whole library to do justice to Black ecological sagacity, was that my computer screen was often obscured by the copious, spontaneous tears that flowed as I read and bore witness to the beauty that is Black people's reverence for the earth. Immersing myself in the stories of these notable Black environmentalists was among the great honors of my life.

Black Earth Wisdom weaves together the voices of some of today's most respected Black American environmentalists, those who have cultivated the skill of listening to the lessons that Earth has whispered to them. The core of the text consists of sixteen conversations with notable environmentalists, whose exclusive interviews have been adapted, edited, and interwoven by theme. While the interviews took place one-on-one, each chapter brings together the ideas of two to three earth-listeners who speak on similar subject matter as if they were together synchronously in a panel discussion. My questions were reverse engineered based on the salient points made by the interviewees during the one-on-one dialogues. In all cases, the combined conversations conclude with the speakers responding to a version of the question, "What do you hear the earth saying to humans at this time?"

The book opens with an historical timeline of Black people's contributions to ecological thought and practice from 4000 BP to 1980, rendered in the form of a *mojuba*, a Yoruba prayer of homage. Then, in section one, "Spirit," we deepen our understanding of the ecological crisis as a spiritual plight. We explore the need for a new covenant between humans and the earth through conversations with Ifa priests Awise Agbaye Wande Abimbola, Yeye Luisah Teish, and Awo Enroue Onigbonna Sangofemi Halfkenny. Ibrahim Abdul-Matin and Chris Bolden-Newsome share Muslim and Christian perspectives on environmental stewardship. We close with an eco-spiritual perspective on the queer earth from Toi Scott and adrienne maree brown.

In section two, "Wilds," we explore the relationship between Black people and open space. We come to understand sky as a primary source for human wisdom with Dr. Lauret Edith Savoy, Rue Mapp, and Audrey Peterman. T. Morgan Dixon, Teresa Baker, and James Edward Mills discuss the use of purposeful walking as a tool for resistance. Angelou Ezeilo, Dr. J. Drew Lanham, and Dillon Bernard discuss the importance of making space for the rising generation of Black youth to access the wilds.

In section three, "Soil," we investigate the importance of land tenure and agrarianism through conversations with Dr. Carolyn Finney, Latria Graham, and Savi Horne. Farmers Greg Watson and Pandora Thomas share their knowledge of agroecology, and Dr. Claudia J. Ford and Dr. Leni

Sorensen describe how they keep the oldways of cookery and herbalism alive. We close with a conversation with seed keepers Aleya Fraser and Ira Wallace, who explain their work saving seeds and their stories.

In section four, "Defense," we lean into the pain of environmental racism and capitalism's assault on our lands and waters. Sharon Lavigne and Dr. Dorceta Taylor speak about the role of industry in toxifying Black communities. Dr. Ayana Elizabeth Johnson and Chris Hill make clear the threats to the oceans and aquatic ecosystems. Queen Quet and Colette Pichon Battle discuss the impact of rising coastal waters and ocean-born storms on their homelands. All speak to the work happening to defend who and what we love.

We conclude with section five, "Witness," where we explore the role of artists, writers, and storytellers in bringing ecological truth to light. B. Anderson, Toshi Reagon, and Yonnette Fleming speak about their role as musicians singing the earth's songs. Kendra Pierre-Louis and Steve Curwood share about their media work educating the public on anthropogenic climate change. Alice Walker and Dr. Joshua Bennett speak about the Black eco-literary tradition and the role of Black people as witnesses to the living earth.

Black Earth Wisdom is bookended by the work of two powerful Black poets who have been entrusted with the earth's whispered secrets. Dr. Ross Gay's foreword invites us into the delight of ecological awakening, and Naima Penniman's closing poem translates Mama Nature's instructions in skillful verse. A directory of Black environmental organizations, books, media, and other resources for the reader's further learning is also provided online at blackearthwisdom.org.

Throughout the text the imperfect English words—nature, environment, and earth—are used to describe the intricate web of life of which we humans are part. Rendered in a colonizer language, these words imply that we are set apart from the rest of earthbound life, when in fact, we are tethered to it in an inexorable tangle of belonging.

Black Earth Wisdom is a conversation between African diasporic people who are carrying on our ancient ancestral practice of listening to the earth to know which way to go. As Dr. George Washington Carver offered, "I love to think of nature as unlimited broadcasting stations, through which God speaks to us every day, every hour . . . How do I talk to a little flower? Through it I talk to the Infinite. And what is the Infinite? It is that silent, small force . . . that still small voice."[7]

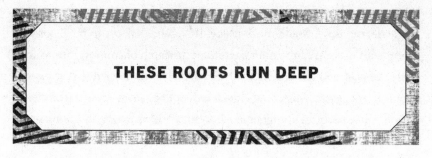

THESE ROOTS RUN DEEP

A Prayer of Homage to Our Earth-Listening Black Elders

The *iba or mojuba* is a prayer of homage that is recited to open morning devotion in traditional Yoruba households, a practice that has spread across the African diaspora. We pour water or alcohol on the ground as an offering, and turn our hearts toward our ancestors, to our respected elders and teachers, and to the benevolent forces of nature. In that spirit, this chapter is an extended prayer of homage to our Black ancestors and elders who have made their love for the earth known in a way that has echoed through time, informing contemporary ecological stewardship and justice work.

The roots of modern environmental thought run deep and wide in the history of Black people, many of whom did not see nature as something separate and pristine, but rather viewed humans as an integral part of nature. Harm to the earth would harm the people; harm to the people would harm the earth. Our ancestors and elders helped develop regenerative farming, practiced herbal medicine, advanced the field of ornithology and entomology, demanded access to land and ecological services, administered national parks, catalyzed the environmental justice movement, and more.

As we pray together, we acknowledge that we can honor and learn from these ancestors, even when aspects of their work are not in alignment with moral decisions we would make today. Reverence asks us to be in conversation with history, not to omit narratives in search of comfort, nor to replicate the past without critical analysis. We also acknowledge that paying tribute to Black earth-listening elders does not negate or erase the immense ecological wisdom of Indigenous peoples worldwide. Paying homage to Black eco-lineage is a "yes-and" act of veneration.

Some of these revered ancestors, elders, and communities are honored herein with *oriki* (praise stanzas), which are presented along the timeline of their births. In the folk spirit of call and response, you are invited to respond to each oriki with *Iba se* ("I give reverence"). With each *Iba se*, pour a bit of water onto the earth to quench the thirst of those who came before us and upon whose shoulders we stand.

Iba se

BANTU WATER SPIRIT WORSHIPPERS (CA. 4000 BCE–PRESENT)

Speakers of Zulu, Xhosa, and Karanga/Shona, and other Bantu groups, believe that water is the essence of both spiritual and physical life, and that rivers and pools are home to water spirits who protect water sources and keep them alive. Religious taboos ensure that only healers and those pure of heart approach sacred water pools, and that they do so singing, praying, and making offerings of white beads. It is strictly taboo for anyone to harvest aquatic plants or to kill crabs, snakes, frogs, or waterbirds, who are messengers of these designated waters. Custom provides a minimum buffer of distance between residential dwellings and the water's edge. The people of Mvoti valley, South Africa, honor a weekly day of rest for the spirit *iNkosazana*, during which the river cannot be touched or disturbed. Bantu traditionalists continue to fight to protect their sacred pools from emerging threats from mining, plantation forestry, and hydrological manipulation. For example, the Zimbabwean prophetess Ambuya Juliana spoke for the *njuzu* water spirits when she led a 1990s movement opposing the large-scale damming of rivers.[1]

Iba se

WEST AFRICAN SACRED GROVE PROTECTORS (CA. 3000 BCE–PRESENT)

Among the Akan of Ghana, the sacred forest groves are the dwelling places of spiritual beings known as *abosom* or *asamanfo*, children of the supreme being Onyame. One such sacred grove outside Kumasi, called Asantemanso, is the place believed by the Ashanti to be the location where the first human beings came forth from the ground. Community members elevate a forested area to a sacred grove through a process of consecration. A specific area is identified as a point of contact between the invisible and human worlds, and the spiritual entities are invited into a ritualized alliance. *Dracaena arborea* (African dragon tree) is planted as a boundary tree to mark the edge of sacred groves and reinforce its separation from the ordinary.[2] Sacred forests, called Nkodurom and Pinkwae by the Ashanti, are oases of conserved biodiversity, as they constitute the only relatively intact forests in severely degraded landscapes. They are home to the West African mud creeper, the black heron, and three species of turtle (green, olive ridley, leatherback), with over 80 percent of the region's turtle nests occurring in sacred groves.[3] Not limited to Ghana, 2,940 sacred groves have been enumerated in Benin, where species richness is higher in these groves than in government-protected forest reserves.[4] Sacred groves across the continent of Africa are foundational to eco-systemic and cultural preservation.[5]

Iba se

SUB-SAHARAN AFRICAN ORIGINATORS OF CROP ROTATION (CA. 3000 BCE–PRESENT)

Farmers in western and southern Africa originated swidden agriculture, also called the bush-fallow system or shifting cultivation.[6] In the swidden system, short periods of agricultural production (one to two years) are followed by long fallow periods (six to twenty-five years). During the fallow period the forest regrows, sending its deep roots into the soil to recycle nutrients, build up organic matter, and store carbon. The roots prevent erosion, increase the infiltration of water, and reduce runoff.[7] Swidden practices sequester nearly 750,000 tons of carbon per 7,500 acres, while the burning only releases 400 to 500 tons,[8] a ratio that puts industrial agriculture to shame. Swidden agriculture uses the forest as a "cover crop," a technology that was adapted in the modern organic movement to use annual crops as cover. Traditional pastoralists, such as the Fulbe of Labé in Futa Jallon, also developed rotational grazing. This practice involved pasturing livestock on land before converting it to rice and crop cultivation, which made the soil exceptionally fertile. In areas of low human population density, these rotational systems are unparalleled in their sustainability.

Iba se
SUB-SAHARAN AFRICAN ORIGINATORS OF POLYCULTURE (CA. 3000 BCE–PRESENT)

Polycultures are mixtures of several mutually supportive species planted together, which help to conserve soil fertility, reduce pest pressure, and increase agrobiodiversity. The Hausa farmers of Nigeria developed at least 156 systematic crop combinations, including no-till polycultures of grains, legumes, and root crops planted on ridges. The Abakaliki farmers of Nigeria used their hoes to construct mounds and then planted crops on distinct parts of the mound based on the water and space requirements of each; they planted yams on top of the mound, rice in the furrow, and maize, okra, melon, and cassava on the lower parts of the mound.[9] They also intercropped egusi melon with sorghum, cassava, coffee, cotton, maize, and bananas, because a biodiverse cultivated community disoriented harmful pests and created a ground cover that suppressed weeds.[10] In Ghana, farmers have developed several polycultures of vegetables and fruit trees. A few among the vegetable combinations are okra, tomatoes, and peppers; carrots, pawpaw, moringa, and lettuce; cabbage, pepper, and onion; watermelon, garden eggs, and pepper; cucumber, okra, onion, and pepper. A few among the fruit tree combinations are citrus, pigeon pea, sweet potato, platina, coco yam, and native timber species; mango, sweet potato, pigeon pea, banana, cassava, and native timber species; cashew, ground nuts, maize, and native timber species; cocoa, pigeon pea, coc yam, cassava, plantain, citrus, avocado pear, and native timber species.[11] Polyculture is a foundational technology in the modern "permaculture" movement, which often fails to credit the Black agrarians among those who developed these technologies.

Iba se

BANTU TERRACE AND MOUND BUILDERS (CA. 3000 BCE–PRESENT)

The Ovambo people of northern Namibia and southern Angola understand that fertility is not always an inherent quality of soil, but rather something that can be nurtured through mounding, ridging, and the application of organic matter. When the colonial government attempted to force the Ovambo farmers off their land, offering them equivalent plots with "better quality" soil, the farmers countered that they had invested substantially into building their soils and doubted that the new areas would ever amount to their existing farms in fertility. The practice of the Ovambo is to demarcate the field, clear brush, then build raised rectangular mounds about ten feet long, five feet wide, and one foot tall. The pathways double as irrigation ditches. The Ovambo farmers add ample amounts of manure, ashes, termite earth, cattle urine, muck from wetlands, and other organic matter to increase the fertility of their mounds. This system concentrates fertile topsoil, aerates soil, and prevents waterlogging. The Ovambo farmers also integrate a rotating fallow after a few seasons' harvest of millet. During the fallow, cattle and goats graze the brush of the resting cropland, recycling nutrients in their deposits of manure and urine that replenish the soil.[12] In Kenya and Tanzania, farmers use a practice called *fanya-juu*, meaning "throw it upward" in Kiswahili. These farmers revive degraded land by recovering soil from the bottom of the slope and throwing it uphill to form terraces, or steps of roughly level land. The practice of *fanya-juu* results in soil organic matter levels 35 percent higher than conventional farms, and

25 percent higher crop yields than conventional farms.[13] These systems of mounding and terracing revive soils and reduce water erosion, and are widely practiced by modern regenerative farmers.

Iba se

THOSE WHO GREEN THE SAHEL DESERTS (CA. 1000 BCE–PRESENT)

Farmers in the western Sahel created the *ẓaï* or *tassa* method of agriculture, which involves digging pits in the earth to catch water and concentrate organic matter, making it possible to farm in the desert. In the 1980s, Yacouba Sawadogo of Burkina Faso innovated on the genius of his ancestors by filling the pits with manure and compost to attract termites, whose tunnels further decompose the organic matter. At the time there was a mass exodus from his community after severe droughts slashed food production and turned the savannah into a desert. Millions of people starved. Sawadogo dug *ẓaï* pits to capture rainfall and nutrients for his millet and sorghum crops. He found that his grain yield increased; additionally, native trees started to grow out of the *ẓaï*. These trees anchored the soil, buffered the wind, and helped retain soil moisture. They also provided mulch for the crops and fodder for the livestock. As others adopted Sawadogo's technique, water tables across the Sahel began to rise for the first time in decades. Sawadogo explained, "My conviction, based on personal experience, is that trees are like lungs. If we do not protect them, and increase their numbers, it will be the end of the world."[14] His leadership is transforming the Sahel desert into a landscape of green.[15]

Iba se

AFRICAN WOMEN COMPOSTERS (1320 CE–PRESENT)

African dark earth is a fertile anthropogenic compost invented by women in Ghana and Liberia at least seven hundred years ago. The creation of dark earth involves the combination of several types of waste: ash and char residues from cooking, bones from food preparation, byproducts from processing palm oil and handmade soap, harvest residues, and organic domestic refuse. African dark earth has a high concentration of available calcium and phosphorus and has a liming effect on soil chemistry, making the soil less acidic and nutrients more available. African dark earths store between 200 percent and 300 percent more organic carbon than other soils; this increase supports better carbon sequestration and climate healing. These soils contain two to twenty-six times the amount of pyrogenic carbon of regular soil, a carbon compound whose long persistence in soil contributes to greater fertility and climatic stability. West African farmers continue to produce and use dark earth today. The elders in the community measure the age of their town by the depth of the black soil, since every farmer in every generation has participated in its creation.[16] The work of farmers of African dark earth paralleled that of farmers in Egypt during Cleopatra's (b. 69 BCE) reign. She is believed to have decreed that earthworms were sacred due to their role in soil fertility, outlawed touching or harming them, and instructed certain priests to study their habits. According to a study by the US Department of Agriculture in 1949, the great fertility of the Nile River valley was the result of the activity of earthworms. The researchers found the worm castings from a six-month period to weigh almost 120 tons per acre, approximately ten times the amount of castings on soils in Europe and the United States.[17]

Iba se

GRANDMOTHERS WHO BRAIDED SEEDS (C. 1550)

Women of the Upper Guinea Coast braided African black rice (*Oryza glaberrima*) into their hair as insurance, while trapped within the bowels of slave ships bound for Suriname, Brazil, and the Carolinas. Linguistic and botanical analysis places the domestication of African rice in the Malian wetlands between 3,500 and 4,500 years ago. From there, African rice diffused across the region from Senegal to Côte d'Ivoire, and inland to Lake Chad. Along with rice, which was held as sacred, these mothers carried with them thousands of years of plant domestication and ecological knowledge. They kept alive our seed heritage of sorghum, millet, okra, molokhia, cotton, sesame, black-eyed pea, eggplant, melon, sorrel, and other African crops.[18]

Iba se

CAESAR AND ENSLAVED AFRICAN HERBALISTS (C. 1650–1865)

Enslaved African women were the chief herbalists in the antebellum American South. Plant medicine formed the basis of rural health care for both Black and white households, and Black herbalists treated community members across racial lines. Enslaved people had intimate knowledge of the pharmacological and spiritual powers of the local plants and animals, much of which was taught to them by Native Americans or learned through experimentation. Enslaved doctors gathered and prepared flag root, jimsonweed, garlic, calamus root, arrowroot, dogwood, snakeroot, pokeweed, peach leaves, sassafras, privet root, mayflower root, and cotton root, among others.[19] For example, Caesar (b. 1682) was an accomplished Black herbalist who developed a cure for enslavers who believed they were poisoned, using plantain and horehound as the active ingredients. In a rare act, the South Carolina General Assembly of 1750 awarded Caesar his freedom and an annual stipend in exchange for his recipe and a commitment to continue developing medicine. They published his cure-all poison remedy in the May 1750 issue of the *South Carolina Gazette*.[20] For Black herbalists, the forest was experienced as a liberatory space, one where they could gather medicines and edible wild plants, meet up with lovers, and engage in spiritual practices. It was said that these herbalists could read the forest like a book by old age. The forest was a place where, in the words of the historian Sharla Fett, "spiritual power intensified and the social power of slavery waned."[21,22]

Iba se

GULLAH JACK AND OTHER ENSLAVED CONJURERS (C. 1650–1865)

Enslaved Black folks carried on their earth-based religious traditions, even as they syncretized with white Christianity. Rites such as baptism by immersion, libation to the earth, spirit possession, worship in forest groves, and ring shouts have distinctive African roots.[23] People enslaved at the Woodboo and Pooshee Plantation in South Carolina kept alive a Kikongo tradition of revering water spirits called *simbi*. They believed that every spring had a guardian spirit, and if the water were disturbed or destroyed, the *simbi* would depart and the waters would permanently dry up.[24] Enslaved construction workers at the Wye Plantation in Maryland buried their protective amulets at the entrance to the greenhouse they built, hid their sacred thunderstones in the roof, and cultivated sacred medicinal plants at the edges.[25] Gullah people kept alive "seekin rituals," a religious conversation process whereby the seeker goes into the wilderness to experience visions, pray, and encounter nature spirits. In 1822, Gullah Jack, a traditional African priest of great repute, helped direct one of the country's most notable freedom plots, the Denmark Vesey uprising. Significantly, the religion of enslaved Africans did not differentiate material and spiritual reality as sharply as white Christianity did. Spirits inhabit the world alongside people, plants, and animals, rather than transcending it, making humans therefore part of nature.

Iba se
AUNT CLARA DAVIS (B. 1845)

Aunt Clara Davis was enslaved on an Alabama plantation of about five hundred acres with one hundred other captive workers. Among the earliest nature writers in America, Davis offered,

> *White folks, you can have your automobiles and paved streets and electric lights. I don't want them. You can have the buses and streetcars, and hot pavements, and high buildings, cause I ain't got no use for them no way. But I'll tell you what I do want. I want my ole cotton bed and the moonlight nights shining through the willow trees and the cool grass under my feet as I run around catching lightning bugs. I want to hear the sound of the hounds in the woods after the possum,*

and the smell of fresh mowed hay. I want to see the dawn break over the black ridge, and the twilight settle, spreading a sort of orange hue all over the place. I want to walk the paths through the woods and see the rabbits, and watch the birds, and listen to the frogs at night.[26]

Slavery did not succeed in severing all Black people's connection to and reverence for the earth.

Iba se

GREAT DISMAL SWAMP MAROONS (1680–1865)

Cooperative groups of Native Americans, Africans, and African Americans fleeing the colonial frontier and enslavement practiced *petit marronage*, the establishment of free communities in harsh and inhospitable terrain. They navigated panthers, water moccasins, rattlesnakes, floods, and mosquitos to make homeplaces in the swamps of Virginia and North Carolina. For ten generations, they operated an anticapitalist system of communal labor. They built at least two hundred habitable islands in the swamp, which was home to thousands of maroons, and kept almost completely isolated from the mainstream US population. Additional maroon communities existed in the swamps of Louisiana, Alabama, and Florida.[27,28]

Iba se

BRISTER FREEMAN AND ZILPAH WHITE (1744–1822)

Well before Henry David Thoreau made a home at Walden Pond, Zilpah White, her brother Brister Freeman, and another former slave, Charlestown Edes, built homes in Walden woods. About fifteen Black people eventually moved to Walden woods, clustering their dwellings into a small neighborhood. Among them, the only landowners were Freeman and Edes, who jointly purchased an acre of land in 1785. In order to provide for their families, they worked as subsistence farmers and in the wool and textile industry. Conditions were harsh, and they lived on the edge of starvation. In an act of resistance that Thoreau duplicated while at Walden,

Brister Freeman did not pay his poll tax. Town officials used his tax debt as an excuse to take away Brister's property, thus denying him the right to participate in town meetings. Thoreau recalled Freeman in "Former Inhabitants" in *Walden*, where he was held up as a heroic figure. Brister's Hill is a few hundred feet from Walden Pond, and it was one of Thoreau's study sites later in his life. Thoreau's studies of forest succession on Brister's Hill resulted in his posthumous essays "The Succession of Forest Trees" and "The Dispersion of Seeds." "Walden was a Black space before it was a green space," according to professor Elise Lemire.[29,30]

Iba se

PHILLIS WHEATLEY (1753–1784)

Phillis Wheatley Peters was seized from Senegal/Gambia, West Africa, when she was about seven years old, enslaved as a domestic in Boston, and permitted to learn to read and write. She became one of the best-known poets in pre–nineteenth century America. Her volume *Poems on Various Subjects, Religious and Moral* (1773) was published in London, making her the first published African American poet. Wheatley wrote about the divine in nature, and influenced the thinking of the transcendentalists, namely Ralph Waldo Emerson and Henry David Thoreau. An excerpt from one of her nature poems intones, "All-wise Almighty Providence we trace / In trees, and plants, and all the flow'ry race; / As clear as in the nobler frame of man, / All lovely copies of the Maker's plan. / Infinite *Love* where'er we turn our eyes / Appears: this ev'ry creature's wants supplies; / This most is heard in *Nature's* constant voice, / This makes the morn, and this the eve rejoice; / This bids the fost'ring rains and dews descend / To nourish all, to serve one gen'ral end . . ."[31,32]

Iba se

YORK (B. BETWEEN 1770 AND 1775)

York, son of Old York and Rose, was an enslaved explorer on the Lewis and Clark expedition (1804–6) and is understood to be the first African

American to have seen the Pacific Ocean. He supported the expedition by hunting, navigating, paddling, portaging, shelter-building, and spotting novel species. At the end of the journey, York was denied the freedom he had been previously promised. He subsequently defected from the colonial project and went to live among the Apsáalooke (Crow) people of what is now Wyoming, where he built a family and became a leader in the community.[33]

Iba se

JOHN EDMONSTONE (EARLY 1800S)

Born into slavery in British Guiana (present-day Guyana), John Edmonstone was trained in taxidermy and ornithology by Charles Waterton, a naturalist, in 1812. He assisted in Waterton's tropical expeditions, hunting and cataloging bird species. When the plantation owner moved to Scotland, where slavery was outlawed, John Edmonstone was freed. He built a career as a "bird stuffer" and began teaching taxidermy to students from Edinburgh University, including Charles Darwin in 1826. Darwin used these skills in his famous voyage of HMS *Beagle* to the Galapagos, where he cataloged finches and began to theorize evolution by natural selection. Edmonstone also did ornithology work for the Royal Museum of the University in Scotland.[34]

Iba se

HARRIET JACOBS (1813–1897)

Born into slavery in Edenton, North Carolina, Harriet Jacobs escaped to freedom in 1842 and went on to write an autobiography, *Incidents in the Life of a Slave Girl*, which is arguably the nation's first work of environmental justice literature. Environmental justice is when environmental benefits, like clean water and green space, are equitably enjoyed by all, regardless of race or identity, and, similarly, when the burdens of environmental harm, such as pollution and climate disaster, are equitably borne. Jacobs wrote that her political status as a slave disproportionately exposed her to environmental harms, like biting insects, poisonous reptiles, stale air, extreme heat, and unrelenting cold, some of which left her with ecophobia and permanent physical disabilities. She contrasted this with Romantic conceptions of nature, which held that nature should exist as a safe haven for all.[35]

Iba se

HARRIET TUBMAN (1820/22–1913)

Abolitionist, suffragist, and freedom fighter, Harriet Tubman used her intricate knowledge of the natural world and ecological confidence to make thirteen rescue missions to the South to free approximately seventy humans from bondage. She navigated by the stars and used birdcalls, like that of the barred owl, to communicate to refugees whether it was safe to come out of hiding.[36] Tubman was a master herbalist and wildcrafter who used her knowledge of plants to keep her passengers safe on the Underground Railroad. Tubman employed paregoric to quiet babies on the journey north, among other herbs that were taught to her by her grandmother. During her service in the Union Army, she famously cured a soldier who was near death from dysentery by digging up some water lilies and cranesbill to make him a medicinal infusion.[37,38,39] For Tubman, true freedom was marked by the opportunity to plant her own trees for the benefit of her own community. She recalled that when she was enslaved as a child, she had been forbidden to eat the fruit of the trees she had been made to plant. She said, "I liked apples when I was young, and I said, someday I'll plant apples myself for other young folks to eat. I guess I done it." Indeed, Tubman planted an apple orchard at her house of freedom in Auburn, New York, which bears fruit to this day.[40]

Iba se

SOLOMON BROWN (1829–1906)

Solomon G. Brown was a natural historian and the first African American employee at the Smithsonian Institution, where he worked continuously from 1852 until 1906. During his tenure, he educated himself in the field of natural history and prepared the maps and scientific diagrams that were used in important museum lectures. He launched his career as a scientific lecturer in 1855 at the Young People's Literacy Society and Lyceum, where he spoke on entomology to a large, educated, and multiracial audience. He became immensely popular for his self-illustrated lectures on subjects ranging from insects, to geology, to the scientific advances of the day. For decades, he enthralled audiences on the greater DC lecture circuit. Several trees are planted at the Smithsonian to honor his legacy.[41]

Iba se

FREE SOIL MOVEMENT (1848–1854)

Among the Free Soilers, whose framework included opposition to the westward expansion of slavery, was Frederick Douglass (b. 1817/18). Douglass critiqued capitalism's alienation of workers from the land and expropriation of the commons, arguing that "liberty achieved its truest expression when free people mixed their labor with nature in the pursuit of self-reliance." Paying tribute to the agrarian ideal, Douglass advised Black people to own land, forgo urban wage employment, and turn toward agriculture as a means of true independence.[42] In an 1873 speech, he remarked, "The grand old earth has no prejudice against race, color, or previous condition of servitude, but flings open her ample breast to all who come to her for succor or relief." Further, Free Soilers argued that the land itself could be tainted and cursed by injustice. James Pennington (b. 1807) attributed the exhaustion of the soil in Maryland to the "bad cultivation peculiar to slave states."[43] Henry Bibb (b. 1815) argued that "honest farmers tilling their soil and living by their own toil" contributed to the beauty of the landscape in the free North, writing, "I am permitted to gaze on the beautiful of nature, on free soil . . . the green trees and wildflowers of the forest; the ripening harvest fields waving with the gentle breezes of Heaven."[44] Lewis Clarke (b. 1812) concluded that slavery "curses the soil, the houses, the churches . . . it curses man and beast."[45] Martin Delany (b. 1812) took this cause further by seeking free soil on the continent of Africa. He led an emigration expedition to the Niger River area in 1859, reverently inventorying cultural and ecological features, and signing treaties with Yoruba chiefs to acquire property for a new Black nation.[46] Consistent with the African conception of humans as part of nature, Free Soilers believed that the oppression of people on the land had cursed the American soils themselves. Redemption of the land could be achieved through emancipation, and absent that, free soil would be sought across the ocean.

Iba se

ALBERY WHITMAN (1851–1901)

Born into slavery in Hart County, Kentucky, Albery Whitman became a poet and pastor and was widely lauded as the "Poet Laureate of the Negro Race" during his lifetime. He was among the first to publicly advocate for Black-Indigenous solidarity, and he supported the Seminole attempt to maintain control over the Twasinta region of Florida. Further, Whitman viewed nature as a book written by a divine hand, and believed that humanity relied on nature as a teacher. In his poem *Twasinta's Seminoles; or, Rape of Florida*, he intoned, "Oh Does not Nature teach us primal bliss? / Who has not felt her lessons in his youth / And having felt, who can forget forsooth? / The voice of birds, the toil and hum of bees, / And air all filled with sounds, sweet or uncouth / Dark heights, majestic woods and rolling seas / Have been my teachers, and my teachers still be these."[47]

Iba se

BOOKER T. WASHINGTON (1856–1915)

Booker T. Washington was among the founders of Tuskegee Institute, an enduring Black institution of higher education that initially focused on rural skills and scientific agriculture. Tuskegee's publication, the *Negro Farmer*, encouraged organic farming methods, rather than the use of pesticides, advising, "Turn chickens and turkeys into the orchards to help destroy insects . . . guinea, ducks, and geese are also splendid insect hunters."[48] Washington himself believed in the psychospiritual benefits of proximity to nature, writing, "There is something about the smell of the soil . . . a contact with a reality that gives one a strength and development that can be gained in no other way." He claimed to feel "a nearness and kinship" to the plants in the vegetable garden. He promoted independent Black agrarianism, saying, "No country can be very prosperous unless the people who cultivate the soil own it and live on it."[49]

Iba se
GEORGE WASHINGTON CARVER (1864–1943)

Dr. George Washington Carver was a pioneer in regenerative agriculture as one of the first agricultural scientists in the United States to advocate for the use of leguminous cover crops, nutrient-rich mulching, and diversified horticulture. Carver was dedicated to the regeneration of depleted southern soils and turned to legumes, such as cowpeas and peanuts, as a means to fix nitrogen and replenish the soil. He believed that the cowpea, a crop indigenous to Africa, was indispensable in a crop rotation, noting that a soil's "deficiency in nitrogen can be made up almost wholly by keeping the legumes, or pod bearing plants, growing on the soil as much as possible." In addition to promoting cover cropping, Carver experimented with and advocated for compost manuring to address the deficiencies of the Cotton Belt soils. In 1902 he spoke at the annual convention of the Association of American Agricultural Colleges and Experiment Stations about his use of swamp muck, forest leaves, and pine straw to fortify soils. He believed that the forest was a "natural fertilizer factory" containing trees, grasses, and debris that produced "countless tons of the finest kind of manure, rich in potash, phosphates, nitrogen, and humus." Carver worked to persuade farmers to dedicate the autumn and winter seasons to the collection of organic matter. He advised farmers to devote every spare moment to raking leaves, gathering rich earth from the woods, piling up muck from swamps, and hauling it to the land to be plowed under. Carver was a practitioner of "scientific spiritualism," and received his conservation instructions from his time in communion with natural objects under investigation. He believed that humans were junior copartners of God, that scientific study was guided by God, and that our right to exert control over the natural world was contained by the moral and spiritual framework in which nature had independent value as God's creation. He said, "Unkindness to anything means an injustice done to that thing . . . the above principles apply with equal force to soil."[50]

Iba se
CHARLES YOUNG (1864–1922) AND THE BUFFALO SOLDIERS (1866–1951)

Charles Young was the first Black US national park superintendent and a colonel with the Tenth Cavalry Regiment, an all-Black regiment also known as the Buffalo Soldiers. The Buffalo Soldiers administered Yosemite National Park in 1891 and 1913, managing hunting and timber harvesting, preventing forest fires, and planting the park's first arboretum. The Buffalo Soldiers created the first infrastructure in Sequoia and Kings Canyon National Parks' rocky terrain, constructing a wagon road to the Giant Forest and the first trail to Mount Whitney. Under Colonel Young's leadership, the park convinced private landowners to sign contracts agreeing to sell adjacent tracts of land to the public commons.[51] The Buffalo Soldiers were also engaged in combat. The US military's use of Black soldiers to fight unjust wars of expansion against native people on the plains, and those soldiers' complicity in the campaigns, was horrific and abhorrent. It's of note that military service was one of the few ways that Black people could escape the oppressive life of sharecropping in the Jim Crow South.

Iba se
CHARLES HENRY TURNER (1867–1923)

Dr. Charles Henry Turner was a zoologist, scholar, and the first African American to receive a PhD from the University of Chicago. Without the benefit of a professorial appointment, research assistants, or a formal laboratory setting, Dr. Turner made crucial discoveries in the field of animal behavior and became the first African American to be published in the prestigious journal *Science*. He worked with a variety of species including ants, bees, cockroaches, crustaceans, moths, pigeons, spiders, and wasps. Dr. Turner developed enduring techniques to measure learning in invertebrate species, and he initiated the first controlled studies of color vision and pattern vision in honeybees. He extensively studied the anatomy of the avian and crustacean brain, discovered a new species of aquatic invertebrate, and demonstrated that social insects are intelligent and can modify their behavior based on past experience. He wrote, "Ants are guided in their home-going neither by tropisms nor other forms of reflexes nor by a homing instinct, the probability is that they learn the way home . . . Ants are much more than mere reflex machines; they are self-acting creatures guided by memories of past individual (ontogenetic) experience."[52]

Iba se
WILLIAM EDWARD BURGHARDT (W. E. B.) DU BOIS (1868–1963)

While Dr. W. E. B. Du Bois is well known for his cofounding of the NAACP and leadership in the Niagara Movement, his contributions to the ecojustice literary tradition are less well known. In his essay *Of Beauty and Death*, Du Bois describes Acadia in vivid reverence, writing,

The mountains hurl themselves against the stars and at their feet lie black and leaden seas. Above float clouds—white, gray, and inken, while the clear impalpable air springs and sparkles like new wine. The land sinks to meadows, black pine forests, with here and there a blue and wistful mountain. Then there are islands—bold rocks above the sea, curled meadows; all the colors of the sea lie about us—gray and yellowing greens and doubtful blues, blacks not quite black, tinted silvers and golds and dreaming whites.[53]

He went on to explain that while Black people are "endowed with a keen, delicate appreciation of nature," the conditions of segregation often barred them from accessing the nation's most beautiful landscapes.[54] He admonished white people for appreciating an illusion of pristine nature, an imaginary picturesque postcard, while ignoring human suffering and oppression. White people could not bring themselves to see that the suffering of racialized people marred the landscape, so they distorted their vision, avoided reality, and clung to an environmental mirage.[55]

Iba se

ZORA NEALE HURSTON (1891–1960)

Zora Neale Hurston was an anthropologist and author who advanced ecofeminist theory and offered people a deeper understanding of traditional, earth-based, African religion. Her novel *Their Eyes Were Watching God*, like much of her written work, is steeped in environmental concerns. Through the lens of ecofeminism, Hurston used natural disaster as a metaphor for the oppressive toll that patriarchy takes on women and the environment alike. Her characters value the earth as sacred, see their bodies as interconnected with the body of the earth, and work toward a livable future for humans and nonhuman beings.[56] During her field studies in New Orleans, Hurston trained to be a Hoodoo doctor, through which she experienced visions and underwent a ritual to become the blood sibling of a rattlesnake. Her complete cultural and environmental immersion led to her emerging critique of environmental inequities and her vision for egalitarian ecological communities.[57,58]

Iba se

NATIONAL ASSOCIATION OF COLORED WOMEN (1896–PRESENT) AND HOME GARDENS (1865–PRESENT)

Home gardening was nearly ubiquitous among Black women, both during and after slavery. Gardens were a source of food, medicine, income, beauty, and recreation. Into the red clay soils of the South, they planted okra, milo, eggplant, collard greens, peppers, gourds, and other vegetables. Flower gardens beckoned neighbors to draw close for sensory pleasure and conversation. Organic practices such as composting and installing bird feeders were common.[59] As part of the nineteenth-century Black Progressive movement, the National Association of Colored Women promoted urban environmental reform. They provided information and resources for home and city beautification, encouraging the planting of trees, shrubs, and flowers. They advocated for their members, who composed 165 clubs in 1903, to have access to public green space.[60] This work laid the foundation for the urban gardening movement that would begin to flourish in the 1960s.

Iba se

LANCELOT JONES (1898–1997)

Born on a sailboat in Biscayne Bay, Lancelot Jones lived out his ninety-nine-year life on the tiny island of Porgy Key in Miami-Dade County, Florida. His father, Israel Lafayette Jones (b. 1858), and mother, Mozelle Albury (b. 1861), purchased Porgy Key for $5 an acre in 1897, cleared the land by hand, and established a pineapple, tomato, and lime farm. Lancelot and his brother Arthur inherited the farm from their parents and maintained the lime business despite two devastating hurricanes. They shifted to fishing, lobstering, crabbing, and offering guided boat tours, holding out against pressures from investors to purchase and develop the islands for tourism. Arthur passed away in 1966, but Lancelot continued to live on the family land, bathing with rainwater, generating electricity with solar panels, and telling visitors about the fascinating ecology of sponges. In 1970 Lancelot sold the family's 277 acres to the US National Park Service, who declared it a national park in 1980. Valuing legacy over profit, his decision to transfer the land to the parks ensured it would be protected for generations to come.[61]

Iba se

HATTIE CARTHAN (1900–1984) AND THE URBAN COMMUNITY GARDEN MOVEMENT

In the 1960s and 1970s, as many urban neighborhoods were experiencing divestment, arson, crime, and neglect, Black and Latinx farmers revived their agricultural traditions and brought vitality to urban spaces by establishing community gardens. Neighbors transformed trash-strewn lots into urban oases with the support of their churches and neighborhood associations. Urban farmers of color removed rubble, planted trees, installed vegetable beds, and built structures for community gatherings. One of the instrumental figures in the urban gardening movement was Hattie Carthan, a Black environmental activist who coordinated the planting of over 1,500 trees in the Bedford-Stuyvesant neighborhood of Brooklyn, New York, in the late '60s and '70s. We also pay homage to Black growers John and Elizabeth Crews, who catalyzed subsistence farming in Detroit, to Rufus and Demalda Newsome, elder leaders in the urban farming movement in Tulsa, and to all the other Black visionaries who helped us find our way home to land. There are now over eighteen thousand urban community gardens in the United States, predominantly in neighborhoods once redlined.[62] Among them is Hattie Carthan Herban Farm, which was established in 1985 to honor Carthan's legacy.[63]

Iba se

EUGENE WILLIAMS (1902–1919)

Eugene Williams was among the first martyrs in the African American struggle for environmental justice. Characteristic of the ecojustice yearning of the times was equal access to environmental goods, including green space and beachfronts. During the brutal heat wave of July 1919, thousands of Chicagoans flocked to the shores of Lake Michigan for relief. Williams was floating on a raft with some friends and inadvertently drifted across the invisible line separating the segregated waters.

A white man started hurling rocks at the boys, striking Williams and causing him to drown. This marked the beginning of the Red Summer of 1919, when white defenders of segregation rioted, using violence and terror in an attempt to reassert dominance over African Americans.[64]

Iba se

NEGRO 4-H WILDLIFE CONSERVATION CONFERENCES AND NATURE STUDY (1904–1960S)

Blending conservation and preservation, Negro 4-H taught young people about agriculture and the natural world. They showed young farmers how to plant cover crops to restore the soil and prevent wind and water erosion, and trained them in food preservation and horticulture, among other things. The peak of Negro 4-H was in 1923, when its 3,001 clubs served 55,971 children. These young people went on camp outings, where they learned wildlife identification, forest management, soil conservation, hunting, bird calls, tree planting, and the recreational enjoyment of nature. The work of 4-H complemented the wider African American nature study movement, which peaked in the 1940s. According to Tuskegee Institute, "The purpose of the work in nature study is to train the power of observation, create an interest in and love for nature, and increase knowledge which will be of service in the future . . . to create in students both an aesthetic and scientific appreciation for Nature, as well as to encourage an active rather than passive attitude towards things in Nature." There were a number of efforts in the Black community to introduce nature study to children during the school day. For example, the Hampton Institute published its *Course in Nature Study for Primary Grades*, focusing on gardening, botany, and tree identification, which was used at African American elementary schools across North Carolina.[65] In 1940, Effie Lee Newsome published *Gladiola Garden: Poems of Outdoors and Indoors for Second Grade Readers*, which included poems that encouraged Black schoolchildren to see themselves as a beautiful reflection of the dark-colored soil, animals, and plants around them.[66]

Iba se

BOOKER T. WHATLEY (1915–2005)

A professor at Alabama's Tuskegee Institute, Dr. Booker T. Whatley carried on the pioneering work of Dr. George Washington Carver in the field of regenerative agriculture. Whatley was one of the original thinkers behind the farm-to-table concept, and he popularized the system of community-supported agriculture (CSA) before that name was widely known. He argued that a small family farm could be financially viable if it adopted diversified horticulture, a pick-your-own operation, and a clientele membership club, which was a farm product subscription service that informed today's CSA models. He suggested that farmers send out a newsletter to their subscribers to update them on picking dates and farming activities so that they would "feel as if the farm was their own." By removing the middleman in farm operations and product distribution, Whatley's ideas made it possible for farmers to rise out of abject poverty while restoring their soil to health. As a plant breeder, Whatley also developed fifteen varieties of muscadine grapes and five cultivars of sweet potato, among others. His organic farming and direct marketing concepts are now in practice globally.[67]

Iba se

FANNIE LOU HAMER (1917–1977)

Fannie Lou Hamer said, "When you've got 400 quarts of greens and gumbo soup canned for the winter, nobody can push you around or tell you what to say or do." While Hamer is best known for her organizing with the Mississippi Freedom Democratic Party, her rebellion extended to food and agriculture. In 1969, Hamer founded the Freedom Farm Cooperative on forty acres of prime delta land. Her goal was to empower poor Black farmers and sharecroppers, who had suffered at the mercy of white landowners. She said, "The time has come now when we are going to have to get what we need ourselves. We may get a little help here and there, but in the end we're going to have to do it ourselves." The cooperative consisted of 1,500 families who planted cash crops, like soybeans and cotton, as well as mixed vegetables. They purchased another 640 acres and started a "pig bank" that distributed livestock to Black farmers. The farm grew into a multifaceted community-support organization, providing scholarships, home-building assistance, a commercial kitchen, a garment factory, a tool bank, agricultural training, and burial fees to its members.[68]

Iba se
BETTY REID SOSKIN (1921–)

At age one hundred, Betty Reid Soskin became the oldest national park ranger serving in the United States. She was actively involved in planning the Rosie the Riveter World War II Home Front National Historical Park and wanted future generations to remember the contributions of women to the nation's history. Of her involvement in this initiative, she reflected, "What gets remembered is a function of who's in the room doing the remembering."[69]

Iba se
TONI MORRISON (1931–2019) AND HENRY DUMAS (1934–1968)

Toni Morrison and Henry Dumas were pioneers in African American ecophilic literature, together with Alice Walker (b. 1944). Morrison's novel *Sula* is a lament of ecocide, chronicling the destruction of forests, brambles, and rivers to make way for the white-run Medallion golf course and suburban development. Shadrack, a character in the novel, "hadn't sold fish in a long time now. The river had killed them all. No more silver-gray flashes, no more flat, wide, unhurried look. No more slowing down of gills. No more tremor on the line."[70] Both Dumas and Morrison discussed the redeeming spiritual power of nature in their writing. Dumas, who was called an "absolute genius" by Morrison, wrote about the spiritual "tainting" caused by urbanization. In *Echo Tree*, he explained, "taintin is when you feel tired, you don't want to do nothing, you can't laugh, and your breathing get slow." Time away from nature would cause a person to become "bino" (albino/white), which meant they were going against the spiritual power of the echo tree, rejecting their ancestral connection, and negating nonhuman natural power.[71] In *Tar Baby*, Morrison explored the primal spiritual power that resides in trees.[72] This echoes the much earlier work of African American poet Maud Cuney-Hare (b. 1874) in her *Message of Trees: An Anthology of Leaves and Branches* (1918), a multicultural anthology that includes eco-poems by Paul Laurence Dunbar, and an intro by William Stanley Braithwaite.[73]

Iba se
AFRICAN AMERICANS IN THE CIVILIAN CONSERVATION CORPS (1933–1942)

Despite being forced to work in segregated units, subjected to racial taunting, and barred from managerial positions, over two hundred thousand African Americans made significant contributions to America's natural resource infrastructure as part of President Roosevelt's Civilian Conservation Corps. Black corpsmen of the CCC remain "hidden figures" in the development of US public lands, having applied their forestry and conservation skills to the establishment of the nation's environmental infrastructure.[74]

Iba se
HAZEL JOHNSON (1935–2011)

Lauded as the "mother of environmental justice," Hazel Johnson was the founder of the People for Community Recovery (PCR). While living in a housing project on the South Side of Chicago, surrounded by landfills and industrial development, her seven children developed lung problems and her husband died of lung cancer. She began to systematically document the chronic health problems affecting her neighbors, as well as their exposures to asbestos, contaminated drinking water, and air pollution, and found that her community had the highest cancer rates in the city. She successfully lobbied the city to test the water supply, which revealed cyanide and other toxins. Under pressure, the city replaced the community's water source.

Johnson was instrumental in passing Environmental Justice Executive Order 12898, signed by President Clinton in 1994, which directs federal agencies to address the disproportionate adverse health and environmental effects of their actions on minority and low-income populations. She was awarded the 1992 President's Environmental and Conservation Challenge Award in recognition of her environmental justice work.[75]

Iba se

MAVYNNE "BEACH LADY" BETSCH (1935–2005) AND ABRAHAM LINCOLN LEWIS (1865–1947)

Abraham Lincoln Lewis, MaVynee Betsch's grandfather, founded American Beach, the second-oldest African American beach in the United States, in Florida in 1935. Betsch became known as "Beach Lady" given her lifelong dedication to protecting American Beach from development and destruction. In 2004, she established the American Beach Museum, which contains the history of the shore and its Black community. As a result of her efforts, the National Park Service added American Beach to its National Register of Historic Places in 2002. Betsch was a vegetarian and a proponent of natural living; she grew her natural locks to be over seven feet long. Upon retirement, Betch gave her life savings of $750,000 to sixty different environmental organizations and causes.[76]

Iba se

LUCILLE CLIFTON (1936–2010) AND JAYNE CORTEZ (1936–2012)

Lucille Clifton and Jayne Cortez were trailblazers in eco-poetics. In her poem "being property once myself," Lucille Clifton, Maryland poet laureate and Pulitzer Prize finalist, established with utter clarity the "bond of live things everywhere" when she wrote, "being property once myself / i have a feeling for it, / that's why i can talk / about environment." Clifton built on the Black understanding of human-as-planet and planet-as-human in "the earth is a living thing," where she wrote, "is a black shambling bear / ruffling its wild back and tossing / mountains into the sea . . ."[77,78] Jayne Cortez fashioned apocalyptic blues poems to decry the multifaceted oppression that was destroying nature and human society. She wrote, "Mr. & Mrs. Crab are not into / Destroying the world / They are crawling to the mud flats / To take in some rotten insects . . ." Cortez lamented eco-crisis, writing, "I got a fishing in raw sewage blue-ooze / I got the toxic waste dump in my backyard blue-ooze."[79] For both poets, Black people were inseparable from nature, and the assault on the environment was simultaneously an assault on their communities.

Iba se

WANGARI MAATHAI (1940–2011)

Dr. Wangari Maathai was a Kikuyu advocate for women's rights, democracy, and ecological protection. Maathai founded and led the Green Belt Movement, earned the first PhD among East African women, served in Parliament of Kenya, and won the first Nobel Peace Prize awarded to an African woman. The Green Belt Movement planted over fifty-one million trees and provided a vehicle for women's political and democratic empowerment. Despite the government's attempts to silence Maathai through public shaming and multiple arrests, she successfully campaigned to stop the sixty-story Kenya Times Media Trust Complex that would have destroyed Nairobi's Uhuru Park and to halt the privatization of public land in the Karura Forest. Maathai believed "you don't need a diploma to plant a tree," and she developed grassroots, community-led afforestation strategies that created economic and environmental benefits for rural women and families. Winner of innumerable awards and honors, Maathai is remembered as one of the greatest environmental and pro-democracy leaders of all time.[80]

Iba se

KEN SARO-WIWA (1941–1995)

A member of the Ogoni people of Nigeria, Ken Saro-Wiwa was an environmental activist, writer, and television producer who spoke out against the environmental damage caused by crude oil extraction in his homeland. As president of the Movement for the Survival of the Ogoni People

(MOSOP), Saro-Wiwa led a nonviolent campaign against the Shell oil company and other multinational corporations that were destroying the lands and waters of Ogoniland. The MOSOP drafted a bill of rights for the Ogoni people, which included increased political autonomy and environmental remediation for damaged lands. He also served as vice-chair for the international Unrepresented Nations and Peoples Organization, which organized massive peaceful marches through Ogoniland. As international attention to the issue grew, the Nigerian government fabricated charges in order to convict and execute Saro-Wiwa and eight other MOSOP leaders. The European Union, the United States, South Africa, Zimbabwe, Kenya, and other countries responded to the execution with outrage and imposed sanctions on Nigeria.[81] Saro-Wiwa's struggle continued after his death, and Shell was eventually forced to pay farmers for environmental damages and leave Nigeria.[82]

Iba se

WADERS AT HAULOVER BEACH PARK, DADE COUNTY, FLORIDA (1945)

Black people were forbidden from enjoying the white sands and blue waters of Dade County's segregated beaches until six courageous Black activists conducted a "wade in" at Haulover Beach Park, defying the racist statutes. Following the action, African American leaders met with the county commissioner and established Virginia Key Beach as a "colored" beach on an island farther south. While originally accessible only by boat, a causeway was eventually built, and the beach became a destination for Black, Caribbean, South American, and Cuban people to enjoy the outdoors. This was an important step in the eventual desegregation of public beaches.[83]

Iba se

BOB MARLEY (1945–1981)

Jamaican singer, songwriter, and musician Bob Marley was a pioneer of reggae and popularized Rastafarianism. Among the practices of most Rastafarians is adherence to a strict vegetarian or vegan diet consisting of local, organic, "*ital*" (living) foods. They prefer traditional herbal medicine over Western modalities, and emphasize the importance of knowing *Jah* (God) personally rather than simply believing in *Jah*. Rastafarian philosophy influenced a generation of Black people's interest in natural living. Rooted in many overlapping values, the influential MOVE organization was founded in Philadelphia in 1972 and also taught strict vegetarianism and the inherent value of all life. The Black veganism movement is growing, and today Black people are three times more likely to be vegan than the general population.[84] Although there are limitations in data that does not distinguish between indigenous methods of sourcing animal protein from Western industrial agriculture, research strongly suggests that a plant-based diet has environmental benefits.

Iba se

JOHN FRANCIS, PLANETWALKER (1946–)

After witnessing the devastation caused by the 1971 oil spill off the coast of San Francisco, John Francis decided to give up motorized transport, a commitment that he kept for twenty-two years. He additionally took up a vow of silence that lasted for seventeen years, during which time he walked across the nation advocating for environmental protection, using his drawings and banjo playing as means of communication. He earned a PhD in land management from the University of Wisconsin–Madison during his period of silence. He was also employed by the US Coast Guard and helped develop legislation on oil spill management, including the landmark Oil Pollution Act of 1990. He ended his vow of silence in 1990, saying "I have chosen Earth Day to begin speaking, so that I will remember that now I will be speaking for the environment."[85]

Iba se

ROBERT BULLARD (1946–)

Dr. Robert Bullard, professor, author, and activist, is widely considered the father of the environmental justice movement. In 1979, Dr. Bullard and his wife, attorney Linda Bullard, took Southwestern Waste Management to court for endangering the health of the majority Black residents of Houston's Northwood Manor. It was the first court case that charged environmental racism under civil rights law. Bullard conducted a study that documented that nearly all of Houston's garbage dumps and incinerators were sited in Black neighborhoods. "Without a doubt," Bullard has said of his experience, "it was a form of apartheid where whites were making decisions and black people and brown people and people of color, including Native Americans on reservations, had no seat at the table." Bullard went on to author eighteen books on environmental racism, and he advocated for the unification of civil rights and environmental movements under the banner of environmental justice. Bullard helped organize the first National People of Color Environmental Leadership Summit, in 1991, where the seventeen principles of environmental justice were developed. He continued to be active in legislative and political campaigns, among them the successful lawsuit to stop a permit for a uranium enrichment plant in Forest Grove, Louisiana. Bullard believes that the movement is "an extension of the first protest against being uprooted from our homeland and brought to a strange land . . . we have to understand the link, the correlation, the relationship between exploitation of the land and the exploitation of the people. The two are inseparable."[86]

Iba se

OCTAVIA BUTLER (1947–2006)

In her eco-apocalyptic novel *Parable of the Sower*, Octavia Butler describes a dystopian future affected by global warming and governmental decline. Shortages of food, water, and basic resources lead to a refugee crisis, drug addiction, and rampant violent crime. The protagonist, Lauren Olamina, believes that spiritual dysfunction is at the root of the environmental crisis and establishes a religion called Earthseed based on the idea that "God is change." After her neighborhood is destroyed by looters, Olamina leads a group of people on a journey to establish a land-based intentional community in Northern California. Octavia Butler's literary work has inspired a generation of Black futurists who dream of establishing eco-communities. Among them are the Earthseed Land Collective in Durham, North Carolina; the EARTHseed Farm in Sonoma County, California; and the Acorn Center for Restoration and Freedom in Covington, Georgia. In her lifetime, Butler received a Hugo Award, a Nebula Award, and a MacArthur Foundation fellowship, among other recognitions.[87]

Iba se

SHIRLEY SHERROD (1947–) AND NEW COMMUNITIES LAND TRUST (1969–1985; 2011–PRESENT)

Shirley and Charles Sherrod helped to found New Communities in 1969, a farm collective owned in common by Black farmers and the first community land trust in the United States. At 5,700 acres, New Communities was the largest Black-owned property to date in this country. Its members raised hogs, grapes, sugarcane, melons, peanuts, and other crops on their land in southwestern Georgia. According to Mrs. Sherrod, "Once white people realized we had the land, they started shooting at our buildings. I mean, we went through so much during our time up there. We even caught a white couple stealing our hogs!" During the severe droughts of 1981–82, New Communities requested emergency assistance from the USDA for irrigation. It was denied while white farmers received relief. By 1980, after repeated droughts and active discrimination on the part of the USDA Farmers Home Administration, New Communities faced foreclosure and lost its land. Its members became plaintiffs in the landmark class-action lawsuit against the federal government, *Pigford v. Glickman*. The chief arbitrator of the case, Michael Lewis, opined that the USDA's treatment of New Communities "smacked of nothing more than a feudal baron demanding additional crops from his serfs." The case was settled out of court in 1999 for $1.2 billion, the largest civil rights settlement in US history. While the average payout was $50,000, New Communities itself won $12 million and used part of the settlement money to reestablish itself on a 1,600-acre former plantation that its members named Resora.[88] Today the struggle for Black land continues, led by the Federation of Southern Cooperatives–Land Assistance Fund, founded in 1967. The federation's twenty thousand members engage in direct action, litigation, and education in defense of land. They sponsored the 1992 caravan of Black and Native American farmers to Washington, DC, to demand reparations for USDA discrimination. Together with the Land Loss Prevention Project and other allies, they fought and won legislative battles to fund the Outreach and Assistance for Socially Disadvantaged Farmers and Ranchers Program (the 2501 program) and the 1890 Land Grant College scholarships. The struggle for Black land builds on the foundational yearning expressed in 1865 by newly emancipated African Americans of Falls Church, Virginia, who said, "We feel it very important that we obtain HOMES, owning our own shelters, and the ground, that we may raise fruit trees, concerning which our children can say—these are ours."[89]

Iba se

BENJAMIN CHAVIS (1948–) AND DOLLIE BURWELL (1948–)

In 1982, residents of the predominantly Black Warren County, North Carolina, began protesting the state's plan to site a hazardous waste dump in Alfton, in which four hundred thousand cubic yards of PCB-contaminated soil would be dumped. Dollie Burwell was among the leaders who organized the initial meetings of concerned local residents. Protesters marched from Coley Springs Baptist Church to the dump site, and then laid their bodies down in the roadway to stop the dump trucks. Sixty police officers responded in full riot gear, arresting Burwell and others. The next day, Burwell invited the Reverend Benjamin Chavis Jr., a United Church of Christ minister, to lead the protests, which grew into six weeks of marches and nonviolent street actions. Over five hundred people were arrested, including the Reverend Chavis. He coined the term "environmental racism" to describe the experience, and ordered a study that documented the extent of the crisis. This study, completed in 1987 and called *Toxic Wastes and Race*, found that race was the number one factor in citing hazardous waste facilities, and that most Black and Hispanic people (three out of five) lived near toxic waste. This study helped to amplify the struggle for environmental justice in the public and political arena. The Warren County protests were a foundational catalyst for the modern environmental justice movement.[90,91]

Iba se

BROTHER YUSUF BURGESS (1950–2014)

Yusuf Burgess grew up in the Marcy Houses in Brooklyn, and would walk himself over to Prospect Park to collect tadpoles in a paper cup and gather acorns. His slogan was "no child left inside," and to that end he founded the Youth Ed–Venture & Nature Network to take urban youth on trips to the wilds of the Adirondacks, the Catskills, and even once to Yosemite National Park. He coordinated the New York State Department of Environmental Conservation's Capital District Campership Diversity Program and worked with young people at Green Tech High Charter School and the Albany Boys and Girls Club. After his death, ninety children who loved him came together to build a community garden dedicated to his memory. Brother Yusuf said, "Many of today's children are growing up in busy cities without nearby parks or 'special places' to experience the beautiful and awe-inspiring. They stand to lose a very important part of what it is to be human."[92]

Iba se

DANA ALSTON (1951–1999)

Dana was instrumental to the development of the modern environmental justice movement and became one of its leaders and staunchest supporters. She served on the National Planning Committee for the first National People of Color Environmental Leadership Summit, in 1991, together with Donna Chavis, Patrick Bryant, Charles Lee, Robert Bullard, Richard Moore, and Benjamin Chavis. Dr. Dorceta Taylor also played a pivotal role in this historic summit, which brought together three hundred African, Latinx, Native, and Asian Americans from all fifty states to strategize on environmental justice and write the platform for the movements. Alston also led a delegation of environmental justice leaders to participate in the 1992 Earth Summit and Global Forum meetings in Rio de Janeiro.[93]

Iba se

ALL OUR EARTH-LISTENING ELDERS

To the revered elders and ancestors whose names we have spoken, and to those whose names were left unsaid. To the farmers, land stewards, scientists, eco-poets, environmental activists, teachers, organizers, and visionaries who held fast to the fundamental truth that Black people are inextricably bound with nature, and that nature is worthy of defense—we thank you. May the words of our mouths, the meditations of our hearts, and the work of our hands honor your legacy.

ASE.

Spirit

IT IS TIME FOR A NEW COVENANT

A Conversation with
Awise Agbaye Wande Abimbola, Yeye Luisah Teish,
and Awo Enroue Onigbonna Sangofemi Halfkenny

When my mother told me to go and fetch firewood, she would warn me, "Don't pick any wood out of the fig tree, or even around it." "Why?" I would ask. "Because that's a tree of God," she'd reply. "We don't use it. We don't cut it. We don't burn it." I later learned that there was a connection between the fig tree's root system and the underground water reservoirs. The roots burrowed deep into the ground, breaking through the water table of rocks beneath the surface soil and diving into the underground water table. The water traveled up along the roots until it hit a depression or weak place in the ground and gushed out as a spring. Indeed, wherever these trees stood, there were likely to be streams. The reverence the community had for the fig tree helped preserve the fig tree and the tadpoles that have so captivated me. The trees also held the soil together, reducing erosion and landslides. In such ways, without conscious or deliberate effort, these cultural and spiritual practices contributed to the conservation of biodiversity.

—WANGARI MAATHAI, *UNBOWED*

I n the Yoruba sacred literature, the Odu Ifa named Ogbe-Odi offers a verse about the consequences of using excessive force in our relationships with other creatures on planet Earth. As the story goes, Mr. By-Force used deception to invite his friends—Grasshopper, Hen, Wolf, Dog, Hyena, Viper, Walking Stick, Fire, Rain, Drought, and Dew Drops—to a collective work gathering on his farm. Each one agreed to attend on the condition that their sworn predatory enemy would not be invited. For example, Hen had a habit of trying to gobble up all of Grasshopper's children, and so Grasshopper wanted assurance that Hen would not be present. Hen wanted assurance that Wolf, who had attempted to devour all of her chicks, would not be invited, and so on. Not only did Mr. By-Force lie about his guest list, but he arranged his guests so that each would be working adjacent to their sworn enemy. He then withheld food and drink, such that the workers would become famished and desperate to eat. When they could not withstand their hunger any longer, they dropped their tools and pounced on one another, gnashing and biting. Fortunately, Dew Drops, the only one among them without an enemy, fell upon them all and brought coolness. Restored to their senses, they started to assist one another in rising to their feet. They embraced one another peacefully and discussed the need to make a new covenant. They agreed that rather than attempt to consume and eliminate all the children of the other creatures, they would eat only what they absolutely needed. Their new covenant was one of moderation and mutual regard. In this verse, Dew Drops is the manifestation of Orunmila-Ifa, the Orisa (Divine Force of Nature) connected to wisdom. The story ends, "Doing things by force has ruined the world of today. Dew drops come and make repairs. Dew drops come and make amends."[1]

The millennia-old verse from *Ogbe-Odi* is powerfully predictive of the way greed, exploitation, and violence are wreaking havoc in the natural world today, a grave breach of the covenant of moderation. We are currently living through the Holocene mass extinction, the most rapid extinction of species in the planet's history and the only extinction event caused by one species—human beings. Industrial human societies have become Mr. By-Force, responsible for the untempered ravishing of Earth's creatures.

Of the 8.7 million species of animals and insects on planet Earth, 1 million are threatened with extinction in the coming decades, which is more than ever before in human history. Amphibian species are most vulnerable, with over 40 percent at risk of extinction. Around one-third of marine mammals, reef-forming corals, sharks, and shark relatives face potential disappearance. We have already lost around 900 vertebrate species due to human activity, mostly because of habitat destruction.[2] There are 21,000 monitored populations of mammals, fish, birds, reptiles, and amphibians, encompassing almost 4,400 species around the world. These populations have declined an average of 68 percent between 1970 and 2016. The more vulnerable species in Latin America and the Caribbean are disproportionately impacted, declining, on average, 94 percent during the same time period. According to the World Wildlife Fund, the rate of population decline "signals a fundamentally broken relationship between humans and the natural world, the consequences of which . . . can be catastrophic."[3]

So that these are not anonymous statistics, it is important to say the names of some of the creatures whose remaining time on Earth may be cut short due to human action. Among them are the African forest elephant, Amur leopard, black rhino, Bornean and Sumatran orangutans, Cross River gorilla, eastern and western lowland gorilla, hawksbill turtle, Javan and Sumatran rhinos, saola, Sumatran elephant, Sunda tiger, vaquita, Yangtze finless porpoise . . .[4] To recite aloud the names of all the earth's threatened species one by one would take about two sleepless weeks.

It is often argued that we should conserve species for their utilitarian value to humans, as providers of ecosystem services, reservoirs of genetic material, and potential sources of novel medicines. While this is a rational frame, there is an alternative philosophy. In Yoruba religion, nature is regarded as a divinity, and all plants, animals, and landforms have intrinsic value as Sacred Forces of Nature. The story in *Ogbe-Odi* presents Grasshopper, Hen, the other animals, and natural elements as sentient and conscious beings, worthy and able of being regarded as equals with humans.

All life on earth shares a narrow band of habitability that extends from the deepest root systems of trees and the dark environment of ocean trenches up to the highest mountaintops. This layer, called the biosphere, is only about twelve miles from top to bottom, comprising only 0.3 percent of the planet's radius.[5] All of the habitats and resources upon which life depends exist in this thin belt of land and water. Perhaps our collective survival depends on a new covenant among the species sharing this life raft.

To learn about the role of Indigenous African spirituality, and specifically the Yoruba religion, in defining that new covenant, we talk to Awise Agbaye Wande Abimbola, Yeye Luisah Teish, and Awo Enroue Onigbonna Sangofemi Halfkenny.

PROFESSOR WANDE ABIMBOLA (he/him) is Awise Awo Agbaye (world spokesperson for Ifa) and special advisor to the president of Nigeria on cultural affairs and traditional matters. Professor Abimbola has served as vice chancellor of the University of Ife (now Obafemi Awolowo University) and the majority leader of the Senate of the Federal Republic of Nigeria. Professor Abimbola is the author of over ten books and many articles on Ifa and Yoruba religion. He has held professorships at Harvard University, Massachusetts; Boston University, Massachusetts; and Obafemi Awolowo University, Nigeria.

YEYE LUISAH TEISH (she/her) is a writer, storyteller-activist, and spiritual counselor. She is the author of six books, most notably *Jambalaya: The Natural Woman's Book of Personal Charms and Practical Rituals*, a women's spirituality classic. She has contributed to forty-five anthologies and magazines such as *Ms.*, *Essence*, and *Yoga Journal*. Her works have been translated into seven languages. She is the Iyanifa of Ile Orunmila Oshun and a member of the Global Council for Ancestor Veneration and the Mother Earth Delegation of the United Indigenous Nations. Yeye has taught at the University of Creation Spirituality, the Institute for Transpersonal Psychology, and the California Institute of Integral Studies. She has lectured at UCLA, Spelman College, and Harvard. She holds an honorary doctorate from the International Institute of Integral Human Sciences, and the title *Yeyeworo* from the Fatunmise Compound in Ile-Ife Nigeria. She has performed in Australia, New Zealand, Venezuela, and Europe.

AWO ENROUE ONIGBONNA SANGOFEMI HALFKENNY (he/him) has been an Ifa priest within the Yoruba Orisa religion for over twenty years and a licensed clinical social worker for thirteen years. He is a consultant, a writer, an artist, and an activist. Born in Boston, Massachusetts, in 1968, Enroue is a multiracial, Black, cisgender, heterosexual man and a father of two who has been married for over twenty years and has been sober for over thirty years. His practice, Healing and Liberation Counseling, skillfully weaves together spiritual health, mental health, and social justice issues to guide individuals, communities, and organizations to develop practices toward liberation.

LEAH: One of the prominent conservation strategies of Western environmentalists is to set aside wildlife reserves and other protected areas where human activity is restricted. Leading biologists argue that at least 50 percent of the earth needs to be preserved for nonhuman creatures if we are to save even 85 percent of remaining species.[6] Yet the idea of forest reserves did not begin with Yellowstone in 1872, which is heralded as "the world's first national park" and "America's best idea." Forest reserves are ancient technologies that have been used by the Yoruba and other African Indigenous communities for millennia. Baba, can you speak to the types of forest reserves among the Yoruba?

AWISE AGBAYE WANDE ABIMBOLA: In ancient times, every town would demarcate an area of forest that nobody was allowed to touch. They knew that over time, the population would increase, and the area would become a city, so from the onset they created the forest reserve. The Yoruba word for forest is *igbo*, and the name for the special area is *etile*, so together the reserve is *igbo etile*. Inside of the *igbo etile* no animals can be hunted. They are safe there.

There is another type of huge forest reserve called *eluju gbogbofo*. This large area is farther from town, and people are not allowed to enter there—not to hunt or do anything at all. The only uses of the *eluju gbog-bofo* are magical. Human beings can go there to turn into animals, and animals can turn into human beings. In these untouched places, meta-morphosis and evolution are possible. In the natural state of the earth, the boundaries between humans and the rest of nature are malleable. There, the boundaries between the human world and the spirit world are not fixed. Long ago, there were certain people living in the tops of the trees in the forest, and the missionaries tried to make them come down. They wanted the boundaries between humans and nature to be fixed. But once boundaries are fixed, there becomes division.

It is hard for Western humans to relinquish the idea that they are in charge of everything. They want to go where they please and do what they want. They want to subdue all the Indigenous people and shift them from one place to another. The broken world we are living in is sustained by brute force. They want to control everything. How can you control everything, when there is so much you can't see with your naked eye or even a microscope? Are you in control of the sunrise and the sunset? The consequences for this behavior are coming. It may not be for ten genera-tions, but it's coming.

LEAH: Yeye, in *Jambalaya* you dedicate a chapter to the worship of divine forces of nature in Indigenous African religion, namely to Abosom of the Akan people, the Orisa of the Yoruba, and the Vodun of the Fon Dahomey people. You describe a "regulated kinship among human, an-imal, mineral, and vegetable life," and warn against the imbalance that arises when too much is taken from the natural world, or when resources are taken and not reciprocated with the appropriate offerings and rituals. Can you further elucidate how Orisa tradition provides guidance on the relationship between humans and other aspects of Nature?[7]

YEYE LUISAH TEISH: In these African Indigenous traditions, especially Ifa, Orisa, Vodun, and Condumble as they are practiced in the Diaspora, there is a core idea that each worshipper is a child of a particular Natural Force. So, as a child of Osun, I am the child of the River. My friend who is a priestess of Olokun is a child of the Deep Ocean. The initiate of Osayin is the child of the Medicine Forest. All of the Orisas are associated with certain places in nature, and this gives worshippers a responsibility to that aspect of nature. I must go to the river respectfully, make offerings, clean up the trash on the riverbank, and pay homage through ritual, because that is the body of my mother Osun. For each Orisa there are also associated sacred animals. My road of Osun is connected to the African vulture,[8] and so I keep my eye on the health of that bird population and on threats of extinction to birds in general. Our mandate to honor the Orisa is not abstract or amorphous; it is embodied and exacting. It imbues our everyday lives with a relationship to the natural world.

LEAH: Enroue, my dear friend, you also have a close relationship with the river divinities and specifically with the river closest to your home. Can you speak to the lessons you have learned by listening to the river?

AWO ENROUE ONIGBONNA SANGOFEMI HALFKENNY: Before being initiated into Ifa, I was first a worshipper of Sango, whose wives are river divinities— Oba, Oya, and Osun. I used to wonder what that was about, as Sango is a divinity of thunder and lightning. I was once sitting by a river on the West Coast near Seattle listening to the tumbling, roaring torrent and realized that it sounded like thunder. There was a shared energy and language between these forces. Even now as a priest of Ifa, the *Odu* of my initiation speaks to a connection with the river divinities and the importance of receiving their icons and worshipping them.

The river is always moving and changing, so it is an embodiment of the spiritual teaching that everything is Change. Our bodies are constantly shifting and renewing. Each moment is different from the one before. The river is an obvious teacher in that way, challenging our assumptions that we can concretize any person or situation. Western scientific and mathematical thinking is very reductive; you look at the parts to understand the whole. The object of study is concretized, frozen, dissected, and taken to the lab out of its context to be labeled and analyzed. Just as we can't understand the human brain by looking at slices of tissue, we can't understand the living, multidimensional being of the river by freezing and slicing it up. Then, it would no longer be a river. In the same way, one interaction with a person does not define the entirety of that person, or of the relationship. A single data point is unreliable. By immersing myself in direct experience in nature, sitting with the river at different seasons, I am taught these lessons.

Rivers are also healing forces. In Nigeria, the Oogun River literally means "Medicine River" and is the Orisa Yemoja. I had a chance to visit the sacred Osun River in Osogbo, whose waters are healing and used to tend to babies. I have been doing a lot of healing and spiritual work at the West River in New Haven, Connecticut, for both myself and my clients. The process need not be elaborate. We introduce ourselves to the river, make offerings, pray for what we need, sit, and listen. We open ourselves up to what these waters have to say to us, how we can heal, how we can be whole, and how we can be free. Learning from the river has been powerful and important.

LEAH: Baba, in a recent lecture you shared that there are sixty-five trees who are worshipped as Orisa in the Yoruba tradition. Can you explain this practice and offer some examples?

AWISE AGBAYE WANDE ABIMBOLA: There are many trees that are worshiped as Orisa, maybe even more than seventy-three. The important idea is that we humans relate to these trees as if they were human. Everything in nature is alive and anthropomorphized without hierarchy. We believe that they have spirits within them that have human capacities—to go to market, to maintain friendships, to get angry, marry, have children, and so on. In the sacred literature of Ifa, creatures in nature move about as human beings. A bird can cast divination for a king, and often does.

Our son Iroko is named after a tree divinity. My father also had the name Iroko. The iroko tree is the tallest hardwood tree in West Africa. When my father's parents wanted to have children and went for divination, they were told that Orisa Iroko would help them to have a child. So they made *ebo* (sacrifice) to the iroko tree and took that name as a family name. When the iroko tree is being worshipped, they dress the tree with a white cloth and offer food. The food offering is consumed by the small creatures and birds who inhabit the tree as their home, and they share the food with the spiritual beings.

Another example would be the tree of Ogun. There is a tree in Oyo town, and on the seventh day of initiation, the *iyawo* (new initiate) dances around the town and ends up at the foot of the tree of Ogun. All of the Ogun community will be present and pray for the newly initiated person. They perform *ebo* right at the tree and hang medicines from the branches. Every Ogun community will have such a tree. A female priest sits at the foot of the tree as the master of ceremonies. Her title is Iya Idi Ogun, which translates to "mother who sits at the foot of the Ogun tree," and is the title that my wife, Iyanifa Michelle Ajisebo McElwaine Abimbola, Iya Idi Ogun Alaafin Oyo, was given by the Ogun community of the Alaafin's kingdom and currently holds. The human feeds the tree, and the tree feeds the human. It is a symbiotic and ecological relationship.

Until humans can accept that trees, mountains, and insects are human, and start to relate and talk with them on human terms, we will not succeed at protecting them. If we simply make legislation that says, for example, don't kill blue whales anymore, we have not changed the underlying attitude. You see humans fishing, and in the course of one day, they harvest two hundred fish and throw them all back dead into the ocean. You see humans mowing down the forests. It is barbaric. It is not true what the Christian Bible says about nature being there just for humans to use and dominate. The way of European so-called civilization is the way of destruction. If we continue to kill and destroy members of our extended family, how can we survive? We cannot live apart from nature. The air we breathe is made by the trees and by the ocean.

This is what the religion of Yoruba is all about. In the final analysis, Yoruba religion is the worship of nature.

LEAH: In Yoruba cosmology there are countless sacred birds, among them the *igun* (vulture), *akala* (ground hornbill), *agbe* (blue turaco), and *odidere* (parrot). The *Odu Irosun Ogbe* discusses the vulture's ascendence to the throne, while the *Odu Osa Meji* makes clear that without the vulture, the offerings and sacrifices of human beings would not reach the spirit world. There are taboos against harming many species of birds, including the Areregosun, who was gifted his beautiful maroon tail feathers from the ocean deity herself. Enroue, you have opened yourself to being a student of birds. What are some of the lessons they share with you?

AWO ENROUE ONIGBONNA SANGOFEMI HALFKENNY: While I was a student at Middlebury College, the forest was a haven away from the people, chaos, and dynamics of that small, liberal, white college environment. The forest was a place where I could inhabit a mystical relationship with Earth beyond what was taught in the biology department, and beyond even my own notions. Outside of the gaze of humans, and beyond the judgment of others, I walked through the back of the graveyard that bordered the campus, along the trail, across some old farmland, and up onto a berm with a lot of evergreens growing on it. I would creep through the grass and sit under the lowest branches of the evergreen trees where I could be hidden from sight and observe.

There was one poignant day when I was watching the songbirds flit about from tree to tree across the meadow, when suddenly everything fell quiet. There was no birdsong, no movement, no rustling, no chirping. I was struck by the absolute quiet and stillness. I sat quietly as well, waiting. Soon, I could see the shadow of a hawk gliding over the tall grass. I watched it pass, and some minutes after its departure, the wave of sounds and movement slowly returned. I realized the hawk was living in a bubble of silence. The small creatures were warned of the hawk's approach and fell silent in advance of its arrival, and the sounds only returned after the hawk was gone. Its existence was in silence, and yet in patient skill, it found a way to catch and eat things and to live. I could draw parallels to my own life—how I was seen or not seen by others. But more importantly, this moment solidified the personal importance of experiences of wonder and mystery in nature. They are what pulled me out of—and have kept me out of—despair, hopelessness, and isolation. I could see that beyond social dramas and interactions with people, there was life. There was life that I was actually connected to, and something here worthwhile to explore.

I continue to be connected to birds as teachers. I live near a wetland and migration corridor for birds, and I get to witness the movement of the starlings, grackles, and others. We also keep a bird feeder to welcome the songbirds and nourish these little beings who flit about ceaselessly. I love learning their names, paying attention to the sounds of their wings, noticing what their body does when they sing and whether the trill is sharp or long. I pay attention to how they respond to each other, and slow down enough to notice differences between the pigmentation on individual birds. It's a practice of patience and silence. It is also a practice of simple joy and beauty.

One of the many lessons that birds share with us is this: Even in the face of predation, habitat loss, and other stressors, birds continue to be birds. They sing, mate, eat, fly, raise their young, and follow the rhythms of the season. They honor the life that is within them.

LEAH: The Yoruba calendar offers us a cycle of the year anchored in reverence for particular nature divinities in their respective seasons. Olokun, ocean deity, is honored in *Erele* (February). Osanyin, plant medicine deity, and Yemoja, river deity, have their festivals alongside Orunmila, deity of wisdom, during the Yoruba New Year in *Okudu* (June). Orisa Oko, farm deity, is celebrated with the first yam harvest in *Agemo* (July.) Oya, Orisa of the storm and winds, has her celebration in *Owara* (October), to name a few. In the Diaspora, the festival calendar may vary, but the underlying principles are consistent. Yeye, how does your spiritual community honor the cycle of the seasons in connection with Orisa worship?

YEYE LUISAH TEISH: At the darkest time and turning over of each year, we have rituals to cleanse away the residual influences of the outgoing year. During our three- to four-day New Year rituals, we go to the ocean to wash ourselves and give gratitude for life on earth. We then do a full bembe drum ceremony where we honor Elegba and ask him to open the door to a new year. We do a divination to get guidance for our community for the year to come.

In the spring, we hold our festivals for Orunmila and Osun, deities of destiny and love, respectively. This ceremony involves bathing in the river. We often have men playing drums around a fire up on the mountain, and the women in the river bathing with a sweet coconut soap that we make together. Our songs are in call and response to the drum, honoring the relationship between the fire and the water. We make beautiful altars, and the people come to celebrate the fertility and promise of spring. The world is renewing itself.

Autumn is the time of the ancestors. In the fall, the veil gets thinner, and it becomes easier to walk into the ancestral village and back again. In 2019, we had a council for ancestral souls rising where we brought together priests from Nigeria, Tanzania, France, Brazil, Cuba, and all over the United States. We gathered on October 31 and went from one place to the next with people saluting their ancestor shrines and sharing their practices. Over a period of nine days, we illuminated the various layers of the soul. The Ancestral Souls Rising Global Prayers have continued online during the pandemic. The importance of ancestor reverence rites cannot be overstated. Whether the Voodoo ceremonies in New Orleans or the Festival of the Bones in Oakland, it is important to make time to participate in communal ancestral reverence.

I also think that it's important to pay attention to what is happening in related, earth-based traditions. I participate in Día de los Muertos, Diwali, the equinox and solstice rituals, and the gong ceremonies of the Buddhists. Each tradition has its own variations based on the land where it was born and the people of that land mass. But the truth is that as human beings we make cultural notions based on universal principles. It's the universal principles that we need to study.

LEAH: When we are still enough, we can hear the voice and lessons of the earth. Enroue, you have a beautiful practice of spending hours on end in nature's wild places listening and learning. I have seen you make offerings of honey and prayers at the entrance to the forest and then proceed into its sanctuary. What have your wilderness teachers—the trees, cattails, phragmites, and other creatures—shared with you recently?

AWO ENROUE ONIGBONNA SANGOFEMI HALFKENNY: The earth is not saying only one thing. Like any relationship, it is multiplicitous and based on the current moment. You and I were together in the forest shortly after my aunt passed away, and we heard the trees crying. As they rubbed their branches together, moaning, the song was a reminder to be here with this wound. The message was to feel and not to fix.

In the wetlands near my home, there are a lot of phragmites growing, which are a perennial reed grass invasive to the area. Prior to the arrival of phragmites, there were mostly native cattails growing in that wetland. Over time, the phragmites have advanced, making it difficult for the cattails to reproduce. Some of the cattails are on the front lines, watching the phragmites right across the water as they advance and take over. Other cattails are far from the juncture, and maybe they do not even know that they are losing out. Yet in all cases, how does the cattail respond? They continue to fully be a cattail. Even though in ten years they may all be gone, they continue in their expression of the fullness that is life. They do not ignore the challenge or engage in futile fighting or turn into something else. The lesson for me is that regardless of the hope or despair of the given moment, my directive is to be fully human. I hope to be able to live and die as the cattail does, to be a person of peace, love, and nurturing, and not of violence or fighting.

Even the phragmite is just doing what it needs to do to live. It did not decide to be an invasive species; it was brought here against its own will, not unlike some of my own ancestors. When we zoom out, we see that all species are just here on Earth trying to live. When a system is stable and something comes in to meddle and destabilize, that is also part of the natural reality of life on earth. We need to think about how to simultaneously minimize harm and to be present with what is.

Being in the rightness of relationship with the earth is also about recognizing that I cause harm, as we all do. I need to eat, which necessitates the taking of life. I am also part of capitalism, which is actively doing harm. Considering Earth as mother or father is in the right direction, but also incomplete, because there is so much more we can offer and receive in relationship to the earth. As a father, I get accidentally hurt by my children in their bumbling. Sometimes there may even be intentional hurt. This does not shut me off from loving them. We are dear to our father-mother Earth, and our harming does not shut us off from that love and that relationship. We are not separate. For me, the answers and meaning are not so much in studying the harm and the oppression. Meaning is revealed in the mystery and magic of the direct connection with the divine in nature, and in being open to the existence of something beyond what I initially think is present.

LEAH: Yeye, what do you think Mama Earth is saying to us right now? What do you hear when you listen in?

YEYE LUISAH TEISH: I think the best way I can answer that question is to summarize an eco-myth that I wrote in response to COVID-19 and in praise to Oya, the Queen of Change. It is called "Eartha's Children." It's about how humans invented war games to subjugate one another based on racial and religious differences, and then expanded that war to the assault on their own Mother.

As I wrote, "They felled the trees in the Ancient Forests and hunted Her beautiful animals almost to extinction. Soon their playthings produced a gray cloud of poison that filled the sky. The creatures in the Ocean, trapped in nets and plastic, cried out in pain. She too cried out as they pierced Her body and drained the black blood from her veins.

"Mother Earth doubled over in pain, stomping her feet and sending tsunamis of warning. She demanded they put down their weapons of war, but only a few complied. She then dawned a Crown of Power on her head and commanded in a booming voice, 'Now hear this: I am Your Mother, Your Queen, and Your Salvation. GO TO YOUR ROOM.' She bellowed, 'Get in there and clean up the mess you've made. Put away those weapons of mass destruction. Take out the trash of fear, hatred, and greed . . . Go into the silence, the stillness within. There you will find your birthright, your humanity, and my Love. Practice humility and respect. Don't make me repeat myself.' The children of Earth complied at last."

You see, we humans have been miseducated to think that if we have money, we can trek into anyone's country, exploit the people, destroy the land, hunt the animals to extinction, and disregard the sacred. All of our societal and personal decisions are impacted by this thinking in the back of our minds that it's alright to exploit natural resources. This simply does not work. There are truths about human life and nature that existed before we were called into this industrial-technological complex. The Indigenous knowledge of our most ancient land-rooted ancestors has been pressed out of most of us.

Our present behavior is species suicide. Mother Earth is forcing our hand now, and we have a choice to change our ways or go into extinction. The pandemic brought us the anthro-pause where we had a glimpse into how nature could flourish without humans trampling all over the earth. Without the cruise ships, the dolphins were having a grand time swimming. Lions were lying about on the freeway in South Africa. We can imagine how nature would flourish if we repositioned our human selves in that flow as another relative in the overall plan of nature, and not as master, dominator, or conquistador. If we do not awaken that relationality, then we humans become the virus.

LEAH: Baba, in *Ifa Will Mend Our Broken World*, you describe several phases of human existence. The serene and all-inclusive age of the world when humans and the rest of creation regarded themselves as brothers and sisters is known as Oba Jomi Jomi (the age of the king who ate water). This was the regime of Obatala, characterized by a peaceful and tranquil period, like water. As society became more settled and populous, there came the age of Oba Jegi Jegi (the age of the king who ate wood). This is the age of iron, belonging to Ogun and associated with war, metal, manufacturing, urbanism, and creativity. It was Ogun who fabricated the iron implements with which violence was done to the rest of creation. We are now in the age of Oba Jeun Jeun (the age of the king who consumes), which is connected to industry, processed food, greed, and exploitation.[9] As we think toward the next age of humanity in which a new covenant can be made, what are its principles? How can we move beyond force and exploitation, and toward reverence and interdependence?

AWISE AGBAYE WANDE ABIMBOLA: There is a verse in *Osa Meji* where Earth herself goes for divination. She is told that she should not be making *ebo* to be wealthy and prosperous, but instead to perform sacrifice on account of her many enemies. Western industrialism and European colonization are the number one enemies of Mother Earth. We should not be the people Earth is doing *ebo* to protect herself from. The verse ends, "We are certainly alive; And we are pleading; That as long as we remain on the earth; The earth may never be destroyed."[10]

Earth herself is a great divinity. All of Earth's creatures and elements are also sacred. There is no functional difference between animals, trees, rivers, mountains, and dewdrops. The only hope for our future is to revive the ancient knowledge that the earth and all creatures of the world deserve respect. The ones who remember this best are the peasant farmers, who are perhaps that last hope for mankind. I think we are in a moment of truth, where people are seeing farming and working close to the land in a new light. Perhaps if we are to survive to our next age it will be Oba Ero Ero, the age of the antidote. Don't be discouraged. Ifa is the medicine that will heal our broken world.

ALL THAT BREATHES GIVES PRAISE

*A Conversation with Ibrahim Abdul-Matin
and Chris Bolden-Newsome*

All living beings roaming the earth and winged birds soaring in the
sky are communities like yourselves. We have left nothing out of the
Record. Then to their Sustainer they will be gathered all together.

—QURAN 6:38

The Abrahamic faiths—Judaism, Islam, and Christianity—get a bad
rap when it comes to environmental ethics and practice. In Genesis
1:28, God said to humans, "Be fruitful and multiply and replenish
the earth and subdue it; have dominion over every living thing." This
anthropogenic directive was seized upon by historians like Lynn White
and Arnold Toynbee to make the case that Abrahamism, with its emphasis on domination and expansion, was to blame for the present-day
ecological crisis.[1] This philosophical underpinning seems to bear out in
practice. Recent studies show that Christians are less likely to be concerned about the environment than non-Christians.[2] In the UK, Muslims are less likely to be concerned about climate change than the general
population due to a faith in the afterlife and divine intervention.[3] Taken
together, Abrahamic monotheism is practiced by over half of the world's

human population, so it is imperative to address the apparent incongruity between creed and earth wisdom.

I have worked to reconcile this troubled ecological report card with my own experience of faith. Growing up, I was a "double PK" (preacher's kid), with my mother, Rev. Dr. Adele Smith-Penniman, pastoring a Unitarian Universalist congregation and my father, Keith Penniman, serving as an itinerant lay service leader for churches across the Northeast. I was devout in my faith, nurturing my own independent practice in addition to weekly church attendance. As a nine-year-old, I would light a candle and sing my favorite hymn before bed: "Here I am Lord, is it I Lord? I have heard you calling in the night. I will go Lord, if you lead me . . ."[4] In this hymn, God identifies as the God of wind, rain, stars, sea, sky, snow, and love. I believed that the divine calling was to serve and protect the earth.

Though we may not be the statistical majority, I am not alone in my understanding of Abrahamic faiths as driving an environmental imperative. There are those who argue that the fundamental Abrahamic teachings, taken apart from the distorting lens of centuries of patriarchy and settler expansion, adhere to an earth ethic.

Present-day Jews are extrapolating the law of *bal tashchit*, the prohibition against the destruction of fruit trees in times of war, to apply to the stewardship of all natural resources and all of nature. Mosques like Park51 at Ground Zero are getting certified as "green" and making explicit the connections between faith and environmental stewardship.[5] The National Black Church Initiative, representing over fifteen million Black Christians, has been working to stop global warming for over twenty years.[6]

It was fascinating to uncover a recent study concluding that, while people of Abrahamic faiths may be less environmentally concerned overall, Black and Hispanic Christians are more concerned about climate change than both white Christians and secular people. Black and Hispanic clergy are also more likely than white clergy to talk about climate change with their congregations.[7] Could it be that Black and Brown people of faith are generally more ecologically concerned than the faith community at large? Could it be that soil-hued people are remembering the original ecological teachings of their respective faiths?

To understand how Islam and Catholicism can inform "right relationship" with the earth, we speak to two devout people of faith, Ibrahim Abdul-Matin and Chris Bolden-Newsome.

IBRAHIM ABDUL-MATIN (he/him) is the author of *Green Deen: What Islam Teaches about Protecting the Planet*. He is also the cofounder of Green Squash Consulting, a management consulting firm based in New York that works with people, organizations, companies, coalitions, and governments committed to equity and justice, and specializes in dynamic, strategic, and focused stakeholder management and partnership development. He sits on the boards of the International Living Future Institute, encouraging the creation of a regenerative built environment, and Sapelo Square, whose mission is to celebrate and analyze the experiences of Black Muslims in the US. He is a bright, playful spirit whose unique voice has helped elevate the environmental vision of Islam and the spiritual opportunity of parenting.

CHRISTOPHER BOLDEN-NEWSOME, originally from the Mississippi Delta, is the oldest son of farmers and justice workers Demalda Bolden Newsome and Rufus Newsome Sr., and a fourth-generation free farmer since emancipation in 1865. In 2010, Chris joined Ty Holmberg in creating the Sankofa Community Farm at Bartram's Garden, a spiritually rooted, African-Diaspora, urban-centered farm and youth development program. In 2012, Chris married seed farmer Owen Smith Taylor with whom he cofounded the cultural preservation and rematriation-focused seed company Truelove Seeds.

LEAH: Dr. George Washington Carver was a devout Christian and had a practice of waking before dawn to go pray in the forest. He believed that nature was God's broadcasting system and credited his conversations with plants as informing his numerous scientific breakthroughs and patents. He explained, "Reading about nature is fine, but if a person walks in the woods and listens carefully, he can learn more than what is in books, for they speak with the voice of God."[8] You both have talked about experiencing God through nature. Can you share a story about this resonance?

IBRAHIM ABDUL-MATIN: I spent my early childhood in the New York boroughs of Queens and Brooklyn, where my brother and I believed that the entire world was a sea of concrete buildings. When I was five or six, our father gave us our first immersive experience in nature, a hiking trip on Bear Mountain. The time for afternoon prayer arrived while we were ascending, and my father stopped to pray. My brother and I were perplexed and asked our father where he was going to pray. Up until then, prayer had always been something done at home or in a mosque. He pointed to a small area on the ground, where he had brushed aside twigs and leaves. Our father related a hadith of the Prophet Muhammad (peace be unto him), "Wherever you may be at the time of prayer, you may pray, for the Earth is all a mosque."[9] In that instant, as we knelt to pray, I understood. The earth is a mosque, and a mosque is sacred; therefore, the earth is sacred. We are all one—all part of the same wonderful fabric of creation.

CHRIS BOLDEN-NEWSOME: I am a practitioner of *in-cultured* African (American) Catholic Christianity particularly, which has provided the pattern for my life and informed my earth practice. So much of Catholic Christianity has its origins within an earth-based African context that existed way before its settling and redefinition in central Europe. The Catholic Church as a whole is catching up to its origins. Starting in 1971, with Pope Paul VI, the church has expressed ecological concern, which amplified to an urgent appeal by 2015, with Pope Francis writing:

If we approach nature and the environment without this openness to awe and wonder, if we no longer speak the language of fraternity and beauty in our relationship with the world, our attitude will be that of masters, consumers, ruthless exploiters, unable to set limits on their immediate needs. By contrast, if we feel intimately united with all that exists, then sobriety and care will well up spontaneously. The poverty and austerity of Saint Francis were no mere veneer of asceticism, but something much more radical: a refusal to turn reality into an object simply to be used and controlled.[10]

At its core, Catholicism—and this reflects the African Spiritual ethos in general, I think—is a practice of deep reverence for the intertwinedness of matter and spirit, and regard for the indispensable role of ancestors, be they blood ancestors, canonized saints, or cultural ancestors like Baba George Carver. At the center of this belief is our understanding that God chooses to connect with creation in Yeshua (Jesus). The essential unity of spirit and matter means that I can't do anything earthly that does not have a spiritual ramification, and vice versa. I show the same respect for the spider and the snake as I do for people. They are valued friends.

LEAH: I am glad you mentioned your respect for snakes. I remember visiting you at Sankofa Farms, and a garter snake crossed our path. Both of us bent down simultaneously to touch the ground and greet the snake. I was coming from a Haitian Vodun perspective at that moment, greeting Damballah, the creator spirit, and was honestly surprised that my Catholic friend would show reverence for a snake. How did you understand that moment?

CHRIS BOLDEN-NEWSOME: When I see a snake in my garden, I feel so blessed, so I greet them in one of their ancient names and thank them. All creatures bring us God's wisdom—they are agents and living sacramentals of the guardian spirits of the land. My father is an evangelical Protestant in the Church of Christ, and he taught me to honor snakes in the garden because they help keep balance in the field by hunting rodents and herbivorous insects. I also learned growing up to honor snakes as a symbol of the resurrection, since they renew themselves through ecdysis. My mother is a Catholic who kept African traditions alive in her faith context, only putting up Black and Brown icons in our home, sprinkling salts in corners and cayenne pepper at the door to ward off evil. Catholic Christianity has historically not shied away from expressing itself through the *paganos* traditions around the world. *Paganos* means country people, or people of the earth, and is related to *paesano*. For example, in Haiti, some Catholic churches pour libations and blow the conch in the four directions before starting Catholic mass. Black Catholicism integrates and expands this spiritual web, which we call the Communion of Saints, rather than erasing our Indigenous ways.

LEAH: The Abrahamic faiths, including Islam and Christianity, have been blamed for humanity's extractive and dominating relationship to the earth. Ibrahim, is this blame misplaced? What does Islam teach about environmental stewardship?

IBRAHIM ABDUL-MATIN: Islam teaches a deep love of the planet, because loving the planet means loving ourselves and loving our creator. There are a number of ecological principles in Islam, among them understanding the oneness of God and creation (*tawid*), seeing signs of God everywhere (*ayat*), being a steward of the earth (*khalifah*), honoring the covenant we have with God to protect the planet (*amana*), moving toward justice (*adl*), and living in balance with nature (*mizan*).

The Western way of being is a digression from these ancient principles, not an enactment of them. Western culture has made humans into a virus, a cancer on the earth, extracting and destroying as we go. This is rape culture, and it is impacting people, impacting culture, and impacting the earth, and is deeply rooted in our economic system. *Khalifah* means stewardship, not being overlords. We are the gardeners who have been entrusted by God to maintain healthy and balanced ecosystems. Everything and everyone in God's creation has intrinsic value.

Mizan is the Arabic word for balance. I often think about our vulnerability being on this planet with just a thin layer of atmosphere that separates us from the harshness of outer space. We have never visualized gravity, yet it is the powerful force that maintains the atmosphere, allowing life to exist. The sun and moon, the rain and wind, the crops and wild plants all exist in a delicate balance. When the balance is disturbed, it's an affront to justice, and all life will speak against the perpetrator before God. Every blade of grass that we have poisoned will speak against us, and every tree we chop down will speak against us. But every place we take care of will speak for us, too. Our deeds are recorded in the natural world and we will be held to account.

LEAH: I think a lot about how separated we can be from the earth in modern times, living behind steel and glass, unaware of the phase of the moon, the height of the sun in the sky, or the weather outside. Islam and Judaism both follow a lunar calendar, which requires an attunement to cosmic cycles. Catholics follow a seasonal cycle of prayer, marking the "ordinary time" of winter, summer, and autumn. I also understand that Muslim prayer practice attunes devotees to daily cycles. Is it also true that the practice of prayer itself connects you both to natural cycles?

IBRAHIM ABDUL-MATIN: Muslims pray five times a day: predawn when the thin red line appears in the sky (*fajr*), noon when the sun reaches a high point (*dhuhr*), midafternoon (*asr*), when the sun starts to go down (*maghrib*), and evening when the sky is black (*isha*). God has given us a tool to anchor and orient to cosmological reality, to connect to the movement of ourselves on this planet in relationship with the sun and moon, and to remind us that we are part of this whole cosmic experience. Rather than feeling small and insignificant, I feel important and part of everything in creation. Ever since I completed Hajj (pilgrimage to Mecca), I have remained committed to consistent prayer and daily recitation of verses of the Quran. Children do what they see their parents do, not what they hear us instruct. I remember my father getting up at 3 a.m. to pray. He was deep in meditation, receiving information from the creator of the universe, and I just sat there and watched without him noticing me. This was one of the most important moments of my life, and a catalyst for my own practice. When I put my sons to bed at night, I recite the Quran and pray, and they get to listen and witness. Now, as they are learning the Quran and developing their own practice, my example of prayer in nature is even more important. I do not want them to think of worship as something set apart or done solely indoors. I want their understanding of faith to always be in balance with the natural world.

CHRIS BOLDEN-NEWSOME: Daily prayer is part of my practice as well. I begin each day at the farm with a land-greeting ritual and pour water libations on the earth. St. Augustine of Hippo was an African who came out of the ancient Nubian church, which was very earth based and required baptisms to be done in living, moving water. They poured libations and honored "Mother Dirt" and the ancestors. So, in that tradition, this is my prayer:

Glory to you, creator, redeemer, sustainer of all of the world,
as it was in the beginning, is now, and always shall be.
World without end. Amen.

Chukwu onye kere ihenyile . . . Chukwu onye kere ihenyile . . .
Chukwu onye kere ihenyile[11]
Pure loving God, I offer this drink in thanksgiving for life.—Ise
To you sweet Mother Earth, from whom I come, to whom I return.
I offer you this drink—Ashe

To you sweet grandmothers—Ise
To you sweet grandfathers—Ise
All my aunts—Ise
All my relations, all those lost to me—Ashe

LEAH: In addition to the daily cycles of prayer, the seasonal cycles of tending crops can connect us with the divine. Chris, can you speak about your work with biblical and ancestral plants and how that is part of your spiritual practice as an African Catholic?

CHRIS BOLDEN-NEWSOME: Castor bean is a biblical crop that we grow at Sankofa Farms. The plant is quite beautiful to behold, repels mice and voles, and is allelopathic. Castor, an African plant, also reminds us of our duty to face difficult work, as described in the Book of Jonah. The reluctant prophet Jonah was instructed by God to go to Nineveh, capital of the Assyrian Empire in modern-day Iraq, to prophesy. Ninevites were enemies and oppressors of Jonah's people, and he did not want to help them, so he fled in the opposite direction by sea. After a stormy ocean and a trip in the belly of a whale forced Jonah to complete his mission, he was bitter and resentful. He sat in the desert brooding, and God provided a *kikayon*, a castor bean plant, to grow up around him and provide shade. It's notable that the castor bean plant is somewhat poisonous, a reflection of the negative and venomous perspective of Jonah. God then took away the castor bean plant, leaving Jonah to swelter in the sun.

Then God said to Jonah, "Are you so deeply grieved about the plant?"

"Yes," he replied, "so deeply that I want to die."

Then God said: "You cared about the plant, which you did not work for and which you did not grow, which appeared overnight and perished overnight. And should not I care about Nineveh, that great city, in which there are more than a hundred and twenty thousand persons who do not yet know their right hand from their left, and many beasts as well!"[12]

We grow the castor bean to remember this lesson on compassion. In honor of our ancestors, we also grow the foods that were part of their lineage—black-eyed peas, okra, cotton, collard greens, taro, and the Gullah black peanut. Our version of the three mo' sisters is sorghum intercropped with sweet potato and field peas. Sorghum is the mother grain, fit and appropriate for this changing climate. These foods become central to our missionary work, as we reevangelize people to their own foods and their own ancestral ways of being. Food is the entry point to reawakening people to who we are. God communicates to us through food, from the Jewish *motzi* (blessing over bread) to the Eucharist, where we partake in the blood and body of Christ as food. Immersing in sacred foods is a step toward reconnecting folks to our collective consciousness, moving past the illusion of death, and opening us up to let the earth teach us. Our gardens should double as shrines.

LEAH: Ibrahim, it was very powerful to hear you speak about your book, *Green Deen*, as a work of translation that would allow environmental movement folks to connect with the Muslim community. You understand that the environmental movement will fail without all of us onboard, including people of faith. One of the compelling parallels that you draw relates to renewable and nonrenewable energy. Can you share a Muslim interpretation of our sources of energy?

IBRAHIM ABDUL-MATIN: We derive the power we use from both renewable and nonrenewable sources. The nonrenewable sources I describe as "energy from hell." These sources include oil, gas, coal, and nuclear energy—sources that extract from deep in the ground. This hell energy is dirty; causes pollution, climate change, and environmental racism; and takes from the earth without giving back. It disturbs the balance (*mizan*) of the universe and is therefore a great injustice (*zulm*).

In contrast, "energy from heaven" is renewable—it comes from above, from the wind and the sun, and from more sustainable consumption practices, including increased efficiency. The call for a green economy and green jobs is about innovating to obtain energy from heaven. One way we can stand out firmly for justice is by ending our reliance on all extractive sources like oil and coal.

In places where the flow of energy is seldom interrupted, like the Western world, we need to start seeing energy as a blessing. You don't squander blessings.

LEAH: Indeed, if we were to see natural resources as blessings, as gifts from God, it would be difficult to justify wastefulness. One of the places where we experience natural resources being wasted and abused is with water. Globally, two billion people are drinking water contaminated by human feces. Nearly half of the world's population lives in water-stressed areas, a condition worsened by climate change.[13] At the same time that Americans waste upward of a trillion gallons of fresh water per year, mighty rivers like the Colorado and the Rio Grande are at risk of running dry due to overuse.[14] How does your faith inform your relationship with water?

IBRAHIM ABDUL-MATIN: There is a hadith that even if you are at a flowing river, you should conserve water. Water is sacred and part of our tradition. Before prayers, we make *wudu* (ablutions) as a ritual purification of the body and the soul. This practice came about among desert people who had to be super mindful about water usage. The Zamzam Well in Mecca is a miraculously generated source of water from Allah, which sprang spontaneously thousands of years ago when Hajar and her son Isma'il were exiled to the desert, parched and despondent. That sacred well flows to this day, drawing millions of pilgrims. Imagine such reverence for water. I believe we need to plan our societies around watersheds, rather than political boundaries. Orienting ourselves to fresh clean water as the organizing principle for building our settlements makes good sense. We need to govern at a regional scale and determine population size and development based on natural resource availability.

LEAH: We have been talking a lot about the reverence that Black People of the Book have for nature—from water to spiders to flowers. But we would be remiss to avoid also talking about the nature-based trauma that Black people have endured. African Americans are 75 percent more likely to live near hazardous waste facilities than other Americans, putting us at heightened risk for lung diseases including asthma, heart disease, premature death, and COVID-19.[15] When breathing the outdoor air in your neighborhood can literally kill you, it's hard to wax poetic about God's creation. Similarly, a history of chattel slavery and sharecropping puts a sour taste in our mouths, even as we recognize the divine sanctity of soil.

CHRIS BOLDEN-NEWSOME: Posttraumatic Slave Syndrome, as described by Dr. Joy DeGruy, is a powerful spiritual, psychological, and physical force. When young people come to the farm, they start making jokes about slavery and making up their own version of spirituals to try to process this trauma. The field was the scene of the crime, so it's not going to be easy coming home to the land. Our trauma is like a grain of sand that gets into a clam. She can't cough it out, so she keeps covering it up. The resulting pearl looks beautiful and it is ours because it was passed down through our mothers, but what's inside of the smooth shine is a lot of deep trauma. We must notice the pearl and recognize how important it is for people to hold on to the pearl. Just as a pearl becomes part of the clam, this metaphorical trauma pearl becomes part of our story, too. If we yank it out, we will kill the clam, and we don't want to do that. We need to figure out how to live with this double consciousness that W. E. B. Du Bois describes, and faith is a part of that liberation.[16]

A lot of people migrated North and became faithless, but I don't know any Black people in the South who don't acknowledge God. When we have faith in God, we know that we were created with an eternal purpose and so we are supposed to be able to figure out how to live well. We recognize that the world and the universe is bigger than this moment, and bigger than any particular condition we find ourselves in. We have a long story, and we are equipped for the days ahead.

LEAH: One of the most powerful stories for me in the Torah, which is shared in the Quran and Christian Bible, is that of Moses coming down from Mount Sinai with the tablets of *mitzvot* (sacred obligation), only to find that his community has started worshipping a statue forged of gold. I interpret this moment as a critique of the lures of capitalism and human supremacy—of the imagining that with our own hands we can fashion something superior to what God has created in nature. Ibrahim, can you share your perspective on the golden calves of our times?

IBRAHIM ABDUL-MATIN: The idols of today are capitalism and white supremacy. We have been brainwashed to think that capitalism and white supremacy are inevitable. We have bought into a scarcity mindset, believing that some people don't deserve food, don't deserve water or home or love. We have been made to believe some people belong in jails and prisons. We need to rewire our brains to think apart from extraction and into regeneration. We need to have an open conversation about the capitalist, white supremacy project and what it has done to us. Representation matters, but it's not enough. I do not want a Black woman leader authorizing a drone strike against people any more than I want a white man to do that, so we need a complete reframe.

CHRIS BOLDEN-NEWSOME: Catholic Liberation Theology teaches me that God exercises the preferential option for the poor, for the "least of these" among us.[17] This means that we need to be transferring power and dignity to the elder who needs help watering her plants, to the creeping plantains just trying to make it through a crack in the sidewalk, and to all those who have been overlooked and swept aside. This applies to marginalized genders and sexualities as well—to women, transgender folks, lesbians, gays, and the whole tribe.

A trans Catholic sister of mine, Mariya, points out that the first Gentile Christian was likely an "Ethiopian" eunuch.[18] He was in Jerusalem for a festival and working for the Queen of Nubia. In today's language, "he" could be understood as being a Black transgender person. Mary, mother of Yeshua, is the venerated mother of the Church and the model for us to follow. So the idea that women or trans folks don't belong is a distortion.

When I say I believe in Sankofa, I don't mean let's go part of the way back. I mean let's go all the way back and pick up what was left behind. Back before our maroon mother in Suriname bound up seeds in her hair while she ran for freedom. Back to our Afro-Semitic roots, and then even further back. Back to the women in Africa who were planting, harvesting, and processing rice and officiating rituals of ancestor worship. There we will see the crucial and essential role of women as connected to the earth in its material and cosmological dimensions. As a same-gender loving man, it has been a deep blessing to build relationships with the "Christian colored ladies" in our Philadelphia neighborhood, some of whom are religiously very conservative. We got to know each other through the work in the garden and built friendships that allowed them to see beyond my being married to another man. Over the years we have bonded ourselves to one another beyond our differences through prayer, singing, cooking, laughter, mourning, and gardening together.

LEAH: You are both people who have cultivated the art of listening to and hearing what Earth has to say. What is she communicating?

CHRIS BOLDEN-NEWSOME: The constant and repeated song of Earth echoes God's song to the cosmos and toward humanity, "I love you and you are mine." As we get more "advanced," we hear that less and less, which is one of the reasons the soil has instructed me that no cell phone calls are allowed in our garden. The earth is not a place of suffering, and only becomes so when we live in conflict with the earth and each other. For example, the roots of this pandemic can be traced back to greed, selfishness, and hoarding. Until we love one another, we will die. This is not a punishment or a curse, but a natural consequence of what our wrong actions are requesting. The earth is constantly reminding us and guiding us back to the divine path, which is love.

IBRAHIM ABDUL-MATIN: Everything in creation is always praying to God. If you are listening and resonating, you will hear nature praying: "Let the fields be jubilant, and everything in them; let all the trees of the forest sing for joy."[19] Sufi saints say they can hear the plants, birds, and trees praising and saying the names of God.[20] We are instructed to walk through nature as if reading the Quran, and to read the Quran as if we are walking through nature. The word *ayat* refers to both verses of the Quran and to cosmic and natural phenomena. Thus, when we destroy the earth, we are silencing voices of praise. I aspire to be like my aunt Dell from Virginia, a devout Christian until the day she died, who sang psalms beautifully while she fried fish, and my dad and the whole family would gather around and resonate. I aspire to be like my father, her nephew, who recited the Quran in the forest. Both of them were in constant dialogue with the natural world. Along with all of nature, humans are invited to be in constant prayer.

QUEER EARTH BIOMIMICRY

A Conversation with Toi Scott and adrienne maree brown

Could we communicate more like manatees, who stay in
communication in all kinds of emergencies, place their bodies in a
way that protects children, touch each other to remember and know?

—ALEXIS PAULINE GUMBS, *UNDROWNED*

nder the darkness of the new moon, and in the wake of devastating
Hurricane Matthew, the soil-hued delegates of Ayiti Resurrect
placed our white taper candles around the base of a majestic elder mapou tree (*Cyphostemma mappia*). The setting was the village of
Bigonet, Haiti, and the ceremony was *Milocan*, a feeding of the *loa*, the
divinities of nature in Haitian Vodun. In order to succeed in drilling a
new water well, replanting hurricane-devastated crops, and running a
holistic health clinic, we would need the support of the same earth spirits
that our Haitian forebears enlisted in the successful uprising of 1791–1804.
In Vodun, trees are considered *poto mitan*, center posts that connect the
physical world to the spiritual world. The two worlds meet at the base of
the tree, and it is at this crossroads that prayers and offerings are made. The
tree is the great connector.

In ecosystems, elder trees also serve as a type of crossroads, connecting kin and nonkin species in an interdependent and mutualistic web.

Known as "hub trees" or "mother trees," these elders share carbon, water, nutrients, and alarm signals through a network of underground fungal mycelium. Fungal threads link nearly every tree in a forest, weaving them together in a wooded superorganism. Resources tend to flow from the oldest and biggest trees to the youngest and smallest, even across species. Though when a mother tree is stressed or sick, the younger trees will reverse the flow of water and nutrients to shore her up. When a tree's death is imminent, it will often bequeath its carbon and nutrients to its neighbors as a parting gift so as not to deprive the ecosystem of the richness bound up in its biomass. The mycelium benefit as well. By fusing with tree roots, they help plants extract and uptake minerals in exchange for some of the tree's liquid sunlight in the form of sugars.[1,2]

Since Darwin's time, Western biologists have viewed nature as a competition between individuals for dominance and survival, a perpetual contest among discrete organisms to proliferate their selfish genes in the next generation. This narrow philosophy placed all living creatures in a ceaseless contest for limited natural resources and provided inspiration for Adam Smith's free market theories, which proposed that societal order would emerge from selfish competition. Scientists also imagined Western society's Christian values of heteronormativity, the gender binary, and patriarchy as informed by innate "natural" inclinations. Emerging knowledge of the mother trees and the forest superorganism have challenged this framework. In recent literature, scientists are advocating for greater attention to the role of cooperation, rather than the self-interest of lone species, to the emergent properties of symbiotic living ecosystems, and to the queerness inherent in the natural world.[3]

If cooperation is as central to evolution as competition, then the theory of natural selection can only remain sound by expanding the definition of the individual. There are countless examples in nature of an individual performing a cooperative, altruistic behavior that seems, at face value, to be detrimental to their own fitness. For example, vampire bats regurgitate their own blood to prevent other bats from starving. Ground squirrels, velvet monkeys, and prairie dogs cry out to warn their peers of predators, even though drawing attention to themselves increases their chance of being eaten. Ants and bees give their lives to protect their colonies. Birds migrate in a V-formation where each bird, with the exception of the first, benefits from the upwash from the wing-tip vertices of the bird ahead, reducing their average energy output by 12 to 20 percent as compared to flying alone. The birds take turns being the hard-working leader to fairly distribute the burdens of flight fatigue among the community.[4] In all the aforementioned cases, these animals are behaving according to kin selection or group selection, where the group, rather than the individual, is the unit upon which natural selection acts to favor beneficial traits.

Plants, animals, and fungi also cooperate across species and sometimes across kingdoms, further undermining the fallacy of ubiquitous lone competitors in nature. Lichens are a symbiotic collaboration between algae and fungi, where the fungi support the algae's survival in extreme conditions in exchange for photosynthate, the sugar that is produced by photosynthesis. Nitrogen fixation is only possible through an interkingdom mutualism between leguminous plants and rhizobia bacteria. Insect pollination, which we depend upon for 80 percent of human food crops, relies upon a relationship between flowering plants and insects.[5] Humans would be unable to digest food without the 10^{13} to 10^{14} microbes living in each of our guts, which match or outnumber the human cells in our body.[6,7] Scientists are now arguing that the concept of the individual organism needs rethinking, and that multicellular organisms and their symbiotic microbes may be regarded as cohesive units acted on by natural selection. Perhaps the entire forest or ocean ecosystem should be regarded as one cohesive unit.

Not only is nature profoundly cooperative, it is also profoundly queer. At least 90 percent of flowering plants have hermaphroditic bisexual flowers that contain both male and female reproductive organs. The Dungowan bush tomato is sexually fluid, with its bright purple flowers alternating their sexual expression. Same-sex intimacy, including court-ship, pair-bonding, affectionate touch, intercourse, and parental activities, has been documented in over 450 species of animals worldwide.[8] Among birds, queer love has been seen in black swans, albatrosses, blue ducks, ibises, mallards, penguins, vultures, and pigeons. Mammals that regularly exhibit gay intimacy include Amazon dolphins, American bison, twenty species of bats, bottlenose dolphins, elephants, giraffes, marmots, lions, polecats, bonobos, gorillas, Japanese macaques, orangutans, monkeys, sheep, and spotted hyenas. There are queer lizards and tortoises. Even among insects and arachnids, dragonflies, fruit flies, and bed bugs have same-sex relationships. Queerness is not a nonnormative exception, but rather a necessary component of many species' persistence and well-being.

If we seek to emulate nature to exist more sustainably as humans—to engage in a practice of cultural biomimicry—then we must recognize that the earth is more cooperative and queer than Western science has postulated. To further explore the idea of cultural biomimicry, we are joined by Toi Scott and adrienne maree brown.

TOI SCOTT (they/them) is a Black and Indigenous earth and wisdom keeper, ceremony holder, diviner, and medicine and prayer maker ded-icated to Afro-Indigenous and trans/nonbinary, queer, and sick and disabled folks of color knowing and understanding their sacredness, med-icine, and power. They are an *artivist*, playwright, spoken word artist, and multimedia artist who compiles and provides on- and offline resources for QTIBIPOC communities. Toi is part of a collaboration of Afro-Indigenous organizers, healers, and growers sharing knowledge, cocre-ating healing spaces, and honoring and reclaiming ancestral land and regenerative land practices, sustainable building techniques, and ways of being while centering Afro-Indigenous trans and queer and chronically ill and disabled folks in Borikén/Puerto Rico and across the Caribbean and Diaspora. Toi has also led anticolonial wisdom shares like the Herbal Freedom School and BIPOC Communiversity and Queering Herbalism medicine shares, which affirm the sacredness, relevance, and futurity of

Indigenous, Black, Brown, two-spirit, trans/gender nonconforming, and queer ancestral healing histories, medicine, science, and technologies.

ADRIENNE MAREE BROWN (she/her) is the writer-in-residence at the Emergent Strategy Ideation Institute, and has spent two and half decades as a movement worker focused on facilitation and mediation toward Black and Earth liberation. She is the author of *Emergent Strategy: Shaping Change, Changing Worlds*; *Holding Change: The Way of Emergent Strategy Facilitation and Mediation*; *We Will Not Cancel Us and Other Dreams of Transformative Justice*; *Pleasure Activism: The Politics of Feeling Good*; and *Grievers* (the first novella in the Black Dawn trilogy), and the coeditor of *Octavia's Brood: Science Fiction from Social Justice Movements*. She is the cohost of the *How to Survive the End of the World*, *Octavia's Parables*, and *Emergent Strategy* podcasts. After living around the world, and in New York City, Oakland, and Detroit, adrienne is rooting in Durham, North Carolina.

LEAH: Toi, your Mbuti ancestors placed supreme importance on the practices of silence and wordless song, which were learned by mimicking the sacred forest around them. Can you talk about this practice, which is both ancient and ongoing in the present day?

TOI SCOTT: I have many Indigenous African ancestors, the Mbuti among them. For the Mbuti, the forest is the supreme being, the sacred source of existence, council, and sanctuary. The Mbuti believe that they are children of the forest, and as such, they listen to and mimic the sounds of the forest as part of their practice. Just as the animals move stealthily to eat and not be eaten, so do the Mbuti move soundlessly throughout the forest. Silence does not imply lack of communication. The forest is always talking, and the quiet pauses between sounds, called *ekimi*, are the source of peace, while the noise, called *akami*, is the source of conflict. Across Africa, there are beliefs that silence makes space for the wisdom of the ancestors, and that silence is a form of spirit speech.[9,10]

The most valued songs of the Mbuti, such as the leaf carrying and honeybee songs, are wordless. The melodies and whispers of the music are powerful and magical. There is overlap between the Mbuti practice and that of the singers of *icaros* in South America. One novice studying the *icaros* said of his teacher, "He revealed to me magical songs, which some call *icaros*, and he showed me something more precious, how to gather music and live in the air, repeat them without moving my lips, sing in silence with the memory of heart." In both understandings, the animals have songs and the trees have songs. They sing their song and want to hear that song sung back through us.[11] In the noisy, wordy clamor of Western life, we miss out on hearing nature's song.

LEAH: *Emergent Strategy* is a cultural biomimicry manual, instructing us to embody fernlike fractal patterns in our societies and to be adaptable like water, among other potent metaphors. In the chapter on interdependence, you quote Black farmer and organizer Karissa Lewis:

> *Ants tell each other where the food is, not hoarding individually, but operating on a principle that the more of them that gather food, the more food they will have as a community. In nature, everything works in collaboration. The hummingbirds and flowers are in such deep coordination that they need each other for survival. How vibrant and alive and successful could our movement be if we moved with such coordination and collaboration.[12]*

adrienne, can you share more about how you understand interdependence as biomimicry and how it can apply in human societies?

ADRIENNE MAREE BROWN: Most of us are socialized toward independence, not interdependence, since we've been fed the value of pulling ourselves up by our bootstraps—of working on our own to develop, to survive, and to win at life. Competition is the opposite of mutual reliance, and we are trained to bring others down in order to get ahead, and to be proud of our individual accomplishments. While competition certainly exists in nature—think of the alpha in mating cycles—it is not the only, or even the dominant, organizing force. There is a connective tissue between all that exists—the way, the Tao, the Force, change, God/dess, life. Birds flocking, cells splitting, and fungi whispering underground all emphasize critical connections over critical mass and the importance of building mutual relationships. This concept builds upon a framework developed by Margaret Wheatley that says that the quality of our relationships matters more than the quantity. A community in an active and authentic visionary relationship is more resilient and impactful than a petition list of names. I'll share an excerpt of my poem titled "Love is an Emergent Process" that speaks to the theme:

i am an ant
who carries grandfather to the grave
in my palms
you lift the next day's meal
enough for everyone we know
we love in this rhythm
leaving home
and returning
on the wind[13]

The quality of our lives and our survival are tied to how authentic and generous our connections are between one another and the spaces we spend time in. Generosity means giving of what we have without strings or expectations attached. At the same time as we practice generosity, we need to lean into vulnerability and ask for what we need. Can you drive me to the hospital? Can you bring in my groceries? Can you hold me while I cry? Can you listen while I feel what I am feeling? Interdependence is not about the equality of offers in real time—that would be transactional exchange. We give freely and ask freely, knowing that at some future time the scales will be balanced. It feels incredible to be loved and cared for, and also to be able to meet an authentic need of someone else. The result is that we feel much more woven into the world, part of a connected fabric of community.

LEAH: The Yoruba ocean god Olokun (Yemoja in the Diaspora) is non-binary and trans, embodying both male and female characteristics and revered as a King Mother. It may not be coincidental that many sea creatures are also queer. Most starfish have both male and female reproductive organs. Lesbian albatrosses partner and parent for multiple consecutive years. Wrasse fish are born female but can change to become male given certain environmental conditions. Teenage orcas gather in male-only sexual groups, and seahorses have both male and female sexual partners. These examples exist amongst an abundance of oceanic queerness. Toi, you have been a trailblazer in the work of "queering herbalism," and you also have a deep connection to the deities of the queer ocean. Can you talk about your relationship to the ocean and how it informs your work?

TOI SCOTT: Yemaya/Yemoja is my mother, friend, and healer, and I've been in relationship with her for a very long time. One of my most sacred places is on the eastern coast of Borikén, in Luquillo, where the river meets the ocean. I give my offerings to the ocean there, and I sing the songs that Yemoja taught me during times of deep crisis and transition in my life. She wants me to sing her songs. She and Oshún and local spirits of the beach and waters have shown me how to work with the healing powers of shells, stones, and the water. At times, I have brought folks to share in honoring her and cleansing in her liquid embrace, to restore harmony and balance.

In Ayiti, the so-called Dominican Republic, I was part of a beautiful ceremony for the ocean spirit Yemoja, where we gathered many folks of many traditions and lineages including Afro-Cuban, Afro-Dominican, Taino, and Mexica queer folks and allies under the guidance of elder priestesses. The ocean welcomes us and sees us as we are. The whole beach was covered with conch shells, and we made beautiful offerings of flowers and fruits to the water.

In West African and Taino traditions, there are different genders associated with the Sea, and as a nonbinary person, I can relate. In fact, a lot of the work I do with my writing and wisdom shares queering herbalism, the Herbal Freedom School, and the BIPOC Communiversity centers BIPOC queer, two-spirit, transgender, gender nonconforming, and nonbinary people and focuses on connecting with our ancestors' medicine and healing. It's also important that we honor our own power and medicine and purpose.

It's said that in the past, queer, two-spirit, gender nonconforming, and transgender folks were often healers in many traditional societies across the planet. Existing between genders—neither male or female, or maybe being both—was thought to be a gift and considered sacred and balanced in some societies. It was believed that they could connect with the spirit realm and serve as messengers of the Creator and, also, as visionaries, dream interpreters, keepers and teachers of spiritual principles, and medicine people. They were mediators and bridges not only between people but also between humans and the spirit world. For example, among the Dagara in Burkina Faso, Sobonfu and Malidoma Somé have said that gay and lesbian people serve as "gatekeepers" between the physical world and the divine. The way they hold masculine and feminine energy allows them to be travelers and guardians of all multidimensional gates, as well as mediators and guides for all genders in their communities. Without them communities would fall apart, not all gates could be accessed, and communication with the other world where we get our teachings about rituals would be difficult.

Queer, two-spirit, and transgender communities are commonly portrayed as victims but look at what those who remember say about our power, medicine, and purpose. In Burkina Faso it's believed that some of us have power over elemental gates! It makes sense that I'd be so connected to Yemaya/Yemoja and Oshún and other water spirits.

One last thing I'll say: In another ceremony in Borikén, we had white tourists come and pick up the watermelon that we had offered to the Yemaya/Yemoja. They carried it off, no doubt to eat it. Some friends involved in the ceremony told them they had to return it to the ocean, that it did not belong to them. They resisted but eventually gave it back. Here is the lesson of the ocean: We humans owe everything, everything. Our debt to the oceans, the source of all life, is immeasurable and unpayable. Yemoja expects us to give back the small bit that we can give.

LEAH: Not only do fungi represent some of the largest and oldest organisms, with the honey mushroom reaching 2,400 years old and covering over 2,000 acres, but they also represent some of the most adaptive and resilient lifeforms. Fungi have evolved the unique ability to digest lignin and cellulose, without which the forests would pile miles high with dead undecomposed wood. Saprotrophic fungi have also evolved the ability to break down a wide variety of human-made toxic hydrocarbons, including petroleum fuels, polychlorinated biphenyls (PCBs), polyurethane, polycyclic aromatic hydrocarbons, phenols, and more.[14] adrienne, these fungal superpowers have inspired your writing on biomimicry. Can you talk about how mycoremediation and other fungal technologies offer humans relevant metaphors for our own community interactions?

ADRIENNE MAREE BROWN: I have a deep fascination with humans and their trauma, and the question of how we clear out what is painful, hurt, and toxic. When you inoculate land that is toxified with the right fungal spores, the fungus can process those toxins completely into inert and harmless compounds. Mycelium helps us to understand that toxicity is part of the cycle of life. Nothing is wasted when it comes to nature.

Everything is recycled and transformed. Trauma in human communities is ubiquitous, and it can cause us to behave in ways that are petty, shallow, and harmful, all to protect our hearts. The thought is that if I can dismiss you and tear you down, then you can't hurt me. We end up isolated, without our intact ecosystem, and unable to survive. Just as fungus recycles toxins, so do we have the essential work of composting trauma so that the harm is not reverberating across generations.

Fungus also teaches us the power of what is happening beneath. Almost all of the action takes place in the mycelium underground, where billions of tiny threads network and collaborate. When the mushroom, the fruiting body of the organism, emerges, it is evidence of something much more complex and expansive taking place outside of view. If we pluck the mushroom, it does not shift what is happening underground. As such, we are reminded not to focus all of our attention on the charismatic leader or the dramatic public disagreement. These visible phenomena point to something that needs attention below the surface. Like threads in a mycelial network, we are all connected to each other at our best and at our worst.

LEAH: Toi, you talk about cassava (*Manihot esculenta*) as an important plant teacher for you. Cassava is the third-most important source of carbohydrates in the tropics but is also blamed for mass paralysis and death.[15] What have you learned by being in relationship with this powerful plant?

TOI SCOTT: Cassava is deep. It has its origins in so-called South America, where in different traditions it's referred to as Mama Cassava. There is a deep connection to the plant across West Africa, the Caribbean, and the Diaspora. In Borikén, cassava, called yuca, is associated with *Yoka Hu* or *Yúcahu*, the divine masculine *cemi*, or spirit, associated with the life energy of the sun and the ocean. His cosmic counterpart is his mother, the *cemi* of the earth and fresh waters, *Atabey*. Together they make up the balanced supreme being *Yaya*. *Yúcahu* translates as "soul of yuca," a tuber that has provided sustenance to the Taino. There is a deep connection to the life cycle of cassava, the sun and the seasons, and Yoka Hu's journey of death and rebirth, which can be seen as having not only agricultural but also spiritual connotations.

Cassava has flowers of both genders and is representative of balance. Connecting back to the relationship between divine masculine and feminine, we see that cassava grows in the ground, Atabey's womb, but is also associated with the sky and life-giving energy of the sun, which are both connected to Yoka Hu. Differing Caribbean traditions honor and respect cassava as either a masculine or feminine higher being. In both African and Indigenous traditions of the Caribbean, cassava is seen as an offering. I was taught by my Taino elders that cassava should be made as an offering to the ancestors and spirit of the North, the direction of wisdom and experience.

Cassava is also a teacher of adaptation and abundance. Cassava is highly drought resistant and can adapt to thrive in harsh climates. The leaves are rich in protein and when sun dried are forage for cattle and chickens, and the tubers are rich in starches and provide carbohydrates for humans and livestock. Learning from cassava can help us to acclimate to changing conditions. The plants traveled from Turtle Island to Africa and back again. Like us, it is a multicultural, transcontinental being.

Cassava is also an early alarm of imbalance in the Democratic Republic of Congo. Cassava contains toxins that produce cyanide, which have to be boiled or soaked away so the eater is not poisoned and does not end up with *konzo* (Congolese Yaka word for paralysis) or other neurological disorders. A full week of soaking in water renders cassava tubers safe to eat. In times of climatic and political balance, farmers are able to grow the least toxic varieties of cassava and have ample time to process out the toxins. In times of war and migration, people are moving fast and have less time to process. They must defend against militia who run them off their farms and pull up and loot the least toxic varieties, while also undermining the stability needed to process the more toxic varieties. Sometimes fleeing families have no choice but to take the toxic varieties that aren't finished soaking or safe for consumption. In times of drought, the plant concentrates more toxins in its starchy flesh. We have seen the rates of *konzo* rise in West Africa as climate change has increased the frequency of drought, and as war and poverty disrupt community life. Cassava is sounding the alarm.[16]

LEAH: When we awaken to the messages that nonhuman living beings are constantly trying to communicate through their example, it's beautifully overwhelming how many truths are hiding in plain sight. I think of the way indeterminate tomatoes need their suckers pruned off, so that they can focus their energy on a central meristem (i.e., purpose) and become more disease resistant and higher yielding in the long run. This is a profound message for me as someone who has been pulled in too many directions and made myself sick with overcommitment. Tomatoes inspired me to do some necessary pruning. adrienne, you take lessons from the most quotidian of nature's teachings. Can you share what you've learned today?

ADRIENNE MAREE BROWN: I am in Detroit right now, and it's wintertime. My whole desk is a little greenhouse full of bromeliads, spider plants, aloe, and others. Throughout the day, I watch them move to seek the light and nourish themselves. It is so easy to turn our attention to what is wrong and what is not working. This can suck our energy and drown us in misery. Let's turn toward the sun and toward nourishment. We can curate what we pay attention to and lift up the artists, nature photographers, music makers, dancers, and creators of joy. We are invited to opt in to the liberation that is available to us. In *All About Love*, bell hooks reminds us that even in conditions of misery, we can make an all-encompassing commitment to do as well as we can. I want to be moonlight at my worst and sunlight at my best, in either case, bringing light into the spaces that I inhabit.

LEAH: Toi, you were once a small child playing in the creek with your cousins, studying flower anatomy with your sister, and enjoying mint from your school's medicine garden. Throughout your life, you have cultivated a practice of listening to nature as a teacher. What do you hear the earth saying to humanity at this moment?

TOI SCOTT: She tells us that our bodies are reflections of the earth. Whatever we do to our bodies, we do to the earth. Whatever we do to the earth, we do to our bodies. So the work is to learn to take care of our bodies as part of our sacred relationship with her. She wants us to come near, and to be more connected to her and to each other. Today she told me to treat the water as we would treat our own blood, and to treat the land as we would treat our own bones. We are reflections of the Earth Mother. She has spoken through the great shaking of earthquakes, the burning of forests, and explosions of volcanoes. All these things are happening, and we have to acknowledge them. It is time to give up our capitalist, destructive ways. The earth wants us to heal with her and to evolve spiritually.

LEAH: And for you adrienne, what do you hear the earth saying?

ADRIENNE MAREE BROWN: The earth is giving us a final invitation. Every species is part of a long dance to determine compatibility with all of life. Each species gets a chance to figure out its unique niche. Humans are struggling to figure out our way to be in relationship with the earth and all her creatures. We are addicted to our extractive practices, which assume access to unlimited resources from a limited earth. The earth produces what is needed, but humans are pulling more than what she consents to. We are oriented to the artificial construct of the nation state, whose borders are not acknowledged by weather patterns or migrating birds. Human survival will involve relinquishing these borders and instead tuning in to watersheds and natural formations of the land.

We have one final chance to figure out how we are going to become compatible with all of life and with the planet.

At this point, human actions will continue to have adverse impacts for at least another thirty to forty years. There will be hurricanes, drought, fire, ice storms, and wild weather. It is time to root down, find some land, some place on this earth to belong to, and get into a deep relationship. There is a shitstorm coming one way or another, and we need to build our land-based communities to survive through to the other side. For some Black folks, this activated homing instinct means a reverse migration home to the South, planting roots with the folks we want to be in community with. The pandemic is our practice round.

Wilds

*A Conversation with Dr. Lauret Edith Savoy,
Rue Mapp, and Audrey Peterman*

> Indeed, a journey through this park and the Sierra Forest Reserve to
> the Mount Whitney country will convince even the least thoughtful
> man of the needfulness of preserving these mountains just as they
> are, with their clothing of trees, shrubs, rocks, and vines, and of their
> importance to the valleys below as reservoirs for storage of water
> for agricultural and domestic purposes. In this, lies the necessity of
> forest preservation.
>
> —CHARLES YOUNG

Dr. *Martin Luther King Jr.* and Coretta Scott King were planning a
vacation to Fundy National Park in New Brunswick in 1960. Anticipating that a public park in Canada would be a welcome and
safe place to seek temporary refuge from the stress and bustle of urban
civil rights work, they nonetheless reached out in advance to ensure they
would be admitted. Harold DeWolf, Boston University professor and
friend of the Kings, wrote to the park innkeeper saying, "Canada's history being what it is, we are confident you would treat them well, but
want to make sure . . . The friends of whom I speak are a fine Negro

minister and his wife." The innkeeper responded, "We feel it would be better *not* to accommodate your friends."[1]

US national and state parks were comparably unwelcoming to Black people. When the National Park Service (NPS) was founded in 1916, Jim Crow laws and local customs kept African Americans on the outside. Even when NPS implemented de jure desegregation in 1945, local ordinances barred entry to Black people in many areas or relegated them to the inferior "Negro sections" of white parks. By 1952, there were 180 state parks in nine southern states available to white people, but only 12 state park areas for Black people.[2]

White supremacy was built into the parks system from the outset. The US national parks comprise eighty-four million acres of land that were stolen from Native communities through forced treaty agreements under the genocidal project of Manifest Destiny. Among these displaced Native people were twenty-six Indigenous groups living in Yellowstone. They were forced out in the 1870s in a settler effort to create, then protect, "uninhabited wilderness."[3] This became the blueprint for the "fortress conservation" strategy that has displaced Indigenous people across the globe, ignoring the fact that Indigenous communities currently protect around 80 percent of the planet's biodiversity.[4]

Some of the founders of the Western environmental movement espoused eugenics and white supremacy. Madison Grant was instrumental in creating the Everglades, Olympic, Glacier, and Denali National Parks as a strategy to strengthen the "Nordic race." Adolf Hitler referred to Grant's 1916 book, *The Passing of the Great Race*, as his "Bible." The first head of the US Forest Service, Gifford Pinchot, was on the advisory council of the American Eugenics Society and a delegate to the International Eugenics Congress. John Muir, who founded the Sierra Club in 1892, referred to Black and Indigenous people as "dirty, lazy, and uncivilized."[5] John James Audubon, famed ornithologist and scientific illustrator and namesake of the Audubon Society, owned slaves and stole human remains for a pseudoscientific study claiming white superiority.[6]

Perhaps Wallace Stegner was off the mark in claiming that national parks are, "The best idea we ever had—absolutely American, absolutely democratic." Despite the fact that 70 percent of people of color participate in the types of recreational activities offered in national parks, Black and Brown people are underrepresented among national park visitors.[7] A 2011 survey demonstrated that Hispanics and Asian Americans each comprised less than 5 percent of visitors to national park sites, while less than 2 percent of visitors were African Americans.[8] Incidents of discrimination against Black people in parks are commonplace, and socioeconomic barriers further impede accessibility. Racial aggression extends to other green spaces. Consider the 2018 incident when a white woman called the police on a group of Black people having a cookout in a public park in Oakland, or the white woman who called 911 on a Black bird-watcher in New York's Central Park in 2020.[9,10]

Despite these systemic obstacles, there are people working toward a conservation ethic that includes Black, Indigenous, and people of color, and that builds democracy back into our relationship to land. We explore these ideas in conversation with Dr. Lauret Edith Savoy, Rue Mapp, and Audrey Peterman.

DR. LAURET EDITH SAVOY (she/her) is the David B. Truman Professor of Environmental Studies and Geology at Mount Holyoke College and a writer of African American, Euro-American, and Indigenous ancestry. Lauret's work considers how this nation's ever-unfolding history has marked the land as well as this society. Her book *Trace: Memory, History, Race, and the American Landscape* won the American Book Award and Association for the Study of Literature and Environment (ASLE) Writing Award; it was also a finalist for a PEN America award and more national honors. Other books include *The Colors of Nature: Culture, Identity, and the Natural World* and *Bedrock: Writers on the Wonders of Geology*, named one of the five best science books in the *Wall Street Journal*. Winner of Mount Holyoke's Distinguished Teaching Award, an Andrew Carnegie Fellowship, and other honors, Lauret is also a photographer and pilot.

RUE MAPP (she/her) is the founder and CEO of Outdoor Afro, a national not-for-profit organization with offices in Oakland, California, and Washington, DC. Rue oversees a carefully selected and trained national volunteer leadership team of eighty men and women who represent thirty states around the US, and a participant network of forty-five thousand people. Through this network, she shares opportunities to build a broader community and leadership in nature. Her important work has generated widespread national recognition and support. In 2010, Mapp was invited to the Obama White House to participate in the America's Great Outdoors Conference and subsequently to take part in a think tank to inform the launch of the First Lady's Let's Move initiative. Outdoor Afro was chosen, out of all the organizations in the Bay Area, to be highlighted and visited by Oprah on her 2020 Vision Tour.

AUDREY PETERMAN (she/her) is a national award-winning author, conservationist, and a leader in the movement to engage more Americans of color in the enjoyment, care, and protection of our national parks and public lands system. Mrs. Peterman and her husband, Frank, drove 12,500 miles around the country in 1995, exploring fourteen units of the national park system. As part of the Next 100 Coalition, she helped persuade President Barack Obama to issue the 2017 Presidential Memorandum Promoting Diversity and Inclusion in Our National Parks, National Forests, and Other Public Lands and Waters. Peterman's books include *From My Jamaican Gully to the World*, *Our True Nature: Finding a Zest for Life in the National Park System*, and *Legacy on the Land: A Black Couple Discovers Our National Inheritance and Tells Why Every American Should Care*.

LEAH: Despite the ongoing marginalization of Black people in national parks, you have had transcendent experiences of belonging and magic in the parks. Can you share a story about your personal connection to these landscapes?

AUDREY PETERMAN: I was forty-four years old when I had that seminal experience of seeing through nature that I was looking into the vast expanse of God. After Frank and I got married, we decided to take a cross-country journey. Our first stop was Acadia National Park in Maine, and as you approach, there is the magnificent Cadillac Mountain that juts up from the forest, almost as if the mountain was a hula dancer and the forest was her skirt. We drove into that expanse of greenery, climbing up the mountain, when I suddenly realized that we had ascended above the clouds. When we got to the top of the mountain, I didn't feel like I was on the same earth that I had inhabited before. On one side was the Atlantic Ocean, thundering onto the shore in a boisterous manner with gulls calling and fishing buoys glistening green and blue. On the other side, I could see calm and placid waters that the sun had dappled golden, dotted with tree islands. I realized I did not need to die to go to heaven. It was almost as if I had been living in a mansion and only ever seen the kitchen, then suddenly tumbled into the grand living room, replete with art and adornments. In that moment, I realized that the same Creator that made this great expanse of beauty also created me. Just as everything around me was beautiful and perfect, I must be beautiful and perfect, too. I stood there feeling infinitesimal and also part of that grandeur, and I fell in love with myself. At the same time, I fell in love with all things, recognizing the face of God in everything around me.

DR. LAURET SAVOY: As a seven-year-old I stood with my parents and a dear cousin at Point Sublime, a remote and hard-to-reach overlook on the Grand Canyon's North Rim. The memory stays sharp because it was part of a journey that marked a path in my life. We had driven hours over rough terrain to watch the sunrise there. No single camera frame could contain the expanse or the play of dawn light. Canyon walls that moments before had descended into undefined darkness soon glowed in great blocky detail. As shadows receded, the Colorado River glinted in the rising sun, just a thin sliver in the far inner gorge. Swifts and ravens flew around us as if emerging from dawn's silence. Those moments at Point Sublime illuminated for the child-me a journey of and to perception, to another way of measuring a world I was part of, yet leaving behind. I've written that "history" began for me then, on *the move*. My parents were returning home to the East Coast. My home lay behind us on California's sunset coast, where I was born at the elastic limit of my father's last attempt to craft a life far from Washington, DC. Erosive forces carved the North Rim's edge, and my family crossed many edges that summer, too. West to East. My childhood home was left for my father's. Before to after. My father had hoped the future in DC would be a return to origins and dignity. But we returned to a city that erupted in flames in the 1968 riots. It was a time of violence and of hate-filled spit aimed at me. To say that the world stopped making sense is an understatement. Yet I learned a lasting lesson: the land did not hate, only people did. Earth never judged or spat.

LEAH: Rue, in addition to parks being a place of personal healing, you have experienced parks as spaces for Black communal healing in the face of racialized violence. Your work with Outdoor Afro has been an incredible catalyst to connect our folks to nature in ways that address trauma. Can you share an example of how you do this?

RUE MAPP: Being an organizational leader is about listening, feeling, and responding to what the community needs and asking myself, "How can Outdoor Afro be of service?" After Ferguson, when there was an outcry on social media and people were spilling into the streets, I had to reflect on how to show up in that moment as a Black woman head of a Black-focused organization. We could feel the violence tightening in the atmosphere and see our folks getting arrested and injured. Nature is my lane, so I started organizing healing hikes. On one hike we brought thirty people into the majestic redwood forest. As soon as we started down the trail, getting farther from the helicopters and riot gear, people began to feel a lightness, freedom, and ability to talk and connect with one another. We were Black people doing what we have always done—laying our burdens down by the riverside. When we came out of that redwood grove, we were present and ready to engage again with community work.

The redwood forest is my favorite biome and my cherished teacher. Redwoods are the world's tallest trees, growing over three hundred feet, and can live for thousands of years. The redwoods grow in familial groves with wide roots intertwined below the surface, which makes them resilient to wind, fire, and other forces of nature despite their stunning height. This serves as a metaphor about how strong we can be rooted together. The historic clear-cutting of the redwoods has a corollary in the displacement and gentrification impacting Black people. The current comeback of the redwood forests is an example of how we can practice community resilience. I sit in the redwoods a lot to think and listen, and it once occurred to me: These trees don't even know that I am Black, and if they did, they wouldn't care. These trees are focused on being redwoods and see me as a human passenger, as a part of nature just like them. Race, gender, and class are not the concerns of trees, so I can be in the grove and free myself from those burdens. The birds will sing no matter how much money is in your account. The flowers will bloom regardless of your political affiliation. We all need a break from those constructs. Nature is a powerful healer. In these spaces, I am free to access deeper expressions of myself.

LEAH: Rue, your model is very powerful, training skilled outdoor leaders to organize outdoor experiences that have included over forty-five thousand people nationwide. You have been able to work with Michelle Obama and Oprah, among others, to change the national conversation about Black people's belonging in the outdoors. Some would argue that Black folks have been estranged from parklands and have lost a cultural connection to nature. How have you kept your work culturally rooted and relevant?

RUE MAPP: Outdoor Afro has always been about more than just getting Black people outside. It's about creating an immersive experience that allows you to be all parts of who you are. My family were first-generation Californians out of rural Texas and Louisiana, and they had what we called *mother wit*—a way of being informed by faith, common sense, and wisdom, and a connection to ancestors and the order of the natural world. While they did not have a lot of formal education, they had a deep and intelligent connection to the earth that they brought with them from the Jim Crow South. My dad would have never called himself a conservationist, but he had a *nature swagger* and moved through land and seasons with so much ease. Wanting to keep that connection strong, my parents established a ranch one hundred miles north of Oakland, California, on fifteen acres with lots of walnut orchards, fruit trees, cows, pigs, gardens, and grapes. It was a living oasis where we brought together people from the church and neighborhood for ceremony, celebration, and exploration. We had baptisms there in the water. We prayed under the canopy of trees or under the stars. We sang, performed, prepared meals, hunted, and fished. It was Blackity Black Black Black! Outdoor Afro has been trying to re-create that without tethering it to a particular place, supporting communities to hold that spirit of being all you can be. That's my truth.

LEAH: *Nature swagger*, as you so beautifully coined, Rue, is certainly a part of our Black heritage. Shelton Johnson, a Black-Native man who has worked as a park ranger since 1986, has done a lot to unearth and promote the role of African Americans in establishing the national parks, notably the Buffalo Soldiers' foundational work in the Sierra Nevada, Yellowstone, and Yosemite. I hope we can delve into Black people's long-standing relationship with the parks, while holding the complexity that the Buffalo Soldiers signed up for the settler colonial parks project as a way to avoid sharecropping and Jim Crow. Lauret, what are your thoughts on the ways Indigenous people and Black people have been erased from belonging in these spaces?

DR. LAURET SAVOY: African American troops were posted at western national parklands over a century ago, when the segregated military preferred to restrict them to remote posts. In 1896, Black soldiers of the 25th Infantry Regiment bicycled eight hundred miles round trip between Yellowstone National Park and Fort Missoula in Montana as an army experiment to learn if bicycles could be used for military purposes. Hundreds of soldiers in the 9th Cavalry and 24th Infantry regiments patrolled Yosemite, Sequoia, and what would become Kings Canyon National Parks. This was when the US Army administered parklands in California's Sierra Nevada. While posted in Sierra parks, these soldiers policed illegal stock grazing, timber cutting, and poaching. They fought forest fires. They built the first park trail to the top of Mount Whitney, the highest point in the lower forty-eight states. And they completed a wagon road to Sequoia's Giant Forest, giving tourists access to the great trees for the first time. But the achievements of African American soldiers as stewards went mostly untold in parks until recent years, when the efforts of people like Shelton Johnson, an interpretive ranger at Yosemite, highlighted them.

What's important to realize is that National Park Service holdings are among this country's most prominent sites of memory. From iconic wilderness parks to monuments, memorials, battlefields, historical parks, and more, their making—and the elements preserved within them—are important pieces of the nation's history, pieces tied to contested narratives about what and who "we the people" are. Wilderness is a key example. As an idea and as preserved land, wilderness never existed apart from human experience or from policies that bound land and people. Take Yellowstone, which Congress made the first national park in 1872. It was supposed to be a "wonderland" set aside as a "pleasuring-ground for the benefit and enjoyment of the people." But to make an uninhabited wilderness park required de-peopling the land in myth and actuality. Crow, Shoshone, the Tukudika band of Mountain Shoshone, Bannock, Blackfeet, Nez Perce, and other tribal peoples would find themselves expelled and dispossessed from what had been part of their homelands. Many would be removed to reservations. Trying to welcome tourists, one early superintendent assured people that "Yellowstone is not Indian country." A later superintendent supervised a report that stated the park's story was "a sequential link in the chain of epochal events" that included "conquest of the savages, and all the epic deeds which achieved at last the winning of the west."[11]

Indigenous peoples would find themselves displaced again and again from traditional homelands that were stolen to become new national parks like Glacier and Yosemite. The Ahwahneechee and related groups were pushed out of Yosemite Valley at different times, starting in 1851. Bit by bit, after Yosemite became a national park in 1890, to well within our lifetimes, Native residents were forced out of the valley even as they tried to have their land rights acknowledged by courts. One glaring irony is that as a real Indigenous presence decreased in national parklands, public narratives began to invoke the myth of the "vanished Indian."[12,13]

LEAH: Lauret, this is a powerful point and makes me think about the juxtaposition of white folks in the mid-1900s expanding their reach into wild spaces, while Black people were increasingly hemmed into urban areas through redlining and racialized restrictive covenants.[14] It seems that acknowledging this painful history is an initial step in reconciling the relationship between the parks and Black and Indigenous people. Lauret, are the parks making any effort to address these historical harms?

DR. LAURET SAVOY: Lack of access and means to travel to parks was long an obstacle compounded by racism. And for years the park system didn't attempt to represent all of the nation's inhabitants, let alone welcome them. W. E. B. Du Bois wrote over a century ago, in his book *Darkwater: Voices from Within the Veil*, of Black people who could afford to visit parks, yet who chose not to because of the Jim Crow racism they'd have to face on their journeys—like being forced to ride in segregated train cars.[15]

More recently national parks have made efforts to serve all people. One way to see this is in how the park system acknowledges migration and movement in the nation's history. Of course, NPS honors migration experiences on the Oregon Trail and at Ellis Island, and now the system also includes the *African Passages* exhibit on Sullivan's Island in South Carolina. The island was a quarantine center when nearby Charleston was the entry port for hundreds of thousands of captive Africans who survived the Middle Passage. There is also the Harriet Tubman Underground Railroad National Historical Park in Maryland and the Selma to Montgomery National Historic Trail, which traces the 1965 civil rights march that began at the Edmund Pettus Bridge. There are many more examples.

In the last few decades, the National Park Service has begun to add broader contexts and ranges of voices to its units. Once, Custer Battlefield National Monument in Montana presented a story of the US losing a battle but winning the war against "Indians." Now, renamed as Little Bighorn Battlefield National Monument, the site presents a more complex history. Here's another example. The memory of Sand Creek, Colorado, has been contested since that early November morning in 1864 when volunteer soldiers attacked a large, peaceful Cheyenne and Arapaho encampment. Most of the troops and white settlers memorialized what happened as a glorious battle against hostiles. To survivors it was a massacre of about two hundred kin, mostly women, children, and elders. The new general plan for the historic site was developed in partnership with Cheyenne and Arapaho tribes, the state of Colorado, and local officials. This site is now the only park service unit with "massacre" in its name. One key goal is to create inclusive programs that help visitors understand the still-contested histories and continuing consequences of that massacre.

LEAH: Do you see access to wilderness as a representation issue, a civil rights issue, or both?

RUE MAPP: Both, absolutely. We missed an opportunity about fifty years ago, when the Wilderness Act and the Civil Rights Act were passed in the same year, 1964. I began asking people who were around at that time, "Were there conversations happening between these two caucuses?" And the answer I heard has always been "No." I've come to believe that had we, at that moment, come together and realized that the crucial conversation is about protecting vulnerable places and vulnerable people, then we might have a very different environmental and conservation movement today.

In Outdoor Afro, whenever we go someplace, we always dig into the history. And we find some amazing stories of Black people in these spaces, who've done incredible things. In the Boston area, we learned about Ona Judge, an escaped slave, and how her community of support around her allowed her to thrive in a way that was pretty unique for its time. We also learned about John Harris, a waiter in downtown Oakland, who tried to use the famous Sutro Baths, was denied, and filed a lawsuit that became the test case of modern civil rights legislation. We often talk about Harriet Tubman, who knew how to move through the wild and through seasons, who understood the vernacular of the wild and could read the signs of the way forward or of danger. It's not just about the natural landscape, but the human relationships to those landscapes. It's important for us to know that we as Black people have had a long-standing presence in these spaces, and feel in our bones and our souls that we belong here.

LEAH: Something that struck me recently was the fact that the national parks contain some of the few remaining places where one can view the night sky unencumbered by light pollution.[16] In the US and Europe, 99 percent of the public can't experience a natural night sky.[17,18] Artificial night brightness prevents trees from adjusting to seasonal variations, sends sea turtle hatchlings off course, and causes birds to lose their way and crash into illuminated human buildings.[19] For millennia, celestial wayfinding knowledge was also part of Black generational knowledge.

Most notably, Harriet Tubman used the Big Dipper—the sky gourd—to guide her journeys northward. Audrey, what is your perspective on the importance of access to the night sky?

AUDREY PETERMAN: I am always mindful of the fact that, before modern times, our ancestors mostly looked at the sky for information. This helped them to plan, to read the weather, and to know what to expect. I attended an astronomy festival in the Badlands National Park and got to learn from an incredible astronomer who had been to space to fix the Hubble Telescope. There I came to understand that we are creatures of both the earth and the cosmos. We got our information from celestial bodies and told stories about the sky for generations. Most of our information now comes from the mouths of other human beings. It's a dangerous game of telephone, where each messenger distorts a bit of the message, and the content devolves over time. It's as if the sky were the primary source, and people are secondary and tertiary sources, and so on. Now that we have electricity, we have stopped looking at the vast expanse above us and lost our access to the wisdom of the cosmos. Learning to read the dark sky is a vital practice in order to live with clarity as we navigate this world.

LEAH: Joanna Macy wrote, "I am not saving the earth; I am part of the earth saving itself."[20] Are we indeed a part of nature? And if so, what is the earth saying to humanity about the direction we need to take for our shared survival?

AUDREY PETERMAN: Yes, we are part of the earth, and the earth is saying, "Wake up from your trance." Humans are the only species that fouls its own nest. The great blue herons and white egrets of Florida are now forced to fish in a canal full of human detritus, while fires rage, hurricane winds blow, and natural disasters abound due to human actions. As someone who has been privileged to visit more than 185 places in America's National Park System, plus scores of national forests and wildlife refuges, I am in support of the efforts to conserve 30 percent of the country's land and oceans by 2030, though if I had my druthers, it would be 50 percent. We are not the only beings in the world, and we need to stop thinking we are in charge, or it will be the death of us.

E. O. Wilson also talked about how we evolved in nature and how it's a biological imperative for us to be outside with the sun beaming down on us and the breeze blowing.[21] Richard Louv wrote about the rising cases of attention deficit disorder (ADD), mental health disorders, and physiological diseases in our children connected to all the time they spend on devices and not outside.[22] Nature is our life support system. I have seen this firsthand in a young man named Juan Martinez who grew up in South Central LA, where going outside meant the danger of being shot; as a result, he had no experience in parks. Through an environmental program he got the opportunity to visit the Grand Teton National Park where he saw stars for the first time, and now he is a National Geographic Emerging Explorer and the first in his family to graduate from college.[23] Mother nature speaks last.

RUE MAPP: I imagine the Earth speaking to us in the words of Celie in the movie *The Color Purple*, "Until you do right by me, everything you think about is gonna crumble!"[24] This is not a threat; it's a reminder to tap into our ancient and ancestral wisdom. We are in a moment where we have created enormous harm through ignorance, and this harm has extended disproportionately to folks who look like us. The earth has thrown us a Hail Mary that it's all 'bout love right now, and that we need to love the earth and each other to sustain life. Nature is an open-source platform, and like a radio broadcast system, it is always transmitting. We just need to stop and tune in so we can hear it. We may then be able to access just a small portion of the full complexity and wisdom of the earth.

DR. LAURET SAVOY: I think Earth does speak, in many voices and in many ways. It speaks in the languages of water, wind, and ice. It speaks in the languages of uplift, eruption, and erosion. It responds to the actions of human beings. What I'm reminded of every day is that human understanding of Earth, and of our place on Earth, began with direct experience. We evolved on and in the land. Landscapes were our original dwellings from which we gleaned crucial information. To read patterns in the land, water, and sky was a skill necessary for survival. Winds and clouds foretold changing weather. Good sites for settlement could be seen in the lay of the land. A terrain's history could be deciphered from its shape, structure, and material pieces—from rock and sediment. Even the texture of a river's surface revealed what lay below.

Earth speaks. For perhaps innumerable tribal traditions, land is the matrix of meaning, indivisible from language and culture. There is reciprocity—mutual life-supporting engagement. But so many people in this nation know little of Earth, and they act as if their ignorance is a right and privilege.

Think of it this way. A child born today enters a world of evermore rapid and extensive environmental change. Ecosystems have never before been so fragmented or degraded; the diversity of life is suffering great losses. Fossil hydrocarbons literally fueled industrial revolutions, including the mechanization of food production. Because of this fossil fuel economy, greenhouse gas levels continue to climb, exceeding the highest atmospheric concentrations since our species evolved. That this issue falls out of the scope of many Americans' concern is a tragedy.

Earth is our origin, our foundation, our material home. We—all humanity and all life—are bound together in time, space, and substance. My child-sense of this began to develop long ago. Once traveling in the realm of geology, I learned to read and listen in the languages of science as well as art and life. To look and see Earth, to hear and listen to Earth, are not just acts of choice. They are a necessity.

SO WE WALK

A Conversation with T. Morgan Dixon,
Teresa Baker, and James Edward Mills

We cannot tire or give up. We owe it to the present and future
generations of all species to rise up and walk.

—WANGARI MAATHAI, *UNBOWED*

Deliberate and purposeful walking has long been a tool for principled resistance among Black people. John Francis, better known as Planetwalker, witnessed two Standard Oil tankers collide in the San Francisco Bay in 1971, dumping eight hundred thousand gallons of crude oil into the fragile lagoon ecosystem. Shaken by the devastation, which occurred alongside the sudden death of a close friend, Francis made an immediate decision to start walking. He swore off motorized transport and traveled on foot for the next twenty-two years. He also spent seventeen years in silence, which he found more honest than the spoken word. Francis wrote, "I feel frustrated that though it is clear to me, I am unable to articulate beyond a single phrase about why I walk. Even more difficult for me to understand is the burgeoning feeling of something spiritual and sacred in the ordinary act of walking. I started to feel that each step taken is part of an invisible journey for which there was no map and few road signs."[1] Through walking, Francis found personal healing and also made an indelible mark on oil-spill management policy and practice.

Ancestor Harriet Tubman also walked purposefully, in her case, for personal freedom as well as the liberty of the seventy self-emancipated people who journeyed with her. Attributed to Tubman are these sentiments on what it means to walk: "If you hear the dogs, keep going. If you see the torches in the woods, keep going. If there's shouting after you, keep going. Don't ever stop. Keep going. If you want a taste of freedom, keep going."[2] In the spirit of Tubman, over forty thousand African Americans walked their daily commutes in protest of the segregated buses in Montgomery from 1955 to 1956. That same spirit infused the Selma to Montgomery march of 1965, the March on Washington of 1963, and the Movement for Black Lives marches of 2013 to the present. Walking is a core technology of Black liberation.

In addition to its liberatory value, purposeful walking has immense trauma healing benefits of particular import to racialized people. In *My Grandmother's Hands: Racialized Trauma and the Pathway to Mending Our Hearts and Bodies,* Resmaa Menakem explains how traumatizing experiences generate energy in the body that must be safely discharged through physical exertion like walking outdoors. In the absence of this release, trauma lodges itself within the body and leads to mental and physical health challenges, and the potential for recapitulation of harm. A nationwide study including over nine hundred thousand people revealed that children who grew up with the lowest access to green space had a 55 percent higher risk of developing a psychiatric disorder, independent of other risk factors like socioeconomic status or parents' mental health history.[3] Access to green space and physical exertion underpin wellness, and are also tools in asserting Black freedom.

To delve deeper into ideas about walking, and access to the open land and sky where we can exercise that freedom to walk, we will be in conversation with three visionary organizers who are shifting the landscape of Black access to the outdoors: T. Morgan Dixon, Teresa Baker, and James Edward Mills.

T. MORGAN DIXON (she/her) is a leader of the largest health movement in America for Black women, @GirlTrek, with over one million members, two major TED Talks, and a viral podcast called *Black History Bootcamp*. Morgan was named among the top 1 percent of social innovators in the world and has received fellowships from Echoing Green (2013), Ashoka (2014), and the Aspen Institute (2015). She is a visiting innovator at Harvard University Kennedy School of Government and currently works from Ghana, West Africa, uniting women and girls worldwide for health justice.

TERESA BAKER (she/her) is an outdoor diversity activist, writer, and founder of the In Solidarity Project, which has succeeded in getting over 185 brands and nonprofits to sign on to the Outdoor CEO Diversity Pledge. She also founded the African American Nature and Parks Experience, which hosts the annual African American National Park Event and the annual Hike Like a Girl event. Teresa has created such projects as the Buffalo Soldiers Trail retracing event from the Presidio of San Francisco to Yosemite National Park and the Women's Outdoor Summit for Empowerment.

JAMES EDWARD MILLS (he/him) is a 2014 Fellow of the Mountain and Wilderness Writing Program of the Banff Centre in Alberta, Canada, and the 2016 recipient of the Paul K. Petzoldt Award for Environmental Education. As a freelance journalist and an independent media producer for more than twenty years, he specializes in sharing stories about outdoor recreation, environmental conservation, acts of charitable giving, and practices of sustainable living. He is the author of *The Adventure Gap: Changing the Face of the Outdoors*, is the co-writer/coproducer of the documentary film *An American Ascent*, and curator of *The Joy Trip Project* platform.

LEAH: Ancestor Wangari Maathai launched a movement that catalyzed millions of Kenyan women to collectively plant over fifty-one million trees, as an ecological force, yes, but also as a strategy for women's empowerment. Morgan, in your work with GirlTrek, I see you embodying this charge. You have engaged walking outdoors as a movement strategy and have inspired over one million women to "rise up and walk." What underpins this approach?

T. MORGAN DIXON: The work of Wangari Maathai and the Green Belt Movement are the prototype for GirlTrek. We studied her when we were building our organization. We studied Harriet Tubman as well. What it comes down to is that, by any means necessary, we have to live. I am not going to ask permission to save my own life. As Black women, in order to save our own lives we have to *disrupt* a system designed to kill us.

In 2011, I learned that 50 percent of Black women are at risk for type 2 diabetes. I was teaching fifth grade at the time and thinking about the futures of the young Black women in my class who were threatened by a silent health crisis. Black women die ten years earlier than any other group of women, and for the first time in history, our daughters have a lower life expectancy than their mothers. I started taking girls hiking on the weekends and talking with them about what barriers stood in the way of them living their healthiest lives. At the same time, my best friend, Vanessa Garrison, was grappling with women in her family dying too early. In starting GirlTrek, we set a goal to get one million women to walk outdoors as a way of taking charge of our health and also taking back our neighborhoods. Walking just thirty minutes a day, five days a week, reduces chronic disease risk by half, and also builds a culture of community and friendship. Now that we have reached a million members, our current goal is to increase the life expectancy of Black women by ten years in ten years.

LEAH: James, you have a powerful story about your impulse to hike a mountain after a traumatic event that shook the nation. Can you speak about this mountaintop transformative experience and how it informed your work to support other African Americans in reaching their own summits?

JAMES EDWARD MILLS: I was working in the outdoor industry in sales and marketing when the Twin Towers fell on September 11, 2001. George W. Bush told Americans to keep shopping, to keep the economy going. I was in the business of selling stuff, and even though it helped people have positive outdoor experiences, it was still just about money. The next month I was at a trade show in Las Vegas, and I decided to climb Mount Whitney. I didn't think about the climb itself as being cathartic, just something that needed doing, and an opportunity for some alone time. When I got to the top, I saw that people had created displays of American flags and handwritten notes pinned with rocks, describing what the events of 9/11 meant to them. It was at that moment that I decided I needed to do something else with my life. I wanted to work toward the outdoors being more accessible to more types of people, and specifically to improve visibility for people of color. Despite advances in so many other aspects of our society, there is a racial divide between those who participate in outdoor activities and those who don't, a yawning chasm I came to call "the adventure gap."

In 2013, I helped put together the first all-Black American expedition to the summit of Denali in Alaska. At 20,130 feet, it is North America's highest peak. The Expedition Denali team started with twenty-six people and homed in on nine folks who completed the climb, ranging in ages from eighteen to fifty-six. I was originally on the climbing team, but because of a diagnosis of osteoarthritis, I had to have my hips replaced. Ultimately, I remained on the team, but as a journalist. We completed several intense training missions together, including ten days on the glaciers of Alaska doing avalanche and crevasse rescue training. During the Cascade Mountains training climb, I remember finally summiting and gazing out at a sea of snowcapped peaks. Even as we were still catching our breath, our team member Adina Scott pulled off her GORE-TEX shell. Underneath she wore a silver-sequined tank top. She asked, "Am I the only one who brought summit bling?" We erupted into a chorus of cheers, high fives, and laughter. Not only was I surrounded by good athletes who had the ability to climb the mountain, but also by dynamic folks who had a passion for the outdoors and a generosity of spirit to return to their communities and tell these inspiring stories to young people.

Like most climbing expeditions, the summit was not the sole goal, but rather one step in a larger mission. One of our climbers, Rosemary Saal, went on to lead the first all-Black American ascent of Kilimanjaro. Everyone who climbed remains friends and has gone on to shake up business, education, and the outdoor industry. In a world where far too few people of color spend time recreating outdoors, our mission was to demonstrate that, despite all evidence to the contrary, Black folks do indeed climb. We do, in fact, have a place in outdoor recreation.

In Dr. Martin Luther King Jr.'s 1963 "I Have a Dream" speech, he talked about freedom ringing from the mountaintops of Mississippi, Colorado, New Hampshire, Georgia, California, and Tennessee. I believe that he was talking about more than lunch counters and buses—that his dream encompassed literal mountains. Perhaps it's not a coincidence that the very next year following King's speech, Charlie Crenchaw became the first Black American to summit Denali.

LEAH: Teresa, you have dedicated much of your career to making the outdoors accessible to Black and Brown people, including founding the African American Nature and Parks Experience. What are some of the most powerful places that you have been able to walk and to facilitate spaces for others to walk?

TERESA BAKER: I don't particularly like being in crowds, so being outdoors, camping, and hiking are necessities for me. Being one with my surroundings and in relationship to the earth grounds me and prepares me for the next battle around the protection of these spaces. Currently, Point

Reyes National Seashore is my favorite place to visit. I often get there at 6 a.m. just as the bobcat, deer, and elk are waking up, and we enjoy the first light together. The giant redwood forests of the California coast are also treasured. There are no words to describe what it feels like to walk among ancient giants, some of them thousands of years old. I can step into one of the groves and not hear anyone, or see anyone, relieved of the pressure to be anyone other than myself. In collaboration with the Save the Redwoods League, I organized a group of people of color to walk in a remote seven-hundred-acre grove of redwoods that had been recently purchased as a preserve. Some of those trees had been around during the Roman Empire and are still growing today.

LEAH: Morgan, it's incredible that you have succeeded in mobilizing over a million Black women to walk, also engaging a culturally rooted strategy. On the TED stage you said, "When Black women walk, things change."[4] Just as Harriet Tubman liberated herself and then went back to liberate her family, GirlTrek is a catalyst for self and community liberation. What was it like for your national team to take a five-day, one-hundred-mile walking journey retracing Harriet Tubman's footsteps along the Underground Railroad?

T. MORGAN DIXON: We started on March 6, 2018, on the Eastern Shore of Maryland where Tubman made her first escape and crossed the Mason-Dixon Line into Delaware on March 10, Harriet Tubman Day. There was a nor'easter when we started,[5] and we got hammered by the wind and sleet. Even with our modern outdoor gear, we were soaked through and freezing. We passed by the former plantations, which are all mechanized now—hack, sort, and sift later—and no longer requiring the precision of fingertips. I could just imagine row after row of me, my people, my foremothers picking that cotton and harvesting those butter beans. There were white people along the way who were rude to us, revving engines and splashing us with muddy slush from their truck wheels. And then there were the sweet gum trees, which drop their thorny balls that tangle in your clothing. I was thinking of our ancestors barefoot or in sandals navigating a forest full of these prickly balls and without winter clothing, bloodied and freezing. It's not a game to be out there. We walked a marathon every day, twenty to twenty-nine miles. There were moments when I broke down crying, felt faint, and thought I couldn't move forward. There were moments of transcendence, too. One time as it seemed my knees would buckle, the wind came and held me up, and it felt like everything that had come before was buttressing me, and I was emboldened, fuller, and bigger.

LEAH: Representation matters, and James, you have made space for the stories of people of color in the outdoors through your documentary *An American Ascent*, as well as numerous print and radio pieces. Now you are gathering and sharing stories on your platform *The Joy Trip Project*. What are some of the inspiring stories of Black folks in nature that you have encountered through this work?

JAMES EDWARD MILLS: Through the course of my journalism career, one of the things that I started doing was trying to tell stories about people who engage in outdoor sports, not exclusively for the purpose of recreation or exclusively for first ascents and highest, fastest, longest, deepest, farthest kinds of accomplishments. I wanted to engage people doing things that actually had some positive social outcome. My all-time favorite is John Francis, an amazing person who was so traumatized by the 1972 oil spill in the San Francisco Bay that he vowed not to use automobiles and started walking everywhere. Then there's Eddy Harris, a Black American guy, who paddled a canoe all the way down the Mississippi River from Lake Itasca, Minnesota, to its terminus in the Gulf of Mexico at the city of New Orleans. He made this trip in 1985, and again thirty years later, documenting the generosity of strangers, the changes to the river ecosystem, and the internal spiritual journey that comes along with paddling. Then there's Carolyn Finney, Monica White, Will Allen, and so many other inspiring people.

LEAH: Teresa, you created the Buffalo Soldiers Trail retracing event, a 175-mile journey, in honor of their legacy. Why do historical representation and historical reckoning matter?

TERESA BAKER: I didn't learn about the Buffalo Soldiers' role in the national parks until I was in my forties. These were men born into slavery whose options after emancipation were essentially to become sharecroppers living in neoslavery or to join the army. Many chose the latter, endured a rugged life far from home, and became the first rangers in Yosemite National Park. I have done a lot of work to bring attention to the story of the Buffalo Soldiers. Sharing these stories is vital in getting the African American community to claim more of the narrative between people and land.

To diversify the outdoors, we must first get to the heart of the issue: the history of our public lands that have systematically been getaways for the privileged. The founding of our national parks, for instance, pushed Native Americans off sacred lands that they'd long inhabited. More recently, our parks were segregated. Take Shenandoah National Park. In the 1930s, signs directed "Negroes" to one area, Lewis Mountain, while the rest of the park—tens of thousands of acres—was designated exclusively for white people. The rule was finally lifted in 1947, but it sent a message to African Americans that has lasted for generations: public lands do not welcome you. That legacy affects how African Americans view our place in the outdoors today. We tend not to venture out to the places that society has deemed "wild spaces," like Yosemite. Staying closer to home offers a sense of safety that these faraway locations don't.

LEAH: Let's home in on the positive social outcomes associated with access to the outdoors. One of the outspoken authorities on this is Akiima Price, who curates programs that feature nature as a powerful medium to connect traumatized and stressed youth to positive experiences. Akiima said of alternative sentencing, "One of my dreams is to get family judges to assign experience in parks for families."[6] Have you experienced nature having this type of transformative power?

JAMES EDWARD MILLS: I am on the board of the Aldo Leopold Nature Center, which is an outdoor experiential education school here in Madison, Wisconsin. We had one multiracial student with a diagnosis of autism and ADHD who had been kicked out of every school he ever attended. Children of color are five to eight times more likely to be disciplined or expelled from school than their white counterparts. This young man was enrolled with us three years ago at age six, has not had a single incident of behavior disorder, and is learning, happy, and energetic. He can snowshoe, explore, and identify trees, rocks, and birds. When you put him in a box like a conventional classroom, it is a harmful and depriving experience. A history of redlining and farmland loss led to forced urbanization for Black Americans, so if we can counter that by offering people of color a place in the outdoors to commune with nature, at least we can lower the heart rate and stress hormones in that moment, and allow them to take a breath. Nature is medicine and allows people like this nine-year-old kid to be himself.

LEAH: As folks who use the power of your own body to move across the body of the earth, you have a lot of time to tune into the messages the earth is sharing with us. What are you hearing?

T. MORGAN DIXON: The earth is genius and has her systems figured out. For example, right now we have Harmattan because it is the dry season. Every year, 182 million tons of dust from the Sahara Desert is picked up by the wind and blows across all of West Africa, the entire Atlantic Ocean, and is deposited in the Amazon rainforest where it provides essential phosphorus and other minerals to the ecosystem.[7] You are welcome, Amazon. Mama Earth is saying to us humans, "Have two seats." Just look at how the world is coming alive after a year of pandemic shut down. On GirlTrek walks we see the birds coming back, the lily pads bigger than we have ever seen. It's not that deep—we just left them alone, got out of the way, and let nature do her genius.

TERESA BAKER: The earth is saying, "Do better by me and do better by yourselves." I think about Harriet Tubman and her deep relationship to the land, almost as if she were a human GPS. She could read the landscape and felt a part of it, which enabled her to guide people hundreds of miles while evading her captors. I can't read the land like that, but I want to learn to rely less on electronics and maps, and instead read the landmarks and terrain. This is what we as a people need to get back to. Our estrangement from the land has damaged our capacity for compassion and humanity. We need to stop taking the earth for granted and protect that which gives us life. I think we need to defer to Native Americans who have protected and taken care of the land for generations, and who acknowledge humans as part of nature. If we had been listening to and following Indigenous ways of forest fire management, then the redwoods of California would not be burning to the ground. We need to be better listeners.

JAMES EDWARD MILLS: I am a bit agnostic when it comes to the universe. So I don't think of the earth as speaking with a voice, but our planet speaks with basic laws like gravity, thermal dynamics, and all the natural processes that organize matter. We will suffer the natural consequences of breaking these basic laws and deprive ourselves of the ability to protect and feed ourselves. Too much carbon dioxide in the atmosphere means the earth overheats and extinction ensues. If we deplete our soil and undermine its ability to grow food, we will starve, and no amount of prayer or sacrifice will save us. It's cause and effect. Just as we treat people how we want to be treated, with love and affection, and hopefully receive that in return, so we need to treat the earth with respect if we want to be held with love, nurturing warmth, and protection.

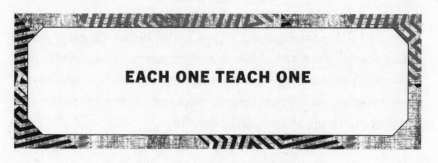

EACH ONE TEACH ONE

A Conversation with Angelou Ezeilo,
Dr. J. Drew Lanham, and Dillon Bernard

The chief moral obligation of the twenty-first century is to build a green economy that is strong enough to lift people out of poverty. Those communities that were locked out of the last century's pollution-based economy must be locked into the new, clean, and renewable economy. Our youth need green-collar jobs, not jails.

—VAN JONES

I n 2010, Maryland approved plans for the nation's largest incinerator to be built near Curtis Bay, in a predominantly Black community already saddled with oil refineries, chemical plants, and sewage treatment plants, and whose residents suffer from high rates of asthma, lung cancer, and emissions-related mortality. The new incinerator would bring four thousand tons of trash into the community every day, releasing copious mercury pollution less than one mile away from two public schools.

As a public high school senior in Curtis Bay, Destiny Watford co-founded the student group Free Your Voice dedicated to community rights and environmental justice. They launched a campaign to stop the incinerator, canvassing neighborhoods, circulating petitions, and organizing protests. When they learned that the Baltimore City Public Schools were under contract to purchase energy from the incinerator, they started a divestment campaign. The school board terminated their contract, and twenty-two other energy customers followed suit, leaving the incinerator with no market for its product. By 2016, the Maryland Department of Energy revoked the permit for the incinerator. Destiny and her fellow students argued that green jobs and renewable energy were immediate needs, and they pushed for the site to be used for a community-owned solar panel farm. In 2016, Destiny won the Goldman Environmental Prize, one of the world's most prestigious environmental awards.

Destiny Watford is among the young, gifted, and Black environmental activists of our times.[1] Other notable youth leaders include Khristen Hamilton of Zero Hour; Nyaruot Nguany of Maine Environmental Changemakers Network; Jerome Foster of One Million of Us; Mari Copeny, or "Little Miss Flint," of Flint, Michigan; Isra Hirsi of Youth Climate Strike; and Vic Barrett of Our Children's Trust, among others. The experience of being just one of a few, or even all alone, as Black activists and leaders in environmental spaces is echoed in the narratives of these committed young people. Though African Americans compose 13.0 percent of the US population, they receive only 2.8 percent of the nation's total environmental science degrees, making environmental science among the least diverse fields of scientific study.[2] Black people compose between 1.0 and 7.8 percent of the environmental sciences and geosciences workforce, and green-collar workers are more likely than workers in other industries to be white and male.[3,4] According to a study by Dorceta Taylor, only 3.9 percent of environmental organizations report their racial diversity data, and of those that do, white people comprise over 80 percent of their boards, 85 percent of their staff, and 96 percent of their senior staff, on average.[5]

Black youth are often excluded from environmental benefits and opportunities from a young age. Patterns of development—including urban sprawl; the construction of roads, pipelines, and transmission lines; and drilling, mining, and logging—have had a disproportionately large impact on Black and Brown communities. Natural spaces are being lost at an alarming rate nationwide—roughly every thirty seconds, the US loses a football field worth of forests, grasslands, wetlands, and other natural ecosystems—and Black and Brown folks bear the brunt of the impacts. Families of color are far less likely to live near places that allow them to get outside safely and access clean water, clean air, and a diversity of wildlife. Seventy-four percent of communities of color in the contiguous US live in nature-deprived areas, compared with just 23 percent of white communities. Scientific studies have shown that people living in polluted areas without sufficient tree cover are more susceptible to developing immunocompromising illnesses such as asthma and COVID-19. Lack of access to urban nature also has devastating mental health impacts, doubling the risk of alcoholism, depression, schizophrenia, and other psychiatric disorders.[6] Black and Latine families with children are the most nature-deprived of any race or ethnicity.[7] As Majora Carter summed up, "Race and class are extremely reliable indicators as to where one might find the good stuff, like parks and trees, and where one might find the bad stuff, like power plants and waste facilities."[8]

In order for our young, gifted, and Black environmental leaders to overcome these barriers and take their rightful place at the helm of earth work, they need resources, support, mentorship, and a platform. There are organizations and individuals committed to the practice of "each one teach one" who are making space for the rising generation of youth leadership.[9] Joining this conversation are three such committed leaders: Angelou Ezeilo, Dr. J. Drew Lanham, and Dillon Bernard.

ANGELOU EZEILO (she/her) is at the helm of a movement to provide environmental and wellness education and career pathways to a new generation, both in the US and in countries throughout Africa. She is the founder of the Greening Youth Foundation, cultivating a generation of youth of color to be stewards of our land and natural resources, and ultimately shifting the demographics of the environmental conservation movement. Angelou was elected as an Ashoka Fellow in 2016 for her work at the Greening Youth Foundation, where she is the former CEO and current Senior Advisor. Angelou also currently serves as vice president of empathy for Ashoka Africa, a global nonprofit focused on social change for the good of all. Angelou is a graduate of Spelman College in Georgia. She received her JD from the University of Florida College of Law. Angelou is a member of the National Center for Civil and Human Rights Women's Solidarity Society and Georgia Audubon boards. She is an advisory board member for Outdoor Afro; the MillionMile Greenway, Inc.; Keeping It Wild, Inc.; and Rachel's Network. Most recently, she coauthored *Engage, Connect, Protect: Empowering Diverse Youth as Environmental Leaders.*

PROFESSOR J. DREW LANHAM (he/him) (BA Zoology 1988; MS Zoology 1990; PhD Forest Resources 1997) is a native of Edgefield and Aiken, South Carolina. In his twenty years as Clemson University faculty, he has worked to understand how forest management impacts wildlife and how human beings think about nature. Dr. Lanham holds an endowed chair as an Alumni Distinguished Professor and was named an Alumni Master Teacher in 2012. In his teaching, research, and outreach roles, Dr. Lanham seeks to translate conservation science to make it relevant to others in ways that are evocative and understandable. As a Black American, he is intrigued by how culture and ethnic prisms can bend perceptions of nature and its care. He is active on a number of conservation boards including the South Carolina Wildlife Federation, Audubon South Carolina, the Aldo Leopold Foundation, BirdNote, and the American Birding Association, and he is a member of the advisory board for the North American Association of Environmental Education. Dr. Lanham is a widely published author and award-nominated poet, writing about his experiences as a birder, hunter, and wild, wandering soul. His first solo work was *The Home Place: Memoirs of a Colored Man's Love Affair with Nature.*

DILLON BERNARD (he/him) is a twenty-one-year-old digital strategist and content producer who uses media and storytelling as a tool for transformative change. Dillon was the director of communications at Future Coalition, a national network of youth-led organizations and youth organizers. Future Coalition coordinated the intergenerational coalition behind the September 2019 US Climate Strikes, which was the largest-ever youth-led climate action in American history. In April 2020, Future Coalition created Earth Day Live to demand climate action on the fiftieth anniversary of Earth Day, resulting in the largest online mass mobilization in history. Since he was thirteen, Dillon has been creating magazines, websites, and media projects, with each project naturally focusing on the intersection of social change and youth empowerment. Dillon is a fall 2020 grantee of the National Geographic Society's Young Explorers program and a 2021 grantee of the We Are Family Foundation's Youth to the Front Fund. Dillon is currently pursuing a bachelor of arts in journalism and design at the New School. He is based in New York City.

LEAH: Angelou, what was your experience as a young Black professional entering the field? At your first position in the environmental nonprofit sector, what were some of the resonances and also some of the challenges?

ANGELOU EZEILO: Prior to starting with the Trust for Public Land, I worked in corporate law, and then with the state of New Jersey on farmland preservation. The rigidity of the government bureaucracy was not a great fit, but I knew that I loved the work of connecting people to the land and wanted to continue in the field. I took a position at the Trust for Public Land, the first environmental NGO (nongovernmental organization) I had worked with, and focused on programs like Parks for People that connected New Jersey and Georgia residents of color to green spaces. I saw the power of what these organizations could do in terms of holding easements that permanently preserved the land. The challenge was that I felt incredibly lonely. There were so few people who looked like me; I had no mentors and few folks of color coming up behind me. I felt uncomfortable in my own skin. The organization would plan events, activities, and retreats through their lens as white people. For example, they organized a staff retreat for program managers at a ranch in California. It was supposed to be bonding time, and the expectation was that I would want to get in a hot tub with a bunch of white dudes drinking beer. While walking through town near the ranch, someone yelled a racial slur at me and told me to "go home." Despite it being important work, I just didn't feel comfortable with the organizational culture. The feeling of not belonging prompted me to ask myself a lot of questions: Who are we trying to reach in this work? Whose voice is heard? This is what eventually catalyzed the formation of Greening Youth Foundation. I wanted the next generation of environmental leaders of color to have community, support, and a culture of belonging.

LEAH: Professor Lanham, you wrote, "I am a man in love with nature. I am an eco-addict, consuming everything that the outdoors offers in its all-you-can-sense, seasonal buffet. I am a wildling, born of forests and fields and more comfortable on unpaved back roads and winding woodland paths than in any place where concrete, asphalt, and crowds prevail."[10] You are so beautifully in tune with the natural world, yet as a Black ornithologist, you have noted that you are a "birding anomaly." How did you fall in love with birds, and what is your experience as a professional in a white-dominated field?

DR. J. DREW LANHAM: I've been birdwatching nearly my entire life. From age seven or eight, I have been in love with birds. I grew up on a family farm in Edgefield, South Carolina, and birds were constant companions and best friends. Often as I wandered in the woods between my parents' and my grandmother's houses, I would look skyward and see red-tailed hawks making lazy circles in the sky, and I'd watch the songbirds flit from one tree to the next. I started to live vicariously through birds. I always wanted to fly and had dreams of free flight. I wondered what the earth must look like from a migrating bird's viewpoint. I would cut out cardboard wings from big, old appliance boxes and make parachutes out of trash bags. As I leapt off of some ladder or roof or hayloft, I was thinking, "This is it, I will take off and fly, and everyone will be envious of me." While gravity always won, my fascination with birds never abated. I don't care how technically adroit or adept we become, try waving your arms for twenty-four hours and flying across the Gulf. You will never overcome the gravity that binds us to the earth the way the hawks do as they ride those thermals at Caesar's Head overlook in Cleveland, South Carolina.

Birds are our bellwethers, our proverbial canaries in the coal mine. Coal miners would bring a canary into the tunnels, and when the bird stopped singing, they knew it was time to get out, and fast, since it indicated the presence of lethal accumulations of carbon monoxide. The birds' singing gives us an indication of our well-being, and there are a lot fewer birds singing now. By some estimates, there are three billion fewer birds singing now than in the last century. I compiled a Christmas bird count at Clemson University for twenty-six consecutive years,[11] and the bird numbers for many species have declined year after year; species that we saw ten years ago are hardly seen now. There are fewer musical notes in the springtime, and that tells us something is amiss. Whole flocks of birds are falling dead out of the air inexplicably. Birds are like libraries offering an abundance of indicators about the well-being of the environment, and if they are not there, we cannot read them—cannot access the information that they are generously willing to give us.

To a rural southern person, the disappearance of the song of the bobwhite quail has been most jarring. It loves the ragged field edges, overgrown ditches, briar patches, plum thickets, and other unkempt corners. During my childhood, I could flush three to four coveys, each with eight to twelve quail, on my daily walk between my grandmother's house and the ranch. As the small farms disappeared, so did the quail habitat. Now you only find them in pine plantations where they are kept alive with supplemental feeding by the Natural Resources Conservation Service (NRCS). We need to talk about the anthropogenic impacts of habitat destruction, climate change, degradation of the soil and water, and air pollution on birds and other living beings. As Marvin Gaye sang, "Birds who live nearby are dying, oh mercy, mercy me."[12] We can't be silent appreciators; we need to be vocal activists.

As a career ornithologist, I've listed hundreds of bird species in hundreds of places, from coast to coast and abroad, from sea level to alpine tundra. But as a Black man in America, I do not fit into the profile of what a birder is supposed to be. Being a birder in the US means that you're probably a middle-aged, middle-class, well-educated white man. The chances of seeing someone who looks like me while on the trail are only slightly greater than those of sighting an ivory-billed woodpecker. In my lifetime, I've encountered fewer than ten Black birders, and I often feel unsafe in the remote rural areas that I must frequent for my work. As Black birders, we are true rarities in our own right.

The wild things and places belong to all of us, and part of my work as an educator is to make oddities become commonplace. As I explain in *Home Place*, the presence of more Black birders, wildlife biologists, hunters, hikers, and fisher folk will demonstrate to others that we, too, appreciate the warble of a summer tanager, the incredible instincts of a whitetail buck, and the sound of wind in the tall pines. Our responsibility is to pass something on to those coming after. As young people of color reconnect with what so many of their ancestors knew—that our connections to the land run deep, like the taproots of mighty oaks; that the land renews and sustains us—maybe things will begin to change.[13]

LEAH: Dillon, you started your work as a storyteller and creative when you were just thirteen years old, and you are the youngest person to be interviewed for this book. You have leveraged your talents to make substantial contributions to the environmental movement. What inspired your concern for nature and led you to use storytelling as the vehicle for engagement?

DILLON BERNARD: Since I was a little kid, I have consistently found myself rooted in feeling protected by Earth. The most powerful thing for me has been reflecting that back by caring for the planet in return. The history of this planet is one that has seen blood, sweat, tears, prayers, joy, and magic. It has been incumbent on me to conjure up those realities in shared vessels to ensure that energy shifts into power. I have been on a long-standing mission to understand who I am and to cultivate authentic connection to the immense power this Earth has.

One of my first loves was the idea of teaching and learning, and the second was the idea of telling stories through media. It is no surprise that these loves have turned into my passion-driven work as a storyteller. For me, storytelling is all-encompassing and includes the stories shared between friends, social media captions, graphics and visuals, etc. At its best, storytelling can be used as a powerful tool for self-empowerment and for transformative justice. Ultimately, it's at the intersection of organizing, policy, data, and storytelling that we see transformative change. We need all hands on deck to usher in the revolutionary change we seek. I have often found that the storytelling piece is underestimated and undervalued as we elevate social change. Unsurprisingly, the success, expansion, and shifting of power across social change relies on shifting the narrative. Storytelling allows us to connect to humanity by amplifying lived experiences while also prompting thoughtful dialogues around root causes and solutions. However, as proven in this digital-first era, the stories we tell can't end there. So often, we find stories of death and destruction amplified by media without the follow-up of concrete and meaningful ways to take action, which only adds to our collective hopelessness and pessimism. We must be intentional to ensure that we don't leave audiences with despair or false hope, but rather leave them with a concrete call to action.

Ultimately, I see myself as a translator. I focus on active listening in Black youth-led environmental spaces. I often spend my days translating policy wonkiness into digestible content, but in order to do so successfully, I rely heavily on other Black leaders to guide what we should say, while I figure out how we should distribute those truths. The most powerful mentors that I have are the other Black young people and allies who have been instrumental in sharing their perspectives. I am particularly inspired by the folks at Generation Green who work at the intersection of Black liberation, climate justice, and environmental justice. The reality is that there are limited Black young people at the decision-making tables across youth-led movements, including climate justice. By creating their own space, Generation Green is shifting the conversation and entering the space with a clear directive to elevate young Black voices.

LEAH: Angelou, you created Greening Youth Foundation to connect young adults with the outdoors and careers in conservation, using culture-based environmental education as an entry point. Since learning about your work, I have been spreading the word among Black youth that I mentor, and they are excited about the opportunities to apply for land management internships and other conservation experiences. Can you share more about the impetus for Greening Youth Foundation and some highlights of your current work?

ANGELOU EZEILO: Greening Youth started as an environmental education class that I led for Earth Day in my son's kindergarten in Snellville, Georgia, which in turn became a student environmental club. The president of the club at the time, then a third-grader, recently reached out to tell me that she is in college studying environmental science, having been influenced by that early club experience.

I grew up in an Afrocentric home where we were taught about our connection to the land. I knew we had a special, deep, and symbiotic relationship with land. Working in environmental spaces, I was seeing a gap between my understanding and the dominant narrative. I wanted to address the misconception that people of color are not interested in the environment. Only in recent years has the data been aggregated to show that people of color are huge supporters and protectors of the environment. You can look at the way votes break down on environmental questions and bond referenda at the ballot box to see that, when asked, Black and Brown communities vote overwhelmingly in favor of protecting the planet and creating more green spaces, and their support spans not just environmental justice issues, but all environmental issues. I find that information to be extremely empowering. You can no longer tell me I only care about food, housing, and education because of my skin color. That's the message I have gotten for too many years: "Oh, the state of the planet isn't your issue, let us worry about that. You keep fighting poverty and racism." Now we are announcing to the world, "Yes, we *do* care about green spaces, healthy food, and climate change."

The mission of Greening Youth Foundation (GYF) is to engage underrepresented youth and young adults in the outdoors and careers in conservation. We not only train youth of color to be stewards of the environment, but also lead them into actual careers in the environment—engaging, important careers that could sustain them for the rest of their lives in a discipline that has traditionally been shut off to people of color. This work has brought us some great successes as an organization; many former GYF interns are serving as park rangers across the nation or doing critical work in other sectors of natural resource management. April Baldwin is one former intern of GYF, and she went on to graduate from Tuskegee University and now works for the National Park Service. These proud moments come so often. When I see a young Black man or woman working in the parks, it's almost always a GYF intern or alumni. We also adapted our curriculum to work with young people in Ghana, West Africa. We certify young adults to be environmental educators in the local schools. We have done some GYF work in Liberia, South Africa, and my now homeland of Nigeria as well. Even as we expand, we are careful to listen to the needs of folks on the ground and have a bottom-up rather than top-down approach.

When it comes down to it, it's imperative that all youth have access to public lands and other environmental benefits. I remember visiting the Grand Tetons for the first time, and something very spiritual happened in that park. Those majestic mountains, so vivid, so looming, brought tears to my eyes. Upon seeing those mountains, you cannot deny that there is a bigger Force—God, Buddha, the divine by many names. How could anything be this beautiful? How could only certain people experience this, and not every child? That was a moment when I doubled down and recommitted to the work that I do. We must make sure that all children have access to wild spaces and that they understand these places are for them.

LEAH: Professor Lanham, you don't spend all of your time with birds. You have made the beautiful decision to share your passion and knowledge with the rising generation through your professorship at Clemson University and your civic engagement with environmental education. Why teach?

DR. J. DREW LANHAM: My mother was an award-winning biology teacher, as well as a homemaker and farm wife. My daddy was a farmer, teacher, and principal of a school that trained the "who's who" of future leaders of the Black Edgefield community. I grew up around dirt roads, orchards, vineyards, gardens, and spring water, but also surrounded by books and encyclopedias.

Lecturing has always come easy to me, and I have given hundreds of talks in the academy and at conferences. While I used to deal in regurgitated factoids and data, backed up by supporting slides of tropical rainforests being slashed, burned, and mowed down, I have shifted my strategy over time. Rather than badgering my audience into boredom and dread like an apocalyptic preacher, I work to inspire a caring selflessness that motivates people to make things better. Like Aldo Leopold, I am someone who "cannot live without wild things,"[14] and I try to transmit from my mouth to the hearts of others the miraculousness of such things as a warbler migrating over hundreds of miles of land and ocean to sing in the same tree once again. I try to invite the brackish bay-marsh tide to rise and the prairie winds to sweep through the crowd. If teaching is preaching, I've become a warmer and gentler pastor, more like the clergy at Mt. Canaan.

I also work to connect students with land-based fields that they may have otherwise ignored. I was teaching an ecology class recently for some of the best and brightest Black students who were looking to attend Clemson. During the break, they took out their candy bars to snack, and I told them that if they could name the origins of the first three ingredients in the bar, I would buy them all more candy. They did not know where the sugarcane, the cacao, or the peanuts came from, or how they grew. Black folks have been disconnected from food—not just from our physiological need for nutrition, but from our psychological need to be close to the soil, the root of us. It is hard to get Black children into agriculture classes because the field is misrepresented by guidance counselors and others, who say there is no future in it. Black and Brown youth are not pushed toward agriculture and the environment, instead limited to engineering and medicine, as if that's all smart Black people can do. Meanwhile more than 90 percent of Black farms have been lost. Education is the most malleable factor of change out there, and if environmental education was lauded at the level of most other STEM/ STEAM (Science, Technology, Engineering, Art, and Mathematics) disciplines, think about the progress that we would make. I am on the advisory board of the North American Association for Environmental Education (NAAEE), which is an imperfect organization doing a very good job of being appropriately uncomfortable as they incorporate an equity agenda. Organizations like NAAEE are working to open pathways for youth of color to get inspired and involved in environmental education.

The fact is that we belong in the wilds. In all my time in the outdoors, I've yet to have a wild creature question my identity. Not a single cardinal or ovenbird has ever paused in dawnsong declaration to ask the reason for my being. As educators, that sense of homeplace and belonging is something we need to foster in Black youth.

LEAH: Dillon, your "each one teach one" strategy is decidedly generational and uniquely impactful. You share information, not in the classroom, but via widespread media platforms. You leveraged media to increase impact during the 2019 US Climate Strikes and 2020 Earth Day Live. I was one of the thousands who participated in the New York City Climate March and was able to witness and be inspired by your work. Can you speak to your experiences curating and amplifying these two historic environmental events?

DILLON BERNARD: As part of the September 20, 2019, US Climate Strikes, my role was to think strategically on how we were maximizing the impact of our reach across social media using the power of content. Through #StrikeWithUs, we saw over forty-five thousand trackable social media posts that garnered over five hundred million social media impressions. For me, what was most important was the shift of the audience from passive audience members to impassioned changemakers, and we did just that. Throughout the day on September 20, I got to feel the energy of 250,000 people participating in New York City, the largest climate mobilization the world has ever seen. At the same time, I also got to amplify the over 1,300 locations that led events that day across the United States. Ultimately, that is the power of content creation in movement building: curating the stories of thousands of people with the goal of inspiring thousands more to take transformative action.

Earth Day Live 2020 was a digital event that occurred as the pandemic-impacted world shifted online, and movement organizing went virtual as well. Dubbed the "largest online mass mobilization in history,"[15] the event commemorated the fiftieth anniversary of Earth Day and reached over five million people. For me, this event marked a moment when it was more critical than ever to be intentional around expanding the base of who we are talking to. It really proved the power that intergenerational movement-building has; all throughout the live stream, young people were passing the microphone to adult allies, and vice versa. To see a wide range of changemakers—including celebrities and youth activists—come together to make a unified statement around a need to tap into the stories that connect us was awe-inspiring for me to witness and help curate.

LEAH: Wangari Maathai said, "We are called to assist the Earth to heal her wounds and in the process heal our own—indeed to embrace the whole of creation in all its diversity, beauty and wonder."[16] Angelou, what has the earth spoken to you about how we are instructed to heal together?

ANGELOU EZEILO: Nature has spoken to me about her incredible healing power in the most personal and traumatic of ways. The stress of starting a company alongside my roles as a wife, daughter, and mother got to be so much that I eventually had a stroke. As I was driving down I-85 with my husband, James, one day, the left side of my face began to droop, sliding downward as gravity tugged. The next thing I remember I was in a hospital room with my terrified family looking down at me. I was an exceedingly healthy thirty-nine-year-old woman, and the only explanation the professionals could give me was that I was overworked and stressed. My psychotherapist reminded me that while I was teaching kids to be stewards of the environment, I also needed to be my own steward. He prescribed twenty minutes of outdoor walking each day. I have kept up this practice, and I have not suffered another stroke.

We have become so disconnected from Mother Nature that I think we lose sight of the gifts she offers to the world. Whether it's the power of the outdoors to heal our ailments or the goodness of the food she produces, we have somehow gotten far away from understanding who she is and how the Creator has presented us with this magical entity so attuned to the needs of the human body. It's no accident that our chronic diseases, our mental state, and our physical instruments are all precisely calibrated to respond to nature in the most positive ways. We are animals, created to live amidst the natural environment and derive everything we need from it. It is tragic to me how thoroughly we seem to have forgotten this.

At the same time, the earth needs healing. She is telling us that she is hurting, and she needs us to understand that in order for her to give, the relationship needs to be restored. Until we heal the relationship, nothing can be right. Before we jump into action plans for emissions reductions or other practical measures, we need to focus on amplifying the respect and reverence at the foundation of the relationship. Humans and the rest of nature are in a symbiotic partnership, and we are not holding up our part of the bargain. Mother Nature says, "I am loving you, but I am not feeling the love from you. I am healing you, but I am not feeling the healing from you."

LEAH: Professor Lanham, you wrote, "I find myself defined these days more by what I cannot see than by what I can. As I wander into the pre-dawn dark of an autumn wood, I feel the presence of things beyond flesh, bone, and blood."[17] What are the things beyond the physical that you are hearing directly from the earth?

DR. J. DREW LANHAM: I've settled into a comfortable place with the idea of nature and God being the same thing. Evolution, gravity, change, and the dynamic transformation of field into forest move me. When I hear the reliable song of the wren with my full attention, with all distracting thoughts melting away, that's joy. The earth wants us to recognize the joy that the world (human society) didn't give us, and that the world can't take away.[18]

And speaking of taking, every day someone is felling more trees to build developments, such that no trees will ever grow in that place again. The earth is a living organism, and each act of destruction of green space and habitat is like excising part of the earth's organismal body. She scabs over and then we cut again. There are only so many wounds a being can sustain. I imagine a time far in the future when archeologists will look at the geological record of the Anthropocene, much like we now investigate the K-T boundary characterized by the mass extinction of dinosaurs. These future scientists will analyze our geological layer and see just plastic and death. The earth says, "Step back, slow down, chill out, and simplify."

I want to take back my forty acres and a mule, and return my hands to the soil. I want to tell the deer that I hunt in the forest, "My ashes will fertilize the trees that feed your descendants. I will give back what I took." We need to unlearn that progress is made of pavement. It's Jedi tricks that society is trying to take the earth from under our feet and get us to settle for whatever can be served up in a Styrofoam box. Growing up, aside from the Crisco and salt that we bought, everything we ate was dug from the ground. If we wanted french fries, we would dig up the roots, scrub, cut, and fry. That was fast food. The other kids would mockingly call us "bama" (Alabama) and "country," and it was not until much later that I understood that we were wealthy. Our wealth was in the five different gardens, the sorghum and sugarcane from which we pressed our own syrup, the hunted game and fish, the clear spring water, and the watermelon, cantaloupe, muskmelon, and string beans. As Black folks, if we say, "those trees have nothing to do with me," or we say "Farming, that is for slaves, I don't do that anymore," well, that's a death sentence.

LEAH: Dillon, as a member of the rising generation of environmental leaders, I think you should have the final word in this conversation. Are you hearing encouraging things when you listen to the earth?

DILLON BERNARD: If the earth could speak, she would tell us to step into our power. If there's anything that they can't take, it's our light. Our existence is powerful, but our commitment to sharing our past, reimagining our present, and questioning our future is revolutionary. To get there, we must step into our individual—and therefore collective—power. The numbers are on our side, as is the passion. There is a thirst to halt business as usual and rebuild the systems that are not serving us. Now, it's all about reckoning with our individual power, and then mobilizing it collectively.

Soil

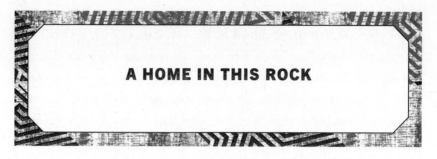

A HOME IN THIS ROCK

A Conversation with Dr. Carolyn Finney,
Latria Graham, and Savi Horne, Esq.

"You see?" the farm said to them. "See? See what you can do? Never mind you can't tell one letter from another, never mind you born a slave, never mind you lose your name, never mind your daddy dead, never mind nothing. Here, this here, is what a man can do if he puts his mind to it and his back in it. Stop sniveling," it said. "Stop picking around the edges of the world. Take advantage, and if you can't take advantage, take disadvantage. We live here. On this planet, in this nation, in this county right here. Nowhere else! We got a home in this rock, don't you see! Nobody starving in my home; nobody crying in my home, and if I got a home, you got one too! Grab it. Grab this land! Take it, hold it, my brothers, make it, my brothers, shake it, squeeze it, turn it, twist it, beat it, kick it, kiss it, whip it, stomp it, dig it, plow it, seed it, reap it, rent it, buy it, sell it, own it, build it, multiply it, and pass it on—can you hear me? Pass it on!"

—TONI MORRISON, *SONG OF SOLOMON*

After 246 years of toiling on the land of enslavers under threat of the lash, recently emancipated African Americans were eager for permanent, secure land tenure. The Black community of Falls Church, Virginia, wrote to the Freedmen's Bureau in 1865: "We feel it very important that we obtain HOMES, owning our own shelters, and the ground, that we may raise fruit trees, concerning which our children can say—these are ours."[1] At the suggestion of Rev. Garrison Frazier and a coalition of Georgia Black ministers, General William T. Sherman confiscated four hundred thousand acres of land from Confederate landlords and allocated forty-acre plots to Black families.[2] Just a few months after forty thousand Black freedmen were settled, Andrew Johnson overturned the order, evicted the Black families, and returned the land to the very people who had declared war on the US. The broken promise of "forty acres and a mule" was one insult in an egregious litany of Black folks being dispossessed of land in the US.

Though forced into the debt peonage poverty trap of sharecropping, Black farmers held on to hope of one day owning their own land. In 1862, the Homestead Act provided federal land grants to Western settlers as a mechanism for transferring 270 million acres of stolen Native American land to white people. De facto discrimination generally prevented Black people from participating. Instead, Black families saved up money and purchased nearly sixteen million acres by 1910, representing 14 percent of the nation's farms. The white supremacist backlash against expanding Black land ownership was swift and severe. More than 4,000 African Americans were lynched between 1877 and 1950. Black landowners were specifically targeted for not "staying in their place," that is, not settling for life as sharecroppers.[3] According to one investigation by the Associated Press, white people violently stole at least 24,000 acres of land from 406 Black people, depriving the Black farmers of tens of millions of dollars and often their lives. For example, Kentucky farmer David Walker and his family of seven were attacked by the Ku Klux Klan (KKK) on October 4, 1908. KKK members burned their house to the ground with one child trapped inside, shot and killed his wife and baby, and wounded the other children. The survivors were run out of town and the 2.5-acre farm was folded into the property of their white neighbor, whose family retains title to the present day.[4]

The US Department of Agriculture (USDA) was also complicit in Black land loss. Throughout the South, USDA agents withheld crucial loans, crop allotments, and technical support services from Black farmers, and excluded them from USDA county committees. For example, Mississippi farmer Lloyd Shaffer went to the USDA office to apply for the programs to which he was entitled. "On three separate occasions, the white FHA loan officer took Lloyd Shaffer's loan application out of his hand and threw it directly into the wastebasket. Once Lloyd was kept waiting eight hours, from the time the office opened until after it closed at night, while white farmers came and went all day long, conducting business."[5] By the 1950s, USDA programs had been "sharpened into weapons to punish civil rights activity." The founder of the White Citizens' Council, an association of white supremacist organizations, drew up a plan to remove two hundred thousand African Americans from Mississippi by 1966 through "the tractor, the mechanical cotton picker . . . and the decline of the small independent farmers." Black farmers who held on to their land used their independence to support civil rights workers, which often made them targets for lynch mobs and local elites.[6] In 1965, the US Commission on Civil Rights, an independent agency created by the Civil Rights Act of 1957 to investigate and report on a broad spectrum of discriminatory practices, released a highly critical study revealing how the Agriculture Stabilization and Conservation Service, the Federal Housing Association, and the Federal Extension Service bitterly resisted demands to share power and resources with African American farmers, leading to a precipitous decline in Black land ownership. In 1983, President Reagan pushed through budget cuts that eliminated the USDA Office of Civil Rights; officials admitted they "simply threw discrimination complaints in the trash without ever responding to or investigating them" until 1996, when the office reopened. In 1920, 925,000 Black farmers owned sixteen million acres of land, 14 percent of US farms. By 1970, the Black community had lost 90 percent of its farmers and its farmland.[7] "It was almost as if the earth was opening up and swallowing Black farmers," wrote scholar Pete Daniel.[8]

Black landowners often do not have access to legal services in order to create wills, so their property is inherited in common by their descendants, who become legal co-owners. Heirs' property is usually not eligible for mortgages, home equity loans, USDA programs, or government housing aid, tying the hands of property owners who want to invest in their land. Heirs' property is also vulnerable to corrupt lawyers and predatory developers because they only need to convince one heir to sell in order to force sale of the entire property; this is known as a partition sale. Developers hunt down distant relatives, often in other states, and offer them cash for their share of the land, then force sale of the entire property at auction. It is estimated that over 50 percent of Black land loss since 1969 was due to partition sales. Today, white people own 94.4 percent of the agricultural acreage in the US. "If we don't have our land, we don't have our family," says Queen Quet, Chieftess of the Gullah/Geechee Nation. "This is the battle we're in now." [9,10,11]

Without enduring, stable land tenure, a community's connection to the earth begins to erode. To understand how land and family are intertwined for Black people, we hear from Dr. Carolyn Finney, Latria Graham, and Savi Horne, Esq.

CAROLYN FINNEY, PHD (she/her), is a storyteller, author, and cultural geographer. Carolyn is grounded in both artistic and intellectual ways of knowing—she pursued an acting career for eleven years, but five years of backpacking trips through Africa and Asia, and living in Nepal, changed the course of her life. Motivated by these experiences, Carolyn returned to school after a fifteen-year absence to complete a BA, an MA on gender and environmental issues in Kenya and Nepal, and a PhD, during which she was a Fulbright and a Canon National Parks Science Scholar Fellow. Along with public speaking, writing, media engagements, consulting, and teaching, she served on the US National Park System Advisory Board for eight years. Her first book, *Black Faces, White Spaces: Reimagining the Relationship of African Americans to the Great Outdoors,* was released in 2014. Recent publications include "Self-

Evident: Reflections on the Invisibility of Black Bodies in Environmental Histories" and "The Perils of Being Black in Public: We Are All Christian Cooper and George Floyd." She is currently working on a performance piece about John Muir while doing a two-year residency with the Franklin Environmental Center at Middlebury College as the Environmental Studies Professor of Practice.

LATRIA GRAHAM (she/her) is a journalist and fifth-generation South Carolina farmer. She is a graduate of Dartmouth College and later earned her MFA in creative nonfiction from the New School in New York City. She received a Bronze level CASE Award for her reporting on immigration policy that stemmed from 2017's Executive Order 13769, often referred to as the "travel ban." After years of traveling the country to cover systemic injustice in underrepresented communities, she recently decided to turn her focus to small towns in the American South at risk of disappearing due to gentrification and Southern expansion. In 2019, she was awarded the Great Smoky Mountain Association's Steve Kemp Writer-in-Residence position, and for two years she has been in and out of conservation spaces, intent on unearthing long-forgotten Black history that she finds crucial to the narrative we tell about the American South. Her work in the region centers on the lives of the enslaved population that lived on the Tennessee side of what is now Great Smoky Mountains National Park. She holds contributing editor positions at *Garden & Gun Magazine* and *Outdoor Retailer Magazine*. Her work has been featured in *The Guardian*, *New York Times*, *Los Angeles Times*, *espnW*, *Southern Living*, *Bicycling Magazine*, and *Backpacker Magazine*.

SAVI HORNE, ESQ. (she/her), is the executive director of the North Carolina Association of Black Lawyers Land Loss Prevention Project. Savi completed six years of service on the National Environmental Justice Advisory Council of the US Environmental Protection Agency. She serves on the boards of the National Family Farm Coalition and the Rural Coalition. Savi is a member of the Coordinating Council of Black Land and Power Coalition and the leadership team of the National Black Food and

Justice Alliance. She is a recipient of the 2020 American Bar Association Section of Environment, Energy, and Resources (SEER) Award for Excellence in Environmental, Energy, and Resources Stewardship. As a state, regional, and national nongovernmental organization leader, she is instrumental in addressing the needs of Black, Indigenous, people of color, and limited-resource farmers and ranchers. Savi is a graduate of the Rutgers University School of Law in Newark (JD) and the City College of New York (BA).

LEAH: One of my all-time favorite poems on the relationship between Black people and land is by our beloved ancestor Margaret Walker. She wrote "My grandmothers were strong. / They followed plows and bent to toil. / They moved through fields sowing seed. / They touched the earth and grain grew. / They were full of sturdiness and singing . . ."[12] Each of you has forebears who were strong and who worked with the soil. What did that relationship to land look like in your family and in your formative years?

LATRIA GRAHAM: In the town of Silverstreet, Newberry County, South Carolina, there is some acreage that has been in my family's possession for five generations, more than a hundred years. At a time when many other African Americans were still sharecroppers, we owned the place we called home. Mary Emma Graham, my father's mother, lived there in her yellow two-story house tucked into a canopy of pines, as did my aunt Molly and uncle Allen, my uncle Charles and May Jane, and my cousins. The green one-room shack where my daddy was born still stood. When I was young, I spent weekends and summers on the farm. At age fourteen, we moved out to the land full time. I worked with my dad growing crops like squash, cantaloupe, and eggplants, and we set up a produce stand. That produce stand was how I paid for public boarding school fees. We knew all about the wild plants, such as yellow root, bloodroot, honey locust, and poke salad, which was the first green of spring. When you were out of your winter stores of preserved food, in the muck season after the snow, poke salad would be the thing that got you through. I remember how my great-uncle Devoe had planted those yellow plum trees in the front yard, and the plums had this indescribable sweet flesh. I remember soaking watermelon seeds in sugar water the night before planting them to make the fruit sweeter, and learning how to process hogs in the old family smokehouse. Farm to table was a way of life, rather than an afterthought.

A lot of my relatives started dying off and leaving the land. We lost my father, Dennis Graham Jr., in 2013 after a battle with kidney cancer that metastasized to his lungs and brain. His death came 364 days after we closed the produce stand. I think he was unwilling to see the anniversary of the end of something he loved so much. My grandmother Mary passed away in March 2020, right at the beginning of the pandemic. I think when they told her she could not have any visitors, she just up and died. I think both my dad and my grandmother died of heartbreak. My father left no will, leaving us with heirs' property. That Vann Newkirk piece in the *Atlantic* about Black land loss—that's not about somebody else, that's what is happening to me.[13] For the last seven years, I've tried to save our stake in the Graham land, paying the property taxes and insurance on my daddy's parcel, but ultimately ran out of money. The land went to the auction block for the highest bidder.

DR. CAROLYN FINNEY: My parents, Rose and Henry, are originally from Floyd, Virginia, by the Blue Ridge Mountains. When my dad came back from the Korean War, he was denied a job as a park ranger in the South, so he wanted to take his family north in search of employment opportunities. He took a job as a full-time, live-in caretaker of a twelve-acre estate in a very wealthy white neighborhood outside of New York City. My father had a twelfth-grade education but understood land—the wildlife, fungus, gardens, foliage, and soils. The owners only came up on the weekends and holidays, so my two brothers and I had free rein to play in the gardens, the woods, and the pond. I grew up with that land as the landscape of my imagination and belonging. We lived in the "gardener's cottage" and were the only family of color in that neighborhood until the 1990s. At age nine, I was stopped and questioned by the police on my walk home from public school for being out of place.

On my parents' fortieth wedding anniversary, my father gave my mother a weeping cherry blossom tree. It's the only romantic gesture of his I can ever remember witnessing. They planted that tree in the garden on the estate. My parents cared for that land for nearly fifty years. When the white landowners passed away and the land came into new ownership, my parents were forced to move back to Virginia, this time to Leesburg. My father always talked about how much he missed the land up in New York. We later learned that the owner who took over once my parents left tore out the weeping cherry blossom of my parents' love. That tree was our memory and legacy, and it was destroyed. They got rid of everything that needed daily tending—the flower beds, vegetable gardens, and fruit trees—all that my father had cared for. When someone buys land, they are not required to know anything about its history, and they have no accountability or responsibility to that legacy of belonging. Privilege has the privilege of not seeing itself.

We later got a letter from the Westchester Land Trust saying that the new owners had put a conservation easement on the twelve-acre estate, touting its ecological value, and thanking the landowners for their conservation mindedness. It was astounding to me that the letter thanked owners who had been there for only about five years but did not mention the family who had cared for the land for fifty years. Just like that, my parents were erased.

I was able to return to the estate this past summer with the land trust and a film crew doing an HBO documentary about my family's connection to that land. Together with the most recent owners, we planted a new cherry tree. Everyone present agreed to become accountable to that tree.

SAVI HORNE: I grew up in the maroon community of Refuge Hill in the District of Exchange, Parish of St. Ann, Jamaica. I was raised by a mighty river. I would scale down the steep escarpment, navigating my small, flexible body and using the shrubs to break my skid. We children would wade across that roaring river and go up on the other side to the ridge where men, women, and children were chipping stone in the quarry for one penny per pound. It was in that village that I developed my formative connection to the earth. My uncle Mack was a yam farmer. He built yam mounds and placed a stake in each one. I remember going out with him one full moon night to those yam hills and sitting still enough that we could hear the sound and see with our own eyes the yam vine creeping up the stake. I have never forgotten that sound and that movement in the night—this generational experience of the sacred yam growing. This scene has played itself out in my connection to the earth, plants, and all people.

In 1995, I was working with a prominent African American NGO in Zimbabwe, where that sacred connection to land was challenged by colonization. At the time, you had twelve thousand Europeans owning 94 percent of the country's arable land and 97 percent of the water rights. Africans were complaining about how inhospitable and infertile the remaining land was, and they were building social activism around their plight. Yet, even in these parched lands, Africans were creating earthen dams to trap water and make things grow. They made compost out of leaves, fruit, and dry soil. I was living in the capital Harare, and my sanctuary was a backyard garden where I would work together with my neighbors to grow food. We grew bananas, cucumber, tomatoes, and mushrooms. We made stews and dried out fruits and vegetables for the seasons when none was available. Through this process of engaging with my African brothers and sisters, we came together as one. They were taught that we American Blacks hated them because of slavery, and so we needed to connect on our own terms and form a new bond. When I returned to the American South, I brought this deepened understanding of what it means to be Black and dispossessed of land.

LEAH: Mama Savi, you often cite the biblical passage that reads, "God gave you the land . . . do not fear or be dismayed." You add, "Dispossession of land becomes an intergenerational pain."[14] The Land Loss Prevention Project (LLPP) has been working for over three decades to stem African American land loss, using legal strategies and community economic development. In your work with LLPP, how do you see land dispossession and reclamation impacting the Black community?

SAVI HORNE: Our ancestors' relationship to the land that they toiled was deep and profound. There were some emancipated people who would leave the plantation and then be compelled to go back because they found that they couldn't live without a particular grove of trees.

This relationship is precious and also tenuous. So much of the land that Black people could afford to purchase was in sensitive and fragile ecosystems, such as coastland, floodplains, or erodible soil—places like Cairo, Illinois, at the confluence of the Ohio and Mississippi Rivers. Families have long used "tenancy in common agreements" to own land together, which is a culturally adapted form of kinship commons that builds upon land tenure systems used in African villages. This adaptive behavior of holding a land title collectively as a family makes sense. We could never trust the white lawyers in the local community, or the white courts, but we could trust our families. So that family was the bridge to the future to continue the legacy of land stewardship. Unfortunately, Western law makes so-called heirs' property very vulnerable. For example, when a climate disaster hits, you need a clean property title to access federal programs or disaster relief. We saw this in New Orleans, which is one large, extended African social system and network bonded by lineage. A lot of homes did not have clear titles, so could not participate in relief programs. Given that our lands are ecologically vulnerable and the issues with title, we become even more susceptible to climate disaster.

In our work with the Land Loss Prevention Project the losses are plenty, but the victories are also numerous, and I never give up. For example, many of our farmers are seeing that their conventional row crop model is not yielding economic benefits, and they do not want to continue in that vein. Yet they worry that sustainable and regenerative farming is not possible when there is no labor to assist them. There was one tobacco farm, heavily in debt and on the brink of going out of business, that we helped stabilize with the assistance of the North Carolina A&T extension and local NGOs so that they could make the transition to sustainable farming. This farm is now ready to pass on to the next generation. Another example was Dorathy and Philip Barker's farm, which they had to reimagine after they lost their original land. They found new land and have moved into aquaponics and fish culture, acknowledging that fish is among the most important proteins in the African world food system. Their work on the tilapia enterprise demonstrates the sheer tenacity and determination of a family farm, and it is a powerful example for the younger generation of Black agrarians. In the midst of failure, they can hold on to hope and rebuild.

LEAH: Sometimes, despite our best efforts across generations, we do become dispossessed of land. In these cases, we may need to keep alive our connection to the soil by focusing on the micro rather than the macro. I think of my grandmother Brownie Lee McCullough, in blessed memory, who lost her family land near Rock Hill, South Carolina, but kept a well-loved strawberry patch and crabapple tree in peri-urban Boston, Massachusetts. Latria, your writing on "ugly trails" strikes me as similarly claiming connection through celebration of the small, marginal, or overlooked details of the landscape. Can you tell us about ugly trails?

LATRIA GRAHAM: I was visiting Atlanta, Georgia, in early spring during African American Nature and Parks' "Hike Like a Girl" weekend. I wanted to hike a new trail, and local folks recommended Arabia Mountain View Trail. It was, honestly, granite gray, monotonous, and in the flight path of one of the world's busiest airports. There was no cathedral of green or stunning sunsets, nothing that would perform well on Instagram. My eyes were starved for beauty. In the midst of pouting about what was missing from the landscape, I slowed down and looked at what was actually there. Right below me there was a profusion of diamorpha, these hardy mountain-adapted plants with red succulent leaves that repel sunlight and hold on to water. Here was a plant adapted to grow in this one particular spot. My curiosity was piqued. Beside the diamorpha, I noticed the little yellow blossom of the Eastern prickly pear cactus. Life is not win or lose, it's win or learn.

In a similar way, I have a practice of staying connected to birds, which are ubiquitous. As a child, my dad fussed at me all the time because I had no patience. To observe and know birds means you have a deep practice in relationship to yourself, because it requires stillness and extended time in observation. Birds can go everywhere, and yet they choose to be with us sometimes and grant us the pleasure of listening to them. I have come to understand that even when you think you don't have any nature around you, the birds prove you wrong. At the Harlem Meer in Central Park you can see the butterbutt warbler (*Setophaga coronate*) show its yellow butt as it flies away. There are red-tailed hawks there, too. Nature can find you, even among the tall buildings. Watching these creative birds make lives for themselves, and adapt to challenging habitats, gives us inspiration for our own survival. Even though I am not religious anymore, it's powerful that the first animal to leave Noah's ark and come back with something was a bird. Birds teach me patience. Birds teach me magic. Birds teach me beauty.

LEAH: Carolyn, in your book *Black Faces, White Spaces* you write beautifully about the deep irony of the Homestead Act, which was propelled by the European belief that "land is a man's very own soul."[15] European colonizers felt that this belief justified their expulsion of Native People and Hispanos from their land, and their exclusion of Black people from secure land tenure as well. You witnessed a similar pattern of European colonial land use in your travels across Asia and Africa. How did your work abroad and at home inform your understanding of "right relationship" with land in this colonial context?

DR. CAROLYN FINNEY: While it's important not to romanticize or amalgamate Indigenous cultures, it's also true that there is a certain understanding and way that cultures become embedded in the landscape. To understand Mount Everest, it is the Sherpas that we need to ask. For the US and European adventurers in the Everest region, the landscape was simply a recreational playground, a proverbial supermarket of resources. The labor, the work lovingly embedded into the landscape, and the care of the land was not recognized.

In the US this "supermarket ideology" has meant colonizers literally trying to wipe out Native people and steal the land. It has meant enslaving Black people. Imagine what a person has to do to perceive themselves as so separate as to make it okay to behave in these ways. It's a form of psychological gymnastics that is required to cause massive harm to people and to nature. This way of thinking underpins capitalism, consumerism, and private property. What is "right relationship"? I cannot answer that for Nepalese people or for Kenyans. But my idea of "right relationship" is a deep commitment to a particular piece of land and to remain connected to that land even if forced to leave.

LEAH: In *Gloryland*, Shelton Johnson wrote, "Wilderness is just a word, and the wind got no use for anything that come out of our mouths except songs or prayers. Only then are we speaking from our hearts and are worth listening to. Otherwise, we should just be quiet and let trees and sky do the talking. The wind's been talking since the world began. I've been listening to it since I was born, and I ain't been bored yet."[16] When you are quiet and let the trees, sky, and water do the talking, what do you hear the earth saying?

LATRIA GRAHAM: I listen to water and the relationship it has to the earth— the ocean is a big talker. The earth is the thing we were formed from and remain tethered to. What happens to earth happens to me. I look at myself as an extension of everything living. I understand that what we take from this ecosystem, we must replenish.

The earth also says to be kind to ourselves and one another, and to show grace. This is something I learned as a farmer, in those moments of frustration when I did everything right, and yet the unexpected happens and the crop is ruined. The impulse toward anger and destruction can be strong in those moments. According to capitalism our inherent worth is based on our output, and there is no grace for mistakes. In a system that forces you to calibrate yourself to these notions of productivity at all times, you can end up doing harm on a widespread level. When you shift to an understanding that there is a larger set of natural systems at play when the hail ruins hundreds of acres of peaches, and that you are not particularly targeted, you are able to connect to grace and even levity.

DR. CAROLYN FINNEY: We need to hone our ability to interpret the different languages through which the earth speaks to us. Scientists who go to the North Pole or Antarctica to pull up columns of ice are reading a language of the earth. When arborists read history through tree rings, they are creating a direct line of communication with nature. Through our chosen practice, we too can cultivate a direct line through which to listen to the earth speak. The ability to hear is honed, as we all have filters and biases through which we interpret. To hear is to make a commitment to being in relationship and building the necessary skills.

This relational framework is not new. As I wrote in *Black Faces, White Spaces*, "Africans and Native Americans recognized that plants, animals, and humans all had a place in the world and should be treated with respect that acknowledged the interdependence of all things. This view contrasted with widespread beliefs among white men at that time who felt that nature should be dominated and exploited for profit and who espoused a form of Christianity that supported the separation of humans from nature."[17]

My father loved the comedian George Carlin and agreed with his basic sentiment that it's arrogant to think we humans can "save the earth" and that the planet will "shake us off like a bad case of fleas" when our time is up.[18] It's not to say that the earth does not suffer at our hands, but that our fear of being small and inconsequential prevents us from comprehending that the Earth is much greater than us. Again, it comes back to relationships. What does it mean to strengthen and center our relationship with each other, and with the earth itself? Even as we feel locked in and complicit with a system, how do we take risks to let go of some things that are no longer serving the relationship and see what might emerge? As Moms Mabley said, "If you always do what you always did, you always get what you always gotten."[19]

SAVI HORNE: Those of us here in this conversation have a special relationship with the earth. We step gingerly and reverently on it. The earth would say to us, "Heal the breach; stop the destruction of your planet home; there is still time to protect and restore the planet through regenerative practice, to stop raw exploitation of resources, and to reverse the breakdown of the moral fiber that binds us to life." Being good stewards of the planet means recognizing that we are not here alone. It means pouring libations to recognize that we stand on the shoulders of our agrarian ancestors. Everything imaginable on our land sprung from their labor, pain, and aspirations for us. When we ground ourselves in an African agro-ecological framework, it helps us fight for economic, gender, and planetary justice. Grounding our meetings and gatherings through pouring of libations and building ancestral altars roots us in our collective responsibility for each other and the planet. The ancestors are working for all of us, not just you or me.

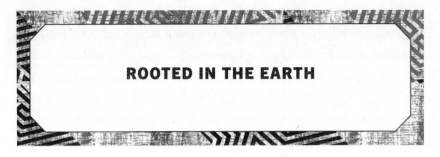

ROOTED IN THE EARTH

A Conversation with Greg Watson and Pandora Thomas

Thinking about and listening to the land can conjure up feelings of stolen dreamspace, stolen lifeforce, and domination. Coming from that perspective, servitude can feel like inferiority. But servitude is grounded in our dignity—it is our birthright to be in service to the land, and it is the only way we can heal our trauma. This dedication does not need to feel oppressive. A true calling to the land invites us to be in genuine service . . . Nature teaches us to be in harmonious relationships—so how do we make our relationship whole again? Until you offer yourself, surrender to be in embodied practice, it will be difficult to recover this relationship. The only way we can receive our Mother's love is to be in service to her. This call is one of reciprocity, and is an exchange of care. Without this care exchange, we don't know the ways the land can nurture us. Even when we don't show up, we are still provided for and taken care of. Imagine what is possible when we show up for the relationship.

—ALSIE PARKS AND WHITNEY JAYE, BLACK AGRARIAN WORKERS
OF THE SOUTH COLLECTIVE (BAWS)

A dangerous mythology prevails that Black people's relationship to land is circumscribed by chattel slavery and has no connection to the global organic and regenerative agriculture movements. The truth is that for thousands of years Black people have had a sacred and sustainable relationship with soil that far surpasses our 246 years of enslavement and 75 years of sharecropping in the US. For many, this period of land-based terror has devastated that connection. We have confused the subjugation our ancestors experienced on land with the land herself, naming her the oppressor and running toward paved streets without looking back. We do not stoop, sweat, harvest, or even get dirty because we imagine that would revert us to bondage. As Black farmer Chris Bolden-Newsome explains, "The Land was the scene of the crime."[1] I would add, "She was never the criminal." Part of the work of healing our relationship with soil is unearthing and relearning the lessons of land reverence and agrarian innovation from the past. Part of healing racism in America is to give credit where it's due to Black, Indigenous, and Asian peoples for their contributions to regenerative ways of tending agroecosystems.[2]

Our ancestral grandmothers in the Dahomey region of West Africa braided seeds of African black rice (*Oryza glaberrima*) into their hair before being forced to board transatlantic slave ships. They also brought with them okra, molokhia, levant cotton, sesame, black-eyed pea, and melon seeds. They stashed away amara kale, gourd, sorrel, basil, tamarind, and kola as insurance. This seed was their most precious legacy, and they believed against odds in a future of tilling and reaping the earth. They believed that we, their Black descendants, would exist and that we would receive and honor the gift of the seed.[3]

With the seed, our grandmothers also braided and carried their ecological and cultural knowledge to the Americas. African people, expert agriculturalists, created soil testing systems that used color to classify fertility, and examined texture by feel to determine detailed particle size classifications.[4] Egyptian farmers in Cleopatra's kingdom developed the first vermicomposting systems, operating under the decree that citizens would face harsh punishment for harming any worm.[5] Ghanaian women built African Dark Earths (AfDE), a compost mixture of bone char, kitchen scraps, and ash that built up over generations. Offering an abundance of organic carbon, AfDE were used to fertilize crops and establish successional home gardens.[6] African farmers developed dozens of complex agroforestry systems, integrating trees with herbs, annuals, and livestock.[7] They built terraces to prevent erosion and invented the most versatile and widely used farming tool, the hoe.[8] African people invented the world's initial irrigation systems five thousand years ago and watered the Sahel with foggaras that are still in use today. They were early domesticators of work animals and established rotational grazing systems for livestock that created fertile ground for grain crops. Our ancestors created sophisticated communal labor systems, cooperative credit organizations, and land-honoring ceremonies. On Turtle Island, Black agriculturalists like Booker T. Whatley, George Washington Carver, Fannie Lou Hamer, Shirley Sherrod, Ralph Paige, and Harriet Tubman brought us Community Supported Agriculture (CSA), organic and regenerative farming, cooperative farms, community land trusts, and Black herbalism, respectively. Even as the colonizers of this land ravaged the soil of 50 percent of its carbon in their first generation of settling, Black farmers used ancestral techniques like mounding, deep mulching, plant-based toxin extraction, and cover cropping to call the life back into the soil.[9] Our ancestral grandmothers braided all of this wisdom and more into their hair and brought it across the Middle Passage. It is our heritage.

The struggle to hold on to a sacred relationship with land continues in the Black farming community today. Take the example of Pembroke Township in Illinois, founded in 1860 by self-emancipated slaves, and once the largest population of Black farmers north of the Mason-Dixon Line. They grew hemp, vegetables, and fruits organically and biodynamically for generations. Pembroke farmers like Frederick Carter and Dr. Jifunza Wright Carter of the Black Oaks Center continue to farm and work on the front lines of environmental protection. Most recently, they led a campaign to stop a natural gas pipeline slated for construction.[10] Despite the diligent stewardship work of Black agriculturalists, white-led environmental groups like the Nature Conservancy have seen Black farmers as an obstacle to their conservation goals in the savannah. When farmers raised concerns about a conservation land grab that would bar them from their ancestral practices of foraging, hunting, and horseback riding in the marshlands, employees at the Nature Conservancy referred to their protests as "melodrama."[11] Like Black farmers across the US, those in Pembroke struggle to hold on to what little land remains in their families.

Greg Watson and Pandora Thomas are among the thousands of Black farmers carrying on our ancestral legacy, and they have powerful personal stories to share about "right relationship" with land.

GREG WATSON (he/him) is director of policy and systems design at the Schumacher Center for a New Economics. He is currently leading an initiative to reimagine Buckminster Fuller's World Game Workshop. Watson has focused on understanding systems thinking as inspired by Buckminster Fuller and applying that understanding to achieve a just and sustainable world. In 1978, Watson organized a network of urban farmers' markets in the Greater Boston Metropolitan Area. He served as commissioner of agriculture in Massachusetts from 1990 to 1993, and from 2012 to 2014. In 2012, he launched a statewide urban agriculture grant program. Watson gained hands-on experience in organic farming at the New Alchemy Institute on Cape Cod. He served as executive director of the Dudley Street Neighborhood Initiative, a multicultural grassroots organization for which he initiated one of the nation's first urban agriculture programs. Watson founded the Cuba-US Agroecology Network (CUSAN) in 2015.

PANDORA THOMAS (she/her) is a passionate global citizen whose work emphasizes the benefits of applying ecological principles to social design. For the last ten years, her earth service has included being a care partner for her mother; cofounding the Black Permaculture Network; working as a coalition member of the Toyota Green Initiative to support African Americans in understanding the benefits of adopting sustainable lifestyles; directing Pathways to Resilience, a permaculture and social entrepreneur training program for formerly incarcerated folks; working with the Urban Permaculture Institute in Marin City to support the People's Plan process; and serving as an advisor, codesigner, and facilitator with Women's Earth Alliance's Grassroots Accelerator Program. Her lifelong commitment to honoring ancestral legacies of earth stewardship, centering the contributions of people of African Ancestry, and reclaiming our shared earth care journeys is culminating in her most recent gift to the planet, the EARTHseed Permaculture Center and Farm, the first all-Black owned and run farm in Sonoma County. EARTHseed's programming will elevate the earth stewarding contributions and legacy of peoples of African ancestry throughout the Diaspora. She is also currently a co-owner of the Urban Permaculture Institute and a Senior Climate Innovation Fellow with the Movement Strategy Center Climate Innovation Team.

LEAH: Yrsa Daley-Ward wrote, "I was raised pulling food out of the earth. I know where joy comes from. How to make it."[12] Greg, can you speak to experiences in your early life that connected you to the joy that can be pulled from the earth?

GREG WATSON: I grew up in a Black neighborhood in Cleveland, Ohio, on the shores of the Cuyahoga River and Lake Erie. The lake's polluted waters were eutrophied, suffocating the chemically poisoned fish, and the Cuyahoga was polluted with so much flammable effluent that someone could flick a cigarette off a barge, and the river's surface would erupt into flames. I remember huge plumes of black smoke. Randy Newman's song "Burn On" was about the Cuyahoga, and we were the butt of many jokes.

My connection to nature and the living world was forged in the environment. We lived with our grandparents who were from a farming community in Trenton, Tennessee, in Gibson County, and part of the Great Migration. My grandmother's name was Josephine Wade, but everyone called her Big Mama. We had a tiny postage stamp of a backyard, but Big Mama got the most incredible production out of her vegetable gardens and the two fruit trees—an apple and a peach. The basement was filled with canned tomatoes, and she kept a crock on the back porch where she fermented dandelion wine. She had to have known that my brother Butch and I were sampling it every once in a while.

My friends and I were super nerdy and fascinated with the lives of insects. We gathered living insect specimens in jars converted into terrariums, wrote labeled cards with information from the encyclopedia, and built a movable insect museum that we wheeled around on a wagon. It was very popular with the neighborhood kids. My best friend, Mike, even had a pet praying mantis that he walked around on a string. We found ways to make the most of a Cleveland childhood.

LEAH: Pandora, you also credit your upbringing and lineage with your connection to the earth. How do you understand permaculture as related to the principle of Sankofa, of going back and fetching our stories in order to move forward?

PANDORA THOMAS: I credit my Black and Native ancestors. Both sides of my family have farmers dating all the way back through my lineage on the African continent. My mother's family specifically was part of the sharecropping legacy in the South, which led to a destructive relationship with the land, but that didn't stop her from teaching me about the natural world after they migrated north. I was raised seeing myself as a seamless extension of the earth, so I grew up loving and honoring all living things, and knowing that they were all connected.

Then I discovered permaculture. And because permaculture is a design system rooted in the idea that we are from and part of the earth, I got really excited about it. Environmental education teaches us to "go into nature." Permaculture teaches us that we are nature. The only challenge was that even though permaculture design is based on practices of Indigenous peoples from all over the world, including my own people, it had mostly been white folks of means who were spreading it.

I have been blessed to be able to study permaculture in communities around the world from which it originated, including in Venezuela, Cuba, and across Latin America. Permaculture's asset-based approach resonated deeply with me. I was a kindergarten teacher and knew that the children were not empty vessels. They already had knowledge and were bringing as much to the lesson as I was. So it is with the earth. We build on and respond to what's there, rather than tilling and clearing a bare template. We design as if nature made it, as if the earth did it. Take for example the modernized water system, which is based on "pave, pipe, and pump." What if we turned that on its head, capturing and storing water, and teaching it to walk where it needs to go? We can start with the resources and knowledge already existing in the place, and then bring external expertise and materials only as needed.

Industrial farming is a destructive practice—we are forcing the earth to create bounty however we determine. Permaculture talks about a permanent form of agriculture where we can right that relationship by understanding the type of environment that best nourishes crops and not taking more than we need. The three central ethics of permaculture are "earth care, people care, and fair share." So for example, if I'm growing corn, I want to grow a bountiful crop so that there is enough for corn to just survive as corn, for corn to be eaten by animals, and for corn to be eaten by humans. That corn is functioning within the larger cycle of an ecosystem.

Permaculture sees the problem as part of the solution. As Bob Marley said, "The stone that the builder refused will be the head corner stone."[13] When embarking on a project, we develop a deep relationship with the site, and we use on-site resources to make a way out of no way. This is commonsense grandmother wisdom. These principles mirrored the teachings that I had grown up with, and therefore embodied Sankofa.

LEAH: Given that the majority of African Americans live in cities or small metropolitan centers, a focus on urban agriculture makes sense for those concerned about the continuation of Black agrarianism.[14] Anecdotally, we have found that around two-thirds of our aspiring farmer trainees at Soul Fire Farm have urban agriculture backgrounds and are looking to make the leap to rural spaces. Alongside trailblazers like Will Allen and Rashid Nuri, Greg, you have done groundbreaking work to promote urban agriculture. Can you talk about the urban farming journey, from Cuba to Dudley Street?

GREG WATSON: I was serving my second term as the Massachusetts commissioner of agriculture, and we had just established a statewide urban agriculture funding program. A colleague asked me about the best examples of urban agriculture that could serve as models. My son Travis, a self-taught student of the Cuban revolution, directed me there. The powerful thing about urban farming in Cuba is that it grew out of necessity after the collapse of the Soviet Union and the US embargo, which curtailed oil supplies. The average Cuban lost fifteen to twenty pounds in that time period, and some were near starvation. They had to figure out how to grow food without chemical fertilizers and pesticides. Their solution pulled everything together—permaculture, agroecology, annual agriculture, vermiculture, and abundant composting. We saw urban agriculture plots everywhere, including some with large acreage like Vivero Alamar Cooperative Farm. While it arose out of necessity, it was fully embraced, and Cubans became some of the most articulate and passionate advocates of organic farming. The social organization was also notable. Women were the lead organizers, and they formed cooperatives so they could reap the shared financial benefits from selling produce at markets and co-ops. Farmer-to-farmer sharing of information was their form of an extension service. One farmer would try out a new technique, say an application of pest control. If it didn't work, the other farmers would supplement the food and crops lost in the sacrifice test plot. If the experiment succeeded, the farmer would share the technique with others free of charge.

I got to Boston in 1967, a few years before the Boston Urban Gardeners (BUG) was established.[15] The community gardens they helped organize were part of the struggle to gain access to land and resources as a community. We did not want a UK-style allotment program where the government maintained control of the land. My mentor was Mel King, the strongest advocate for agriculture in the Massachusetts legislature and Boston's first Black mayoral candidate. He was a quintessential networker who took an inclusive rainbow approach to organizing, getting to know everyone face-to-face. Consistent with this approach, we raised money through potlucks and dances to purchase our land. We put the land into a community land trust run by just two staff and an intricate and supportive web of volunteers. When topsoil was needed, BUG cofounder Charlotte Kahn led an effort that convinced Lt. Col. Tony Grosse to enlist members of the US Army Reserves 642nd Battalion to cart topsoil from a biomedical park construction site in Worcester all the way to Boston. That was the power of organizing.

After serving my first stint as commissioner of agriculture, I was convinced by the board of the Dudley Street Neighborhood Initiative (DSNI)—a resident-led and resident-driven community organizing and planning nonprofit—to serve as their executive director. I was there for four years, and I really should have paid them for the privilege to serve. It was more than a graduate degree in life. DSNI was governed by a thirty-member board of directors including equal representation of Cape Verdean, Latino, African American, and white residents. Their attendance at the monthly meetings was impeccable. There was always a potluck with good food, and it felt like family when we came together. Board seats were hotly contested, and elections were monitored. It was true self-governance. In a neighborhood that had been ravaged by divestment, arson fires, and dumping, they were charting the future of their community, and they knew the power the land could give. DSNI gained eminent domain authority, purchased vacant land, and decided to establish collective control by establishing a community land trust. Residents owned their own homes, and the community owned and leased the land. The vision was to create an urban village; we worked on housing first, then urban agriculture and economic development. In collaboration with the Food Project, we tore down a defunct commercial garage and replaced it with a ten thousand square foot greenhouse. The youth worked with architects and students from MIT to design Commons North and Commons South, an area where people from outside the community had been selling drugs and engaging in prostitution. They wanted to see if they could design the crime out without relying on policy. Members of the neighborhood did what professional planners could not. They showed that development and displacement are not synonymous. The community chose the land trust model. It was not forced or ordained. It allowed for everyone to stay.

LEAH: As a teen at the Food Project, I worked in some of the community gardens and farmers' markets in the Dudley Street neighborhood, so it's powerful to hear the backstory of their formation. Pandora, you also have an ambitious project to get land into the hands of the community. Can you talk about EARTHseed?

PANDORA THOMAS: I was in seminary at Union Theological feeling fed up and frustrated by colonial education, especially its inability to hold religious diversity or the old dark-soil, rootsy, earth-centered Black forest church spirituality that was my home. Then my professor Dolores assigned Octavia Butler's *Parable of the Sower*, and I realized that Lauren Olamina's journey to Earthseed was the journey of my own life. EARTHseed Farm and Community is what I was put here to do. After decades of learning and dreaming, EARTHseed Farm was established in March 2021. We are a fourteen-acre solar-powered organic farm and orchard located on the ancestral lands of the Coast Miwok and Southern Pomo Peoples of the Federated Indians of Graton Rancheria in Sonoma County, California. We are grateful to have the permission and blessings of the Graton Rancheria Tribe to be on the land and operate the farm. There was already a mature orchard of apples, pears, persimmons, plums, pluots, guavas, and mixed berries on the land that we are shifting over to a diverse food forest based on Afro-Indigenous permaculture principles. We are building a Fibershed arts program, greywater recapture systems, heritage cropping, and a culinary program. The hope is that learners will arrive at EARTHseed and immediately see the African legacy of the practices that we demonstrate. As people with long histories of displacement, it is important to know that we have this earth, this place that can hold us over time. It is important that we work to heal the rift between Black folks and our nonhuman kin.

LEAH: Greg, as someone who has been in this work for decades and is respected as an elder in the movement, what advice do you have for the rising generation of Black farmers and earth stewards?

GREG WATSON: Getting back to the land is essential, but not everyone needs to be a farmer. Black farmers in the South were cheated out of their land, resulting in the current situation where 98 percent of agricultural land is white owned. The top two farm owners in this country hold millions of acres; it's way out of balance. Initiatives like the Justice for Black Farmers Act, which would create a pull factor for Black folks to return to the land, are part of the solution. We need to be aggressive and get it done, and it is young and energized folks who are the practical visionaries we need. Some are farmers, while others are focused on sophisticated political solutions. For example, Charles M. Blow calls for a reverse migration to repopulate the South and establish a Black political majority in a number of states.

It is also important to be open to innovation as we consider the appropriate technologies that allow us to provide food, energy, and shelter in environmentally sound ways. Our designs will not be exact replicas of nature, but will draw on the principles of nature in the spirit of biomimicry. Aquaponics is one example of that. At the New Alchemy Institute, where I worked and played for over three years, we raised hydroponic plants in tandem with fish, whose waste enriched the water that nourished the plants. We converted polluted water into nutrient-rich water. Nature does not think in terms of externalities. Pollution is a valuable resource in the wrong place. There are some health officials who say that produce in contact with fish waste is a no-no, and others who think soilless agriculture is not appropriate, but we need to overcome that. It is possible to grow enough food on one-tenth of an acre to feed thirteen people with no chemicals. New Alchemists demonstrated that it is possible to build a greenhouse bioshelter in the Northeast with no backup heat and to raise tropical fish, fig trees, and banana trees (designing in "the extreme" to punctuate the bioshelter's full potential). Being open to innovation and entrepreneurship is important. Words of caution: It was city residents of color who laid the groundwork for urban agriculture, including zoning for commercial farms in the city. But now we have an influx of nouveau riche coming in with capital and building vertical farms, freight farms, and other high-tech, capital-intensive innovations. We will not be pushed out and exploited again.

LEAH: Arguably, the people who spend the most time in direct contact with the earth are those most able to hear the messages of the earth. In our society, farmers are the people with the most contact hours with Mama Earth. When asked what the earth says to her, Germaine Jenkins of Fresh Future Farm, South Carolina, wrote:

> As a Black farmer, I make waves with soil. Moving earth with my fingers. Grounding. Reconnecting. Remembering. Resurgence. Power. Dewdrops, wind, sweat, heat, rain, songs of birds, insects, and breathing swirl in rhythmic harmony. Parables of reaping and sowing and counting chickens manifest before me. Ancestry flows through flesh and

bone; its wisdom becomes my inner voice. My heirs are now branches, embarking on their own journeys with the land, each layered with a unique story. Nature's library is always teaching. Land in the South feels like a giant altar charged with a thousand ancestors.[16]

When you listen to the earth, what do you hear?

PANDORA THOMAS: She cries a lot. I don't conceive of natural disaster as the earth coming to get us, but rather, the earth speaking to us. When the water encroaches, it's a communication to move inland. Our Native ancestors looked at the birds, insects, and critters migrating. We looked to the sky and saw that it was the time in the cycle for us to move on. The Earth wants us to slow down, listen, and consume less. She needs us to be doing a lot less driving and flying, less designing of things to exist so many steps away from their source. She needs us to be in a deeper relationship with nonhuman beings and outside of human-built structures. We, too, are animals. If you tore your skin away, you would be the same collection of muscles and bones. We, too, are trees. When I look at the Santa Cruz redwoods, I see that their skin looks like mine, and I feel more beautiful. Redwoods brought me to my true tree nature, understanding that I am a tree in human form. The trees remind us to go back to our roots and to hold the complexity of our relationships.

GREG WATSON: Full disclosure, I think the earth does speak. I am a believer in the Gaia hypothesis that the earth has an intelligence that transcends our intelligence. By extension, our intelligence is part of the earth's intelligence. She tells us that we humans are here for a special reason, and it's not to dominate or to be passive, but to be a constructive partner in the process of planetary evolution. The challenge is that we have to reconcile our understanding of and commitment to local social and ecological systems alongside the planetary systems. There is a global aspect that we have to understand. If we are to achieve peace and realize our full human potential, it will require an unprecedented degree of global cooperation. Even as we focus locally, we need to keep our eyes on the whole earth. For example, there is no way we can build enough solar panels and wind turbines to achieve international greenhouse gas emissions goals if every country does it alone. There are simply not enough resources, and we would be mining minerals unsustainably. We need a 100 percent renewable-energy-powered and globally interconnected energy grid—originally proposed by Buckminster Fuller—that takes advantage of the fact that half of the world is always in daylight and that somewhere on earth the wind is always blowing. The earth will be around to maintain the conditions necessary for life, and she would love for humans to be part of that. But if our consciousness can't keep up, she is fully prepared to say that humanity was a noble but failed experiment, and she will go back to the drawing board to come up with another thoughtful, mindful cospecies to collaborate with her.

OLDWAYS

*A Conversation with Dr. Claudia J. Ford
and Dr. Leni Sorensen*

I need to hear the bumping of pestles making percussion with
sunrise and twilight. I need the scratch of grating tubers and the
grinding of spices on stone. I need the sonic world of the ancestors,
lullabies said while babies are fed, bawdy songs as the land is
smoothed for planting. I need to understand the sound of the wind
in the rice and the complexities of the yam mounds intercropped to
save space. I need the rustle of the oil palm fronds so I can hear the
generations speak.

—MICHAEL W. TWITTY, *THE COOKING GENE*

I t was 1999, and I was working a summer internship at the Farm School
in central Massachusetts, where I was on the livestock-care rotation,
mucking stalls, milking cows, and slinging hay bales. A group of
Boston elementary school students came out for a multiday field trip,
and I had the enthralling assignment of teaching them to milk the cows
by hand. As I sat on a stool next to one young Black boy, coaxing warm
milk from the cow's udder by way of demonstration, he became very
pensive and asked, "Doesn't meat come from cows, too?" I responded
gently, anticipating a deep conversation about the cycles of life, "Yes,

some people do eat cow meat and the meat of other animals as well." Brow furrowed, he followed up, "Well, which one do you squeeze to get the hamburger?"

The comment was funny and charming, but also tragic. Many of us have become so disconnected from our food that our children do not know that carrots grow underground, much less have a connection to their ancestral foodways. A litany of recent scientific studies has verified the long-term health value of traditional African diets, which are rich in leafy green vegetables, roots, tubers, fish, legumes, and fermented whole grains.[1] Researchers put twenty middle-aged African Americans on a traditional African-heritage diet and twenty middle-aged rural South Africans on a typical American diet. After two weeks on the African-heritage diet, the African American study participants showed more diverse healthy gut bacteria, increased levels of butyrate—an anticancer chemical—and reduced inflammation of their colons. On the other hand, the African study participants on the American diet showed greater production of bile acid and lessened diversity of healthy gut bacteria.[2] As younger populations of Africans drift from traditional to nontraditional lifestyles, signs of metabolic syndrome, such as increases in weight, blood pressure, and cholesterol, are becoming more prevalent.[3] In the US, home cooking has declined overall in the late twentieth century, but non-Hispanic Black people cook at the lowest rates of any demographic group.[4] Only one in five African Americans has a diet rich in fruits and vegetables.[5] Furthermore, as a result of US food apartheid—where Black and Brown communities are flooded with highly processed, government-subsidized commodity foods—rates of diabetes, heart disease, and other diet-related illnesses are catastrophic.[6] In the face of these alarming trends, there are committed chefs and cooks like Chef Njathi Kabui, Michael Twitty, Bryant Terry, Edna Lewis, Jessica B. Harris, and Dr. Leni Sorensen who have refused to let our foodways slip through our fingers.

The Black American community's relationship to our wild food and medicine ways has also been under assault. During enslavement, foraging provided Black people with a means of survival and economic health. In an effort to keep African Americans on the plantation, Southern states enacted criminal trespass laws during Reconstruction that made it illegal to forage and hunt, thereby undermining economic self-sufficiency. European settlers also forbade Turtle Island Indigenous communities from gathering food and medicine on their ancestral lands, and the Indian Removal Act and the Dawes Act further extricated Native people from their homelands and coerced them into colonist-style agriculture. Today, foraging is banned or discouraged in most US cities, impacting residents' ability to span the "grocery gap" with fresh-harvested nutrition.[7,8] Yet, Black foragers persist. Folks like Alexis Nikole Nelson, who hosts the wildly popular @blackforager social media accounts, are inspiring a generation to fall in love with garlic mustard, dandelion flowers, and serviceberry. In the words of Robin Wall Kimmerer, wild foods like serviceberry—called *Boʒakim* in Potawatomi—have a "wild, complex chemistry that your body recognizes as the real food it's been waiting for."[9]

In traditional African communities, there is an exiguous distinction between food and medicine, both being gifts from the natural environment. According to the World Health Organization, over 80 percent of people on the continent of Africa rely on traditional medicine as their primary health therapy, with much of this medicine being gathered from uncultivated lands. This ancestral way of being in healing relationship with plants was carried across the Atlantic with enslaved Africans. Priests, herbalists, and magicians, initiated into their trade back in their homelands, pursued their vocation to the extent possible in a hostile American setting. African-based herbal medicine, spiritual healing, and their associated plant pharmacopeias have persisted in some Black American communities. An average of 17.4 percent of African Americans retain their relationship with herbal medicine, despite centuries of assault on the practice.[10] We offer our gratitude to Black herbalists like Amanda David, Adaku Utah, and Karen Rose, and ethnobotanists like

Dr. Claudia J. Ford, who are among those keeping our sacred plant-medicine traditions alive.

It is an honor to be in conversation with two keepers of the oldways, midwife and ethnobotanist Dr. Claudia J. Ford, and chef and culinary historian Dr. Leni Sorensen.

DR. CLAUDIA J. FORD (she/her) has had a career in international development and women's health spanning four decades and all continents. She is a midwife and ethnobotanist who studies traditional ecological knowledge, women's reproductive health, and sustainable agriculture. Claudia is a tenured professor and Environmental Studies Department chair at the State University of New York at Potsdam, where she teaches sustainability, gender studies, ethnobotany, traditional ecological knowledge, environmental literature, and environmental justice in classrooms and workshops. Claudia serves on the Soul Fire Farm Institute board, joining a team committed to ending racism and injustice in the food system. Claudia has a BA in biology from Columbia University, an MFA in creative nonfiction writing from Vermont College of Fine Arts, an MBA in health administration from Antioch University, and a PhD in environmental studies from Antioch University. Claudia is also a writer, poet, and visual artist. As a single mother, she has shared the delights and adventures of her global travel with her four children.

DR. LENI SORENSEN (she/her) was born in California in 1942, was a member of the 1960s folk music recording group the Womenfolk, farmed for eight years in South Dakota, and is the mother of four and the grandmother of seven. Throughout all those years she cooked, taught cooking, and talked about food, at one time catering to movie crews and at another starting a tamale business. After moving to Virginia in 1982, she majored in history at Mary Baldwin College and earned her MA/PhD at the College of William and Mary in American studies. She worked for over thirty years as a university lecturer, museum consultant, hands-on presenter, and researcher with a focus on African American slavery, American agriculture, and women's work in colonial and postcolonial America. Retired from six years as the African American Research Historian at Monticello, she now continues to lecture, consult, and write on issues of food history, and she teaches home provisioning and rural life skills from her home in Western Albemarle County. She publishes an e-newsletter from her website and is working on digital presentations to reach more people.

LEAH: Mama Claudia, your connection to plants and their physiological and spiritual medicine has been passed down through your lineage. How were your grandparents and great-grandparents connected to the plants in their Virginia home, and how has the connection transcended generations and geography?[11]

DR. CLAUDIA J. FORD: Hayden Brown was my grandmother's father and I knew him well, as he lived until I was seventeen or eighteen. He was the elder head of the family, a farmer, and an herbalist; he was always out in the fields. One of the plants he loved to use was fireweed, which was a tonic for longevity. He mixed the plant material into moonshine to make a tincture and then stored it in jars. If we children had a stomachache or other ailment, Great-Grandpa would be sent out to pick the fresh plants, and then they made tea and we drank it. Even as my mother kept a running commentary in the background about old-fashioned people and their country ways, it was a normal part of growing up.

His daughter, my grandmother, Elsie Vivian Hill, was the oldest of six, and they called her "Big Sister" until the day she died. She was the head of the family, no doubt, and was responsible for moving the extended family back and forth between our land in Newport News, Virginia, and Harlem and the Bronx in New York City, driving in tight caravans to be safe across the Jim Crow South. I remember how she would transform when she stepped back onto the land that she grew up on, which had been passed down for seven generations. She put on her country clothes and apron, took off her shoes, and started running around the farm planting things, tending the goats, pumping well water, gathering medicinal herbs from the backwoods, cleaning leaves off the graves in the family plot, and bringing fresh food to distant relatives. My mother, the city girl, would be fussing, moaning, and complaining. But the country was where my grandmother came alive. The land was the geography of her heart, and it was good to us.

Even though my grandmother only had one child, unusual for her generation, she kept hundreds of houseplants in her immaculate third-floor, walk-up, three-bedroom apartment in the Bronx. Every single possible space in that apartment, from the fire escape to the bathroom, was covered in plants; it took hours just to water them. Each plant had a name and a particular location based on the sunlight. She sang church hymns to them, prayed over them, and loved them. Grandma would take a bit of mayo and carefully polish the leaves of the succulents. She had a thick century plant on the kitchen windowsill that she told me bloomed only once every one hundred years, and it happened to open its yellowish blossom while I was visiting her home from college one time. Her tiny backyard garden was a similar tornado of beans, corn, tomatoes, herbs, fruits, vegetables, peach trees, and grapes. The plants were her children, her friends, and her confidants. In her, I witnessed the possibility of finding connection with the natural world even in our urban cells.

LEAH: Dr. Sorensen, how did you come around to home cooking and gardening? What were the formative experiences in your childhood that made you interested in foodways?

DR. LENI SORENSEN: I grew up in Logan Heights, San Diego, in the late forties and early fifties in an overcrowded section of town that was a destination for migrant and immigrant communities, including Black Southerners, Mexicans, and Japanese people. Each came with their own accents, language patterns, and social customs. There were sixty-eight kids packed into my second-grade class. My mom was a white Unitarian communist, and my stepdad was Black; at that time interracial marriage was illegal, so almost no one let their kids play with me. I was scared and intimidated, but unimpressed by the other kids, so I spent nearly all my time in the refuge of the small Carnegie Library. I was a voracious reader, devouring every book in the children's section, and then convincing the librarians to let me into the big section where I pored through stacks of *National Geographic*, *Life*, the *Post*, and *Ebony*. Perhaps because I was a hungry little girl, one of the things I loved to read and learn about was people who produce their own food.

Our Unitarian church was the first to refuse to sign the Loyalty Oath, and many parishioners were called up before the House Un-American Activities Committee. The church did a lot of fundraisers and activities to support poor and working people, and they talked in a very respectful way about agriculturalists. I was trained to see Mexicans, Southerners, Africans, and South Americans who could produce food from the land as qualitatively superior to the rest of us. Even if they had more children than teeth, or couldn't read or write, they deserved respect as food producers.

Martha Gonzales was my friend in third, fourth, and fifth grade. Her mother still made tortillas by hand every day, with beans and salsa cruda to complement. This fascinated me, because my daddy Roberts, who grew up very poor in New Orleans, always made cornbread, beans, greens, and rice. These two cuisines were almost identical in ingredients but tasted different. I could, and did, eat either five days out of seven.

After his mother died, Daddy Roberts left school in the third grade to take care of his four siblings while his father worked. Daddy was taciturn, and he expected you to comply when he told you what needed to be done. He taught me how to cook by Southern Creole standards, and he had some real fixed notions about gravy. On Fridays in the summer, we would go around to the church fundraising dinners, where the church ladies and men set up their card tables on the sidewalk and put out their stuff. You could choose barbecue chicken, ribs, fried fish, smothered green beans, or cornbread, all from different kitchens and all featuring the same core ingredients. This gave me a deep sense of this community's foodways, and how agriculturalists tend to eat the same thing over and over and over again.

LEAH: You are a student of plant stories, Mama Claudia. As a midwife and women's health practitioner, your relationship with plant medicines that support reproductive health is both personal and scholarly. My heart is stirred by your stories about blue cohosh (*Caulophyllum thalictroides*) and cotton (*Gossypium sp.*) in connection with Black and Native child-bearers. How have our people been in relationship with these plants?[12]

DR. CLAUDIA J. FORD: I have a very personal connection with blue cohosh. I started in women's health as a teenager, and by the time I was twenty, I was attending births and ultimately became a midwife. We used blue cohosh to stimulate and support parturition, especially when labor had slowed. When I started doing research about plant medicine and culture for women's health, this plant came up in the historical research almost immediately. *Caulophyllum thalictroides* was used by Narragansett, Cherokee, Chippewa, Iroquois, Menominee, Meskwaki, Mohegan, Ojibwa, Omaha, Ponca, Potawatomi, and other Native healers to assist with childbirth and menstrual health. The knowledge of the curative powers of this plant circulated between Indigenous, African, and European Americans at a time when childbirth was a really scary thing and the safety of mother and baby was far from guaranteed. As a descendant of slaves who were ripped from their home place, I will never be native to a place. Yet I know my people have traditional ecological knowledge. One of the goals of my research was to understand how ecological knowledge is related to place, but also something you carry as a people.

Enslaved Africans brought with them their knowledge of midwifery, Cesarean section technology, herbal medicines, and other effective medical practices. Among their knowledge of medicinal plants was the many properties of cotton. The root of the cotton plant stimulates uterine con-tractions and was used as an abortifacient. Enslaved women were often forced to submit sexually to planters, owners, and enslaved and free Afri-can men in order to increase the enslaved population. As I wrote in "Pain Pollen: The Story of Cotton," "African women urgently put cotton to use as a means of exercising some control over the inhumane and heinous breeding practices of slave owners. Even as enslaved women bloodied their hands picking the masters' bolls, they used the roots of the plant to thwart unwanted conception."[13]

LEAH: Dr. Sorensen, I first saw you speak at the 2017 Black Farmers and Urban Gardeners Conference in Atlanta, where you offered the keynote. I was sitting next to our then farm manager, Larisa Jacobson, when you admonished the gathered farmers for offering the best harvest of the land to the market, rather than prioritizing home provisioning. You said that the highest-quality, freshest, most delicious crops should go directly onto our family tables. Larisa and I looked at each other, guilty as charged, and we have not thought about farming the same way since. Can you explain your relationship to "home provisioning" and its importance?

DR. LENI SORENSEN: I had a lot of experience catering, making tamales, baking my own bread, hand-milking cows, and teaching cookery by the time I met my husband, Kip, through an ad I placed in *Mother Earth News*. He had grown up on a 160-acre farm in Flandreau, South Dakota, where they raised milking cows. He was an ex-con who didn't have any money, but he knew how to do some real stuff. Together, we decided to go all-in for traditional, hand-scale farming. We moved to a northeast South Dakota farm where we lived rent free in exchange for taking care of 3,500 acres with cattle. We established a huge garden in an area where the cows had grazed for over a decade, then pigs for ten years, and fi-nally had lain fallow for ten years. That amazing rich ground could grow weeds that were taller than me, and I'm five feet nine. That land is where

I learned winter gardening. We raised animals for home provisioning as well. Someone gave us a whole flock of old hens in exchange for us fixing her porch. I learned how to induce molting, and we had eggs. A neighbor discovered that his pigs had rhinitis, which is not contagious but can cause them to not flourish. He gave us those pigs, and we raised them and butchered them; that was my first butchering. Our friend arrived at 10 p.m. one night with an antelope they had hunted and asked if we wanted it. I told him to hang it in the basement, and that became my first experience skinning a wild beast. I preserved the meat by canning it. Neither Kip nor I was squeamish, and we didn't mind blood and guts. I could never bear letting any food spoil or go to waste, so I had to learn how to do these things on the spot. From there, we moved back to the place where my husband was born and started farming pinto and great northern beans, tending a four-acre truck garden, and raising sheep, pigs, and Jersey cows. We also had two babies born at home.

All the while, I have also been reading about history, both global and American history. I wanted to understand what our Black forefathers and mothers knew how to do, but more so, how they knew what they knew. I consider our forebears to be professional agriculturalists, despite others battling with me over the term. They were not merely peasants. Farming was their primary occupation, and they were experts. Yes, they worked under slavery, under the lash, under the most horrid umbrella of repression, but that does not negate what they knew as farmers. All seventeen slave states had a similar deadly weekly rationing system, consisting of a peck of cornmeal, a pound or two of salt pork, some salt, and a little molasses once in a while. Enslaved people had to figure out how to provide the rest for themselves, and also provide for the big house. At Monticello, we have a detailed three-year record of the crops bought by white families from Black families—hundreds and hundreds of dozens of eggs, scores and scores of young chickens, bushels of vegetables. Black agriculturalists were not tabula rasa. For example, they knew that the time to plant corn was when the oak leaves were the size of a squirrel's ears. This is because oak leaves burst forth in between other tree species—after the eager willows and before the conservative black walnuts. Oak leaves are the size of a squirrel's ears just after the last frost, which means that an attentive farmer can trust that it is safe to put the corn seed in the ground. They knew how long it would take to bring a cow or pig into season, and when to bring your sow in from pasture so she could give birth. It takes skill to pick cotton, which is why those who mastered the skill could slide over and help those who were slower pickers. Their knowledge was at least as good as the farmer's almanac.

This is true of the cooks as well. Rarely do white people acknowledge how well James Hemings, Edith Hern Fossett, or Frances Gillette Herns cooked for the Jeffersons. We know that they acquired culinary expertise under the guidance of French chefs. We have reports of the excellence of the food from those who ate at the Jefferson table, with misplaced credit to the Jeffersons. By any measure they were professional chefs who learned to make fantastic and beautiful meals that exceeded the requirements of elite dining. I respect James Hemings for not poisoning those SOBs and for carrying on doing what he did with excellence, even without the response or respect of white people.

I am now living and teaching in Virginia at our family's farmstead where my husband's ashes are buried. Kip and I tended the same garden plot for over three decades, transforming the soil from the usual Albemarle County red brick clay to a deep, dark friable brown loam. I grow as much of my own food as possible. Among my favorites are the tart, old-fashioned firm tomatoes that host a healthy population of parasitic wasps who keep the hornworm under control. With two hot-water bath canners and one steam canner, I can process almost thirty jars of tomatoes in a single afternoon. I love to grow parsnips, and I dig them out in January at their sweetest. We have one beautifully generous persimmon tree that bears sixty to one hundred persimmons in a year. I love the bitter bite of greens, like mustards and collards, that offer a richness of texture—a mouthfeel—that I find superior to the sweets and salts that dull the American palate.

I named our mountain farmstead Indigo House and in the spirit of the dictum "each one teach one," I pass on foodways, home provisioning, and rural life skills. It may be an urban myth, but I once heard that the average American family does not have three days' worth of food in their homes, making them more vulnerable to emergencies. That's scary, and I want my work to help change that.

LEAH: Herbalist, educator, and artist Ayo Ngozi wrote, "Our human approach is what it is—sometimes reverent, generative, and expansive, too often disrespectful and extractive. It's fine to be an herbalist, to be a teacher. It's good to read our books and harvest the plants for our medicine. But, and, the earth is the temple and the deity, the shrine and the marketplace. This work is a kind of priesthood, but it is nature, and not humans, that determines who are her priests."[14] Mama Claudia, you have also talked about the earth as sentient and have invited us into "kincentric relationships" with nature. Can you explain this understanding?

DR. CLAUDIA J. FORD: The term "kincentric ecology" comes from the research of Enrique Salmón and other Indigenous thinkers.[15] There is an understanding that all earth forms are relatives, part of an extended ecological family with common origins and ancestry. This is not the Western way, though subtle aspects of this framework survived in my lineage, and my grandmother would certainly speak to plants as her relatives. When you know that you are related to a being, your neurons fire differently. The love for someone you call your grandmother, brother, sister, or child engages your whole being, including your nervous system, into a compassionate and generous mode. So, if we have a kincentric point of view, then we extend our capacity for compassion out to all living things. A mother will lift a car off of their child, should circumstances necessitate it. We understand the psychological and physical shift, the superpower of love, creating strength and protection. How cool would it be if we felt that way about all the living earth, if we simply could not bring ourselves to hurt the earth? This is the Indigenous way of thinking, and it still exists in many places.

From a kincentric frame, we are also invited to remember that just as we love earth beings, we are also loved by the earth. As a Black person who suffers daily from the pain of discrimination and bias, from the onslaught of daily news of racial injustice, from the pain, grief, and trauma of our history, it was a revelation to me when I first internalized that the earth is not against me. I was on a birthday vision quest in South Africa, having lived there for ten years. I went to the mountains in the Western Cape and spent four solo days fasting among the snakes and scorpions. I had an epiphany about my own fear of nature, and I realized that while people and society might intend to harm me, nature was not out to hurt me. While we need to be respectful, careful, nonharmful, and attentive, it's not as if the snakes are lurking in the shadows waiting to attack. My relationship with nature is one where she says, "I see you, I love you, you are okay, I am not judging you." I never get a microaggression from a tree. I have to remind myself of that truth. Nature is not, and never was, against us.

LEAH: Dr. Sorensen, you have said that you are "about as spiritual as a stainless steel pan,"[16] so I won't ask you what the earth says when she speaks to you, but I will ask you what advice you would give to the rising generation around being in "right relationship" with the earth.

DR. LENI SORENSEN: On the most immediate scale, every Black person with land needs to have a goddam will that clarifies their legal relationship to that land. I have seen the travesty scores of times: When all the children went up to Chicago, leaving Daddy behind in Jackson, Mississippi, and when he dies without a will, the law states that all the heirs need to be notified and they need to agree to do something, in the interim paying taxes on the land while everything is in probate. Since the siblings aren't talking to each other, and none of them want to live in Mississippi, the acres don't mean anything, so they stop paying taxes and the land goes up on the annual auction list in the newspaper. Of course, in this racist system, the white guy next door can get a bank loan and buy up those acres. And then the Black family wants to cry rip-off! Because I am old and crotchety myself, I am good at talking to groups of elders about why it's important to have a will and how to talk to their children about what they want done with the land. Maybe one of the children wants it, and an arrangement can be made to let them pay over time or just inherit it for free. Even if none of the children want it, we can talk about bringing in a young apprentice who will farm for two, three, four years for free rent, and then be positioned to buy it. This is what happened with siblings Matthew and Althea Raiford of Gilliard Farms. Their grandma was a bright, sensible woman who made a damn will, and she left the land to her descendants who would carry on farming the land and not sell it off.

We can't really begin to talk about how to farm the land, our ecological values, or anything else, until we have the land. So land retention is the place to start. Back when I was in Canada in 1971, I asked Black folks around me whether they were thinking about land. And they said, "No, we just got off the plantation." Even though they were born in Seattle, and their mother was born in Chicago, and their grandmother was born in Memphis, making them three generations off the plantation, they still had a deep feeling of ugliness about the land. It's good to see the current reclamation of land among the younger Black generation.

This way of life is not about self-righteous positioning or the serotonin high you get when you buy three tomatoes and six bunches of arugula at a farmers' market, paying more for the produce than the gas it took to get there. It's not about gurus or speculative philosophy. A lot of folks putting forth lofty ideas about the food system have clearly never grown a tomato in their lives. Folks need to figure out how to incorporate baking bread into their lives or keeping a garden, and giving up their cherished, privileged, elitist notions about urban life. I know this is a loaded statement. And if the young, woke generation wants to come after me, this is my address!

LEAH: Mama Claudia, you have lived and worked in eleven countries over the span of thirty years, and more recently rooted down in the Northeast woodlands. Over the course of these experiences, what have you heard the earth saying to us as human beings?

DR. CLAUDIA J. FORD: I have been so fortunate to have seen so much and to have been let in so deeply. My children went to school in the Dominican Republic, Belize, Bangladesh, Thailand, Cambodia, Angola, South Africa, Swaziland, Zambia, Germany, and the US. I often found myself sitting on the floor talking with mothers about our families while my children and theirs were running around. I witnessed extreme material poverty, especially in Bangladesh. In traveling back and forth between the US and whatever country I was in, I recognized that we misname wealth here. The people with their hands in the dirt, those who know the origin stories of their animals and food, who have relationships with other women, and who honor their grandmothers, had a spiritual wealth that was missing in my own life. There is deep spiritual poverty in the US.

Connected to the idea of true wealth are the concepts of generosity and gratitude. The plant world takes sunlight and gives the planet everything it needs, which is the ultimate generosity. Each seed multiplies itself one hundred thousand times, feeds us, and reassures us that we will continue to be fed. What an act of generosity. We are using up and destroying things, and we are not appropriately thankful. Nature is waiting patiently for us to grow up and figure out how to connect to our gratitude.

Apparently, scientists are now finding out that animals and plants have sentience. That makes me laugh, because of course they do. Not only are humans related to and part of all nature, but there is no separation between humans and nature. All beings have sovereignty and sentience.

There is a specialness to the human condition, but it is not superiority. To recognize this truth with humility will fundamentally change how we interact with each other. If we want to hear the earth and speak to plants, we need to slow down. We don't hear because we move too fast, and we are not observant or focused. Our aesthetic forms, such as art, music, and beautiful language, are similar forms of communication to what nature employs. For that reason, our creative skills and practices are very important as we accept nature's invitation back into kinship.

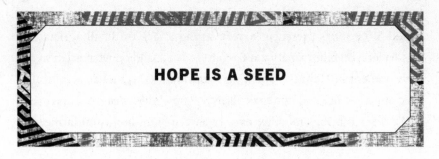

HOPE IS A SEED

A Conversation with Aleya Fraser and Ira Wallace

And so, right before the arrival of dawn, Mama Tjowa took a bundle of the rice that her people brought with them from Africa, and carefully braided the grains in her hair. And then, they ran, far, far away from the plantation, tééé (until) . . . they arrived at a hidden place, deep in the forest, where a lot of trees had fallen. . . . They burned the trees, Mama Tjowa loosened her hair, and shook the rice seeds on the ground. Some time later, rice seedlings grew from out of the fertile soil. Then, they took the harvest even further upriver, and did the same thing again. And today, we plant and eat from the same rice, that Mama Tjowa brought for us to survive.

—ORAL HISTORY OF THE MATAWAI MAROONS IN SURINAME

In the wake of the magnitude 7.0 earthquake* that devastated Haiti in 2010, claiming around three hundred thousand lives and severely disrupting the food system, Monsanto arrived with a donation of sixty thousand sacks of hybrid and GMO seeds. The seeds were treated with fungicides such as Maxim XO and thiram, highly toxic EPA-regulated chemicals that require workers to wear protective clothing while handling them.[1] The Peasant Movement of Papaye, a group of Haitian farmers and a member organization of the international Indigenous-led La Vía Campesina, pledged to burn the seeds at the port. They called Monsanto's presence "a very strong attack on small agriculture, on farmers, on biodiversity, on Creole seeds . . . and on what is left of our environment in Haiti . . . Fighting hybrid and GMO seeds is critical to save our diversity and our agriculture." The United Peasant Movements (G4) of Haiti brings together over twenty-five million rural farmers on a united platform of food sovereignty and coordinates native seed exchanges to keep the local seeds alive.[2,3]

Corporate control of our world's seed supply is a grave concern of earthkeepers globally. Ben Burkett, a Black farmer of the Federation of Southern Cooperatives, emphasized,

> You've got a few companies that want to control all the seed stock of the world, and they've just about got a handle on marketing three of the main commodities: corn, soybean, and cotton. [For us,] it's hard to find seeds that aren't treated with the Monsanto-manufactured Roundup Ready. I've tried to find cotton that wasn't treated, but I couldn't. Now they're working on controlling wheat and rice.[4]

His experience underscores the importance of the work to save heritage seed in our own communities. Just sixty years ago, seeds were largely stewarded by small farmers and public-sector plant breeders. Today, the proprietary seed market accounts for 82 percent of the seed supply globally, with Monsanto (Bayer) and DuPont owning the largest shares.[5]

In the US courts, plants and seed were historically interpreted to be products of nature and, thus, not patentable. However, profit-eager lobbyists persuaded the federal government to pass the Plant Patent Act of 1930, allowing biological materials to be patented. On seed patenting, Vandana Shiva wrote, "Some Western companies remind me of a doctor who performs a C-section and claims he also made the child."[6] Proprietary seed corporations are effectively claiming ownership over the seed developed by generations of careful selection.

Lobbyists also convinced the government to end the widely popular farmer-to-farmer seed distribution programs of the early 1900s, paving the way for consolidation and privatization. Monsanto, founded in 1901, began buying up smaller seed companies and eventually became the first company to genetically modify a plant. Genetically modified seed now dominates the commodity crops. The Food and Drug Administration (FDA) reports that genetically engineered (GE) soybeans comprise 94 percent of all soybeans planted in the US, GE cotton accounts for 94 percent of all cotton planted, and GE corn makes up 92 percent of corn planted. The result has been a decimation of crop biodiversity.[7]

The Food and Agriculture Organization (FAO) estimates that we have lost 75 percent of the world's crop varieties in the past one hundred years, and 22 percent of the wild relatives of certain staple crops. Today, 75 percent of the world's food is generated from only twelve plant species and five animal species. Biodiversity is the food system's life insurance, so this loss puts us at great risk in a climate-unstable future. Holding on to our heritage seeds supports biodiversity, preservation, and global food security.[8,9]

According to Martin Prechtel, "Farmers are the ecstatic lovers of the long history of the seeds."[10] Two Black women seed keepers who guard the living history of the seeds, Aleya Fraser and Ira Wallace, join us in conversation. It is an honor to listen to their narratives.

ALEYA FRASER (she/her) is a weaver and pollinator in the food system at large. She has cofounded multiple land-based projects in the US, including Black Dirt Farm and Stellar Roots Co-op. She currently resides in her ancestral lands of Trinidad and Tobago where she and her husband make cocoa products, support the work of Trinidadian cocoa farmers, and uplift their stories. At the crux of all her passions is increasing the livelihood of land stewards and farmers, so she also works with nonprofits, universities, and businesses through her consulting firm ACRES Consulting to provide technical assistance, education, and advocacy. Aleya holds a BS in physiology/neurobiology from the University of Maryland, College Park.

IRA WALLACE (she/her), author of *The Timber Press Guide to Vegetable Gardening in the Southeast*, is a Central Virginia Master Gardener and a worker/owner of the cooperatively managed Southern Exposure Seed Exchange. Ira serves on the boards of the Organic Seed Alliance and Virginia Association for Biological Farming (VABF), and formerly, the Organic Seed Growers and Trade Association (OSGATA). She was among the lead plaintiffs in *OSGATA et al. v. Monsanto* in 2012–13. Ira was one of nine cooperators with the Southern Sustainable Agriculture Research and Education (SARE)–sponsored Saving Our Seeds Project. She cofounded the Heritage Harvest Festival at Monticello and speaks throughout the southeast.

LEAH: Mama Ira, you are one of the teachers who got us started with seed keeping at Soul Fire Farm. Now we grow for the Truelove and Ujamaa seed collectives, and one of my favorite crops to save is amaranth. Also known as callaloo, or tete, it is considered by the Yoruba to be the first plant to grow on earth and a revered elder to all other plants. Tete is a delicious "superfood" that is also central to our ceremonies. Of all the many seeds that you keep alive, is there one in particular that is close to your heart?

IRA WALLACE: My mother died when I was still young, and I was raised by my grandmother. She taught me how to garden, and I remember her growing southern peas. We liked eating them fresh, when the pod was filled out but they were still green. It was a special thing we got to eat at certain times each year. Whatever your grandmother cooks for you is always the best tasting. As an adult, I still grow some of those heritage beans I grew up with, like the purple hull black-eyed peas. We liked those because they were easiest to shell; some other kinds gave you a lot of trouble coming out of their shells.

LEAH: Aleya, what is one special seed for you?

ALEYA FRASER: I grew my first sorghum when I was farming with Denzel Mitchell in Baltimore County. We got the seed from Blain Snipstal, who got it from a friend in Africa. It was tall and striking and grew amazingly, but I didn't know much about it. It turns out sorghum is both ancient and futuristic, and has done so much to help our people. From what I read, it was a form of market currency at certain points. It was used to make sorghum meal and sorghum beer, and was served as a staple to sustain families. It's drought resistant, cures the soil, pulls out toxins, and builds organic matter. It can be used as biofuel and fodder, and it's so sweet we can make it into molasses and sugar—a powerhouse plant. And the roots are amazing! From that moment planting it on my little urban plot, I saved those seeds and planted them everywhere. I brought it to my one-fourth acre on the eastern shore of Maryland, where I grew those seeds and gave them away. They are now growing in Trinidad. Along the way, I have collected other people's sorghum seeds, which I plant wherever I go and share with others.

LEAH: Mama Ira, you are one of the worker/owners of Southern Exposure Seeds, which offers over seven hundred varieties of open pollinated and heirloom seeds. You also recently helped launch a new BIPOC-led seed project with my cousin, Bonnetta Adeeb. Ujamaa Seeds is providing opportunities for emerging and seasoned growers to raise culturally meaningful seeds and sell them to the public. How did you come into this work and what is your vision for it?

IRA WALLACE: As a seed saver, first and foremost I see the importance of preserving the genetic variation of crop seeds for future generations. As a seed keeper, one of my main goals is to capture the stories of the sage ones before they are gone—before their wisdom is sealed inside of them forever. I am old, and the seeds are older. We need to connect these young people to the seeds before the old seed keepers drop dead and no one is carrying on the legacy. Seeds carry our stories.

Part of the work has been reaching out to see what seeds people are still holding in Black communities. A lot of localized, family varieties are slipping away because many Black people think of farming as a bad thing to do. One of my first successes with seed keeping was our work with a group of African American sorority sisters who grew the Davis and Morgan collard greens collection, including varieties like the William Alexander Heading collard. We ended up sending some of those seeds to Svalbard to be part of a global seed bank so that the varieties important to Black communities are preserved, and so that we are part of writing ourselves back into the story. We have to remember that eating dark, leafy green vegetables is something that Black people gave to Europeans, not the other way around. My grandmother, who knew about eating fresh food, bought into the idea that eating processed foods showed that you were prosperous, and she ended up dying of diabetes.

I have a predisposition toward the collard, as it's one of the things we grew every winter growing up. I once visited an ecovillage in Jamaica where they have collard salad all year round; they massage the young tender leaves just like kale. I have been seriously on the collard trail for almost a decade now. I was able to contribute to the research for the book *Collards: A Southern Tradition from Seed to Table*. The researchers contacted me and Monticello, and they eventually collected ninety accessions of heirloom collards. Southern Exposure Seed Exchange and Seed Savers Exchange got a lot of seeds from the USDA gene bank, and then we grew them out in our seed savers exchange network, evaluated them for germination and uniformity, and were able to regenerate the national seed bank. We are now able to add two to ten new varieties out of that collection every year. It's a lot of collards—purple ones, blue ones, curly and shiny ones. They are fabulous!

To make this work of seed keeping viable in the long term, we need to show that farming is a reasonable way to make a living. Take the example of Clifton Slade. He is a third-generation farmer and extension agent at Virginia State University. Formerly a "big tractor" farmer growing

GMO corn, he switched to organic seed growing after he observed wild-life avoiding the GMO crops. It took me five years to convince Clifton to become a seed farmer because he was concerned about being able to make a living. But now as a seed grower, he can make the same income on two acres that his neighbors make on three hundred. One of his specialty crops is sweet potato slips. Virginia Baker, the heirloom that he grew with his father as a child, had nearly slipped into obscurity before his switch to seed farming. He helped recover this variety to preserve the legacy of that seed for his four children and future generations.

I used to joke about not being able to find Black people in the seed world, and now they are popping out of the woodwork. I was deep in a conversation with a young Black man about okra, and he said that he had never thought about going into botany or seed keeping because he had not seen any Black botanists in the university, and much of the research on seeds was Monsanto-led. I asked Acorn Community to sponsor this young man so he could get a paid seed-keeping internship over the summer. The community gave him a $5,000 stipend through the Utopian Seed Project. I realized then the question was not "whether" but "how." Now with Ujamaa Seeds, the vision of young Black seed keepers working together is even further along.

If you're going to achieve all the things you want, you have to work with other people. Seed saving is a poster child of interdependence and how that can work well. It's an everyday act of resistance.

LEAH: Aleya, we have some Moruga Hill Rice growing at Soul Fire Farm, and I understand you had a part in getting that seed rematriated to our communities. Can you talk about your seed work with upland rice and with Trinidadian farmers in general?

ALEYA FRASER: My ancestors likely came from the Chesapeake region to Trinidad. I was in Trinidad several years ago doing a permaculture class and got connected with ethnobotanist Francis Morean. We visited and interviewed rice farmers in the south of Trinidad and in Tobago. We saw that they were still using the same growing methods, patterns, and processes that our ancestors used. In exchange for fighting with the British in the War of 1812, many Gullah/Geechee people were relocated to Trinidad, which was a mixed blessing. The Gullah/Geechee, who became known as Merikins, were left in the forests of Moruga and set up their own settlements. The wild bush of Trinidad is no joke, and rice farming was an uphill battle. We collected some of the seed that was gifted to us from the Merikin community and planted it at Black Dirt Farm, Maryland. We also gave some to our friends Chris and Owen to distribute through Truelove Seeds. Francis has gone back to Sierra Leone with the seed, and he has talked to the original rice farmers there.

The Merikins have petitioned the United Nations for Indigenous status and to be recognized as maroons. There was upland rice culture in Trinidad at least nine years before the war of 1812, and it was cultivated by African communities that predated the Merikins. However, the Merikins played a major role in the evolution and persistence of the tradition.

Currently, we are working with cocoa farmers in Trinidad. We help them add value to their products and get access to more markets. Dry cocoa beans are cheap at five dollars per kilogram, but if you make it into chocolate, it becomes more financially viable. We support farmers in buying machinery and producing products like cocoa butter, nibs, and chocolate. We formed a cooperative of the farmers, so we can guarantee supply and quantity. We love working with the farmers, amplifying their stories, and learning as we go.

LEAH: Something I love about your approach to seed keeping, Mama Ira, is that it's not just about the seed. It's about the container that brings forth the seed. You raise your seeds in an egalitarian income-sharing intentional community. You raise your seeds as part of symbiotic plant polycultures. Can you explain the setting that brings forth these special seeds?

IRA WALLACE: Acorn Community was founded in 1993 by some of us who had been part of Twin Oaks. We practice nonhierarchical consensus-based decision-making and own all of our resources, land, and money in common. Community living makes it much easier to live simply and extract less from the earth. Think about the fossil fuel use per person, or the space per person, and you see that we are doing pretty well. Our seed business is Southern Exposure Seed Exchange, and we work with seed savers committed to organic, heritage agriculture and independence from corporate agribusiness control. We celebrate people becoming members of Acorn by planting a tree in their honor. This gives them a place here even if they don't stay here for all time.

As I get older, I realize that my role is to share and pass on whatever I can to others. I do things that rely more on my knowledge and less on brute force. I have survived two cancers, and I learned that just because I get ill does not mean I am done. I just see what I can do from the place I land on the other side of healing. Community makes this possible.

As far as how we grow our crops, a portion of our land is devoted to various perennial polycultures, both for the farm and for the wildlife. We want our fencerows to be a nonintrusive area for the birds and a place of beauty to retreat. I was exposed to polycultures from an early age. In my grandmother's garden, we didn't grow our collards, mustard, and turnips separately. They were all mixed in together. By age five, I could tell the young plants apart. They thrived in this style of mixed succession planting that our ancestors passed down to us.

In the annual areas, we have been doing a lot with silage tarps. We grow a cover crop and then mow it down, and we cover the soil with tarps instead of tilling. We use cardboard mulch on paths with hay or wood chips on top. If you soak cardboard in the toddler pool it stays put and doesn't blow away. We trial many annual crops, including twenty heirloom collard varieties, maybe a dozen different kales, winter radishes, purple carrots, winter lettuce, and turnips. We grow amaranth, or edible celosia, which is easy to cultivate and self-sows. This is an important green in the African countryside, where the tradition of eating dark, leafy greens originates. All of these things help make a beautiful landscape full of interesting edible things.

LEAH: Aleya, can you speak to your growing practices as well, particularly the concept of "Afroecology"?

ALEYA FRASER: The idea of Afroecology came to us at Black Dirt Collective through our experience with the agroecology camps, as well as work with La Vía Campesina and the University of California, Santa Cruz, where we experienced teachings in alignment with the ecological framework, but were not seeing our people represented. We were not hearing about Dr. George Washington Carver, Fannie Lou Hamer, or other Black people who we knew were connected to land and movement spaces. As we all know, Blackness is often erased from history. So Afroecology was our stand, our reclamation that we are an integral part of agroecology and cocreators of this movement. We worked together to create this definition:

> *Afroecology is a form of art, movement, practice, and process of social and ecological transformation that involves the re-evaluation of our sacred relationships with land, water, air, seeds, and food; (re)recognizes humans as cocreators that are an aspect of the planet's life support systems; values the Afro-Indigenous experience of reality and ways of knowing; cherishes ancestral and communal forms of knowledge, experience, and lifeways that began in Africa and continue throughout the Diaspora; and is rooted in the agrarian traditions, legacies, and struggles of the Black experience in the Americas.*[11]

Some of our Afroecological practices may have been different from agroecology. We keep elders in our circles so we can learn from them. We place emphasis on political education, and we center artistry, such as music and dancing. We recognize that this information is inside of our DNA, and we learn to tap into intuition so we can look at a seed and intuit what it wants and needs, and how deep it wants to be planted.

This intuition can come from ancestral memory and visions. My family has deep roots in the south of Trinidad, a place called the Gulf of Korea, which is made up of the flat floodplains of a creek. My grandmother is Anistasia Fraser, and her father, George James, was a farmer for the village. He grew corn, sugarcane, rice, and cocoa. She says that I am becoming like him. After a period of fasting, I had a vision where I had his hands, and I saw myself planting corn. The hands were my hands, and then they turned into my great-grandfather's hands. A lot of ancestral memories started coming through, and I was called to come back to these lands. After traveling back and forth for three years, I was here in Trinidad when COVID hit and the borders closed, and I have been here ever since. I got married and had a child. Down here, I have a patch of land where I have the Black three sisters growing—sorghum, pumpkin, and pigeon pea, as well as benne seed. What I am doing now is Afroecology.

LEAH: When you listen to the voice of the earth, and the voice of the seed who is the microcosm of the earth, what do you hear?

IRA WALLACE: Perhaps the earth is saying, "Let me heal. Make some space for that." I have seen healing happen. My first community was on a degraded tobacco farm. With intensive cover cropping and composting, we saw the soil transform from washed out clay to brown clay loam in just four years. I think that if you care about the earth, then envisioning a good life for yourself needs to be in line with a good life for all beings in the more expansive sense of community. We used to say, "Live simply so that others may simply live." This is liberation theology. A lifestyle that will protect the earth and protect the people on it will be simple, and it will be based on using our own energy and that of the sun and renewable sources. That means not having such big houses, not sending goods around the world, and not having so much stuff. Cheap food is not cheap. If you can realize that about food, you see that cheap clothing is not cheap either. The cost is borne by other people and the earth.

ALEYA FRASER: The earth is not dead or dying. She will reclaim balance as she has always done. She holds the power, and she only asks that we connect to and respect her if we want to survive. Humans need to recognize that even though we are powerful beings, we aren't entitled to wreak destruction all over this beautiful earth. Humans are naive in our assumption that a single species such as ourselves can destroy the earth. Mother Earth will shake us off when she grows weary of us. Fear will not save us. Resilience and adaptability is the only way forward. We need to slow down, connect, and get in tune with the rhythm of the earth if we want to increase our chances of survival.

Unlocking our intuition and ancestral memories is crucial. When we connect with the land, our mitochondrial DNA is stirred awake, and the knowledge embedded in it from our uterus-carrying ancestors— knowledge that has been passed down through generations and across the Diaspora—is realized. In the black dirt under fingernails, melanated work under the sun, and calloused hands, ancient rhythms and ancestral superpowers germinate.

Defense

I CAN'T BREATHE

A Conversation with Sharon Lavigne and Dr. Dorceta Taylor

> I like to describe environmental justice as an umbrella, an overarching construct. Then there are various parts that make up that umbrella, including climate justice, civil rights, criminal justice, economic justice, housing justice, and food justice, as well as other important issues that are incorporated into our environment—where we live, play, pray, go to school, recreate, and interact with others. It means equity and distributive justice—meeting people where they are, determining what they need to be safe and healthy.
>
> —DR. ADRIENNE L. HOLLIS[1]

Felix Wynn, *an eighty-five-year-old African American fisherman* in Triana, Alabama, was found to have 3,300 parts per billion of DDT (a synthetic insecticide) in his blood, more DDT than has ever been found in any human being. The Olin Corporation, which produced DDT for the US Army, dumped at least 475 tons of the carcinogenic chemical into the Huntsville Spring Branch from 1947 until 1970.[2] The contamination led to massive fish die-offs, devastated the livelihoods of fishermen, and caused DDT to accumulate in the bodies of the mostly Black residents of Triana, including Mr. Wynn. Residents were not made aware of the presence of DDT in their community until 1979, over thirty years after the contamination began. They promptly organized a lawsuit against Olin, which was settled in 1982, and remediation efforts began.[3] Even as seven hundred Triana residents cashed their $2,300 settlement checks, the underlying health concerns were not resolved. Marvalene Freeman, one of the plaintiffs, said, "Money can't ever buy back our health. It couldn't bring Howard Hughes [a loved one] back to life . . . We're walking dynamite."[4] The contamination of Triana was just one example of environmental racism, which is defined as the "deliberate targeting of ethnic and minority communities for exposure to toxic and hazardous waste sites and facilities, coupled with the systematic exclusion of minorities in environmental policy making, enforcement, and remediation."[5]

The historic efforts of Triana residents represent one of the formative events in the now widespread movement to end environmental racism. Another example of early environmental justice (EJ) organizing was the work of the Northeast Community Action Group of Houston, Texas, to oppose the Whispering Pines Sanitary Landfill that was slated for construction 150 feet from a local public school. Their 1979 lawsuit, *Bean v. Southwestern Waste Management Inc.*, was the first of its kind in the US to charge environmental discrimination under civil rights law. Also salient was the organizing of African American residents of Warren County, North Carolina, together with the National Association for the Advancement of Colored People (NAACP) and United Church of Christ (UCC), to attempt to stop the construction of a hazardous waste landfill in their neighborhood where soil contaminated with polychlorinated biphenyls (PCBs) would be discarded. While these protests failed to prevent the Houston and Warren County landfills from being constructed, they did prompt landmark studies such as the 1983 Government Accountability Office (GAO) study and the 1987 UCC Toxic Waste and Race study, which both demonstrated systematic patterns of environmental racism in siting sewage works, mines, landfills, power stations, major roads, and emitters of airborne particulate matter in proximity to communities of color.[6,7,8]

Local and regional EJ organizers brought their effort to a national stage in the early nineties with the work of the 1990 Michigan Coalition and the 1991 First National People of Color Environmental Leadership Summit. The summit brought together hundreds of community leaders in Washington, DC, to call attention to the disproportionate targeting of Black and Brown communities in the siting of hazardous facilities. Summit attendees wrote a consensus document on the seventeen principles of environmental justice, which affirmed the sacredness of Mother Earth, decried discriminatory public policy, and uplifted Native treaty rights, among other provisions.[9]

While the efforts of groundbreaking EJ activists like Robert Bullard, Hazel Johnson, Beverly Wright, Dorceta Taylor, Peggy Shepard, Bunyan Bryant, Benjamin Chavis, Dollie Burwell, Dana Alston, and others forced the EPA to make major positive changes to its regulations, we still have a ways to go. A 2021 EPA study reported that African American communities continue to be disproportionately burdened with particulate matter pollution and corresponding high asthma rates, inland and coastal flooding due to climate change, and heat exposure.[10] These disparities are exemplified in communities located in Louisiana's "Cancer Alley," who are exposed to emissions from 150 oil refineries, chemical facilities, and plastics plants. The predominantly African American residents of this region experience disproportionately high rates of cancer. They also have high morbidity and mortality from COVID-19, which is linked to exposure to air pollution.[11] Recent national studies show that the Black population continues to be disproportionately impacted by coal-fired power plants, chemical facilities, wastewater disposal wells, and leaded pipes.[12]

Sharon Lavigne and Dr. Dorceta Taylor are two frontline organizers working hard to protect our communities from environmental harm. In conversation with them, we will explore their current EJ efforts and adjacent work.

SHARON LAVIGNE (she/her) is native to St. James, Louisiana, a small country town along the Mississippi River, and a mother of six. Growing up, Sharon lived off the land. She was a special education teacher for thirty-eight years in the St. James Parish school system. In 2018, Sharon founded Rise St. James, a faith-based, grassroots, nonprofit organization fighting for clean air and water, and the eradication of petrochemical industries in St. James Parish in particular. She hosted the first meeting in her den with approximately ten individuals present. Sharon then retired from school teaching to dedicate herself full-time to the fight for environmental justice. In June 2021, she was awarded the prestigious Goldman Environmental Prize for environmental activism in her community. Sharon has become an iconic activist for the eradication of air, water, and land pollution in majority Black communities.

DR. DORCETA TAYLOR (she/her), a professor at the Yale School of the Environment, is one of the nation's preeminent scholars in the field of environmental justice. Prior to her Yale appointment, Dr. Taylor was professor of environmental sociology at the University of Michigan's School for Environment and Sustainability for twenty-seven years. In 2014, Dr. Taylor authored two landmark national reports, *The State of Diversity in Environmental Institutions: Mainstream NGOs, Foundations, and Government Agencies* and *Environmental Organizations in the Great Lakes Region: An Assessment of Institutional Diversity.* Dr. Taylor has published influential books including *The Rise of the American Conservation Movement: Power, Privilege, and Environmental Protection*; *Toxic Communities: Environmental Racism, Industrial Pollution, and Residential Mobility*; and *The Environment and the People in American Cities, 1600s–1900s: Disorder, Inequality, and Social Change.* Professor Taylor received PhD and MA degrees from the School of Forestry & Environmental Studies (now the Yale School of the Environment) and the Department of Sociology at Yale University in 1991, 1988, and 1985.

LEAH: Natalie Mebane, a young Black anti–fossil fuel lobbyist said,

Know your worth. You will be told almost daily that you are not good enough. Your intelligence, your experience, your insights and knowl-

edge will continuously be questioned. You will make people uncomfortable simply by your presence in their space. Once you decide that this is your life's work, do not stop and do not be discouraged.[13]

This message strikes me as especially relevant to you, Sharon, as someone who came into EJ work from a place of direct experience, but without a technical background. Can you share your story of getting involved in the fight for your community's well-being?

SHARON LAVIGNE: I grew up in St. James Parish, Louisiana, on generational family land. My father was a farmer who raised chickens for eggs, a cow for milk, geese, and turkeys, and he grew a large garden, sugarcane, fig trees, and pecan trees. We would get fresh fish and shrimp from the fishermen. We cooked all our food from scratch, things like fresh steaks, butter beans, shrimp, and fried fish. I had so many steaks as a little girl that I don't want to eat that anymore. We had clean drinking water and drank right from the hydrant. We could take a deep breath and fill our lungs with fresh air. We played softball in the yard and spent so much time outdoors among the trees. We had everything a person would need, and we were free from sickness and diseases. I still live on the same land as my grandparents.

When I was in the eighth or ninth grade, the first industry came in. They were called Gulf at the time and are now the Mosaic fertilizer plant. Everyone welcomed it, thinking it would finally put St. James on the map and create jobs. Then, more and more industries came. The school board even sold off our public high school to make way for industry. We counted twelve industries in our community by 2018. Things were changing in the environment as well. Our pecan trees were dying, and there were no pecans to pick anymore. My friends and family were getting asthma and cancer. When you took a deep breath, the smell of the chemicals in the air was overwhelming.

I was in the classroom with my students when I heard that the governor had approved Formosa Plastics coming to St. James. It made me sick. I couldn't even focus on teaching that day. He clearly did not care about our community to put another toxic plant on us like that. He said it would bring revenue for the state and help address the deficit. It was like we in St. James were not even viewed as human beings, only collateral damage.

My sister and cousin had been challenging me to do something about it. I said that I couldn't. I am not a public speaker. I do not have a degree in environmental science. But they fussed at me and said that I could do it. So, I went and prayed to God. I asked him if I should sell my home and land, and get away from the industry, or if I should stay and fight. God told me to stay and fight. That day I was changed into a new person.

In May 2019, I organized our first march to let people know what was happening. I wore a mask that said "RISE" to emphasize that we should rise together on the issue of industrial pollution. It was a five-day, fifty-mile march from Reserve to the governor's office in Baton Rouge. God kept talking to me and telling me to dedicate my life to this. I retired from teaching and started to build the organization Rise St. James. We team up with other organizations to try to stop industry. I was even able to speak at the White House. We won a huge victory in getting the US Army Corps of Engineers to rescind their permit to Formosa and do a more stringent environmental review of the project. This will delay them at least two years and hopefully make them abandon the project.

Some people say that I sound like my daddy when I do the organizing. He was president of the local NAACP and responsible for integrating St. James public schools. I think my daddy is looking down from heaven, proud. When I cry myself to sleep at night thinking about all the people hurting and suffering, my daddy's voice says to me, "Prayer changes things." Harriet Tubman knew this. She prayed, and God showed her the way to freedom.

LEAH: Dr. Taylor, did your childhood also inform your love of the natural world? What were the formative experiences that shaped your commitment to EJ, and how did this commitment manifest?

DR. DORCETA TAYLOR: I grew up in the mountains of rural central Jamaica in the late fifties and early sixties. Our house looked out over a waterfall, which fascinated me. In my community, the chickens started crowing between 4:30 and 5:30 a.m., so nobody slept in. As a girl, I was responsible for taking care of the rose garden and was delighted by the flowers that we grew. On our acreage, there were twenty-five different types of mangoes, as well as many types of cashews, avocados, grapefruits, lemons, oranges, and sugarcane. We did not have a fruit bowl in the house. If you wanted a fruit, you had better learn how to climb that tree and get it, or how to perfect your aim to throw a stick and hit the mango. My milieu was being outside, and I knew every single tree on that land—which ones had the sweetest fruit and which ones were bland. We used the shelter growing method of planting coffee under mahogany trees, and no extension agent had to come to the village to tell us how to do that. From an early age, we learned propagation. My uncle once took an orange tree and spliced in scion from a grapefruit or mango to see if he could get branches of the orange tree to bear other fruit. With no farmers' almanac or radio, we knew when to put out yams, cassava, and potatoes by the moon cycle. Everything was organic and based on our understanding of the soil types and what grows well with other things. We were too poor to afford fertilizers. When we killed a chicken, nothing went to waste. One of our tasks as children was that we would pluck the tender down feathers to make pillows. In my village, we learned to make our own hair and skin products with coconut oil by age five or six. No one went to college, and few finished high school, but we knew all that. We grew up farming and were very tied to the elements.

I got into biology very early on, studying zoology and botany, and realized that so much of what I was learning in school reflected my life growing up. When I was eleven, we moved from rural Jamaica to the big city of Kingston, and I got even more involved in studying STEM. I then moved to the US around age twenty to rejoin my mom, and I entered college. In my environmental course, we were studying pesticide poisoning and how the spraying of chemicals used to control the mosquito population was resulting in people getting cancer. I thought back to my childhood, when workers would come around and spray pesticides to get rid of the mosquito that causes dengue fever. I asked myself, "Were they spraying a horrible pesticide in the Caribbean and parts of Africa that had been banned in the US?" At the same time, I noticed that I was the only student of color in my class. This was shocking to me, because in the Caribbean, whether you were Black or Black-Asian or Black-Indian, we all did the sciences. I felt I was living in two worlds. My experience at home in the Caribbean was that we lived and breathed environmentalism and STEM. I knew if I went to Africa, I could find the same thing. My experience as an undergraduate was that there were no other Black students in my courses, so I began to wonder what it was about the American experience creating this pattern. I asked the professor, "Where are the other Black students?" He promptly told me that "Blacks are not interested in the environment." That one sentence changed my life. I could not believe that Black people and the environment don't go together, or that we don't understand or care, are not interested, or are not good at it. I shifted my focus to look more at the relationship between the environment and people of color in the US and globally.

LEAH: The urgency of the EJ movement arises from the fact that our success or failure is a life-or-death matter. Eric Garner's last words, spoken in 2014 while an officer held him in a choke hold, were, "I can't breathe." We live in a time where there are multiple assaults on Black people's right to draw breath, from police violence to wildfires, and from COVID-19 to chemical pollution. Sharon, can you explain in more detail how industry has been impacting your community's capacity to breathe?

SHARON LAVIGNE: The industries here are taking over our lives by giving us cancer. We can no longer garden. We can't even stand outside because it smells like rotten eggs and something burning. There are plastic pellets in the bellies of the fish. Ethylene oxide is filling up our lungs. Benzene is filling up our drinking water. People are dying of cancer, women are having miscarriages, babies are being born preemies, and the asthma rates are going up. It's all because of industry, and it just makes you want to cry. One of my members at Rise told me that when her route to work took her in front of the chemical plant, she would get strep throat and need to take antibiotics three to four times per year, and when she started taking a different route, her throat cleared up. Another Rise member has a little boy with severe asthma. One lady said she had to bring her child to Tennessee for cancer treatment. Americas Styrenics, a chemical plant that makes Styrofoam, has chemical flares burning in the air every day. I pass by there daily, morning and night, so I posted a livestream and alerted the EPA. They said they will check on it, but yeah right. The plant took over our highway and levee, so we can no longer use it as an evacuation route during hurricanes. We are trying to get the chemical plants to deal with their waste internally and not give off emissions, and if they can't be accountable to these community needs, then to shut their operation down. We at Rise St. James are trying to fight all of these issues, and it's a lot of work. The governor, the secretary of state, and other officials do not seem to care about us. They think we are animals, and that it's okay to just let us be sick and die. We send pictures, videos, and testimony, and they do not do anything. They are just like industry. After the hurricane, industry gave out toilet paper and paper plates, but offered no help for people to rebuild their homes. Meanwhile, they have billions of dollars and enjoy state tax breaks. Where is the empathy? Where is the accountability? It seems the only person that can help us is the good Lord. Still, I believe that one way or another, all of those industries will go down.

LEAH: You were among the early pioneers of the EJ movement, Dr. Taylor. An adage coined at the time was, "We speak for ourselves." What were some of the ways that you developed your voice and message in this foundational time?

DR. DORCETA TAYLOR: While the Warren County landfill is often cited as the beginning of environmental racism and the EJ movement, I beg to differ. We can go back to the 1600–1700s in Manhattan, when they moved all of their slaughterhouses and factories away from current-day Wall Street and placed them in current-day Greenwich Village, a Black neighborhood, and then proceeded to pollute that population to death. In the earliest days of many American cities, we see a pattern of injustices emerge. They removed Native Americans, then they polluted the water and air where Black people lived, and cleaned up the white neighborhoods. This goes back hundreds of years, and we see it in city after city after city.

When the environmental justice movement really broke onto the scene in 1989–90, there were very few of us people of color. Folks like Beverly Wright, Robert Bullard, and myself contributed to the early body of literature on EJ. I was only the second Black student to have been enrolled at the Yale School of the Environment. I broke the Black color barrier last year (2020) by being the first Black faculty to be hired by that school in its 120 years of existence. My Black students were questioning me about the literature, wanting to understand where the experience of people of color in relationship to the environment was being documented. I realized this relationship was not being written about or documented, and I decided to write a short research article on the topic. The article became a 672-page book, *The Environment and the People in American Cities*, which explored urban spaces as the birthplace of environmental activism, including the role of Black nurses saving Philadelphia from falling into complete disarray during the 1793 yellow fever pandemic. I then wrote *Toxic Communities*, which draws connections between residential segregation, zoning, and environmental hazards. I followed up with a 496-page book on the rise of the conservation movement.

Something that struck me in working on the book was that no one was making the connections that were painfully obvious to me. For example, when I was reading bedtime stories to my identical twin girls at three years old, we pulled out a book on Harriet Tubman and the Underground Railroad. I had an epiphany that Tubman was an environmentalist. She had to have been. To understand the natural ecology and the interconnectedness of things, to successfully move through the wilderness at night, and to read the environment to know whether it was safe to go into a plantation and free people, she had to have a deep understanding of the natural spaces she moved through. Tubman not only had an environmental sensibility, but a transcendental way of looking at things. She understood how we are deeply connected to the environment, can absorb knowledge beyond what can be read in a book, and experience nature through instinct. No one had written about Harriet Tubman in an environmental light. It was the same with Phillis Wheatley. A group of Black scholars are now going back into her writing to look at her environmental sensibilities and what she brought to the table decades before Ralph Waldo Emerson developed his widely acclaimed environmental philosophies. Emerson gets credit for being the first doing this work, but he knew of Wheatley, and many people think that he pulled some of his environmental thinking from her. I became very excited about framing environmentalism in this new way so that people of color could see ourselves in it, not as peripheral and being acted upon, but as thinkers and actors bringing important pieces to the table. We are at fault if we do not write our own narratives and histories. When I sit down and write, I do not think about writing to another academic. I am visualizing the reader as someone who doesn't have the opportunity to be in a place like this.

LEAH: Something that strikes me about your work, Dr. Taylor, is how you are in it for the long game. As a movement elder, you continue to work tirelessly as a professor, activist, organizer of environmental internships for students of color, writer, speaker, and so much more. My generation and those after me can be impatient about change. What can you share about urgency and time scale?

DR. DORCETA TAYLOR: My twins are now in their late twenties, and like so many Gen Z'ers and Millennials, they want to see solutions instantly and get depressed about the pace of change. It can be infuriating and insulting to think you can go and fix something quickly, as if those who were already working on it are too dumb to figure it out. Structural change takes time. The good news is that we have come a long way. Back in 1987, when the United Church of Christ put out their toxic waste report, you could count on two hands the number of people involved in the environmental justice movement. We organized the First National People of Color Environmental Leadership Summit in 1991, and there were six hundred people in the room. It was the first time that all of us across the nation got together. We recruited those attendees by going through our rolodexes at a gathering at the University of Michigan in the previous year, and making calls and individual invitations. We spent four days together in DC and hardly saw daylight, working from 8:00 a.m. and supposed to end at 6:00 p.m., but often continuing until midnight. Black, Latino, Native, and Asian communities came face-to-face with one another and saw a big pattern: We were all dealing with toxic facilities, waste dumps, or water pollution. And it was not just happening in Warren County, it was in Mobile, Alabama, and South Central LA. It was highways pushed right through the middle of the community, like the freeway from Lansing to Detroit that could have circumvented the Detroit community, but instead punched right through what was the heart of the Black middle class—the homes of doctors, lawyers, and Motown music. That community has never recovered. This was also true of the Dan Ryan, a fourteen-lane expressway in Chicago that split the Black community from the working-class white community, and in Baltimore, the Cross Bronx, and New Orleans. These highway-impacted neighborhoods remain poor today. We were just starting to look at the racialized patterns of destruction related to water, energy, and residential segregation. Many of the organizations that gathered together in 1991 were not really organizations; they were people sitting at their kitchen table trying to get something done with no funding or staff.

See where we are and what we have been able to do now. These same organizations have staff, people doing the work, and training others. The University of Michigan created the first environmental justice program in the world in 1992. Now just about every environmental program in the country has an environmental justice component. This is significant progress. We look at what's going on with the Biden administration, where EJ is more prominent, and the Environmental Protection Agency is not running away from it. It's a big deal. We look at how Stacey Abrams organized people to get out the vote in Georgia. They didn't just say, "Go and vote." They talked about food insecurity in rural Georgia and asked folks if they wanted affordable fresh foods and grocery stores. They pointed out the smokestacks and talked about pollution. They said, "If you want change, you need to go and vote." They flipped Georgia with that EJ message. Organizers also flipped Michigan by focusing heavily on EJ in Black and Brown communities. Some of my former students, who run the Michigan Environmental Justice Coalition, mobilized the community to canvas and campaign two years before the election, focusing on the Flint water crisis and the energy shutoffs in Detroit.

Their political strategies in Michigan and Georgia echoed the early work of Peggy Shepard of WE ACT in West Harlem, who knew how to connect EJ to electoral politics and how to mobilize people. In the late 1990s, they realized that by controlling the permitting and zoning boards, they could control the siting and distribution of these toxic facilities, so they had to get elected to these local boards. These are massive changes. We are now seeing lots of money coming into communities to do EJ work.

LEAH: Reverend Benjamin Chavis said, "Racism has always been used to justify the rape of the environment."[14] I resonate with this message because it underscores the heart of the Black environmental philosophy that we as people are part of the environment, and that the white supremacist project of capitalism exploits Black people in parallel with exploitation of the earth. In understanding that our fate is bound up with the Earth, how would you describe the messages that the Earth is transmitting to human beings at this moment?

SHARON LAVIGNE: Like the reverend says, industry is hurting Black people and the earth at the same time. I hear the earth saying, "Let me live." Remember that the earth comes from God, and people are destroying the earth—destroying the air, water, and soil upon which we depend. We are directed to take away all of the industry that is harming God's earth. God wants the polluters to see that they are doing wrong. God wants people to open their eyes and to save their own lives. God is speaking, but they are not listening. So, God will expose them and bring down his wrath in a matter of time. For those who are listening, it is time to fight. We need to speak up when we see something is wrong and trust that we can make a difference. We need to find out what is going on in our neighborhoods and do something about it. When I started, I did not know about the environment, or take any classes on it, but I was chosen to do the work. Seek God first, and then he will help you get your facts together and learn what you need to learn so you can make the changes that are needed. You can't go wrong if you do.

DR. DORCETA TAYLOR: I think the earth is saying, "What are you thinking? How can you destroy your water when you have not figured out a way to live without water? How can you destroy your air when you have not figured out a way to live without air? You have destroyed the places where you can walk, where you can think, where you can breathe." It is mind boggling that there is anyone still left on the earth who does not believe we are endangering the planet. It defies any kind of logic that there are people doing so many things to destroy the planet when, frankly, I don't think there is another one to beam up to. We do not have an alternative, and yet we are killing this one home. There is enough space on this planet for all of us. We are just being boneheads. What do we do when the water runs out? When there is no air to breathe? In that case, I think we have about fifteen seconds to live.

I also think it is essential to remedy the deep-rooted hatred some people have for others on the sole basis of skin color. Nothing good will come out of that in the long haul. Fundamentally, we are going to have to figure out how to all work together to save our one home.

ONE BLUE PLANET

*A Conversation with Dr. Ayana Elizabeth Johnson
and Chris Hill, JD*

When you see water in a stream
you say: oh, this is stream
water;
When you see water in the river
you say: oh this is water
of the river;
When you see ocean
Water
you say: This is the ocean's
water!
But actually water is always
only itself
and does not belong
to any of these containers
though it creates them.
And so it is with you.

—ALICE WALKER, "WHEN YOU SEE WATER"

Revered as the deities *Mami Wata* and *Olokun* in Vodun and Yoruba, respectively, the ocean is the four-billion-year-old womb from which all life on earth emerged. Fresh and salt waters together cover

71 percent of the surface of our planet, with oceans containing 95 percent of the earth's water. The ocean is still mostly unexplored and may be home to upward of two million unique species, only 240,000 of whom have been described by science.[1,2] While majestic rainforest trees often get all the credit for providing the oxygen in our atmosphere, the reality is that the oceans are more aptly titled the "lungs of the earth." Ocean creatures, mostly phytoplankton, produce over half of the oxygen that we rely upon to breathe.[3] Furthermore, the oceans absorb excess planetary heat, dissolve atmospheric carbon dioxide, and regulate the global weather system.

Freshwater reservoirs, such as wetlands, rivers, lakes, and glaciers, are also of crucial ecosystemic importance. Wetlands protect human habitat from storm surges and flooding, occurrences that are ever more common in this age of climate chaos.[4] These wetlands are among the most productive ecosystems in the world, sequestering ten times more carbon dioxide than mature tropical forests.[5] More than one-third of US threatened and endangered species live exclusively in wetlands, and nearly half rely on wetlands for part of their life cycle. While often overlooked, glaciers and ice caps are also an integral part of the water cycle. Containing 70 percent of earth's fresh water, glacial melt is an essential source of drinking water and irrigation in the Arctic, Himalayas, Andes, New Zealand Southern Alps, and across the globe.[6]

In Yoruba sacred literature, the *Odu Ifa* called *Oyeku Ogbe* contains a verse about a fisherman named Ode Afawon Yangyan. As the story goes, Afawon was an ambitious and insatiable hunter of aquatic creatures, so he used an outsized net to capture them. He accumulated large heaps of fish and great wealth from the lagoon—more than he could use in multiple lifetimes, but he was not satisfied. He was warned by the ocean deity Olokun to temper his greed, but defiantly went to the ocean to pull out nets full of fish and other marine riches. Offended by his ingratitude, Olokun opened up the door to heaven, and Afawon was swallowed.[7]

Like Afawon, human society is ravaging the life that dwells in waters. One in every four people rely on oceans for their livelihood, and more than

90 percent of global fish stocks are fully exploited or overfished.[8] Agricultural runoff and manufacturing waste has led to over four hundred dead zones worldwide, where oxygen levels are so low that all the fish in that area suffocate.[9] The Deepwater Horizon disaster of 2010 spewed 134 million gallons of oil into the ocean and was just one of the hundreds of spills that the National Oceanic and Atmospheric Administration (NOAA) responds to each year.[10] Microplastics in our sea now outnumber the stars in our galaxy five-hundred-fold.[11] The ocean's absorption of our excess carbon dioxide has led to a 30 percent increase in acidity, causing the shells of crustaceans to dissolve and killing off coral reefs.[12,13] Approximately 35 percent of the world's wetlands have already been lost to human development,[14] and reference glaciers have lost an average of ninety feet of ice since 1970 as a result of anthropogenic climate change.[15]

The story of Afawon is a potent metaphor. Human survival depends, quite literally, on healthy oceans, rivers, glaciers, and wetlands. To better understand our relationship to this marine crisis, we will be in conversation with Dr. Ayana Elizabeth Johnson and Chris Hill, JD, two Black women water experts.

DR. AYANA ELIZABETH JOHNSON (she/her) is a marine biologist, policy expert, writer, and Brooklyn native. She is cofounder of Urban Ocean Lab, a think tank for coastal cities, and cocreator of the podcast *How to Save a Planet*, on climate solutions. She coedited the bestselling climate anthology *All We Can Save* and cofounded the All We Can Save Project. Recently, she coauthored the Blue New Deal, a roadmap for including the ocean in climate policy. Dr. Johnson earned a BA from Harvard University in environmental science and public policy, and a PhD from Scripps Institution of Oceanography in marine biology. She is madly in love with nature and climate solutions.

CHRIS HILL, JD (she/her), is senior campaign director for the Our Wild America Campaign at the Sierra Club. She is an avid adventurer who loves backpacking, climbing, snowboarding, and fly-fishing. Chris serves in leadership roles with Trout Unlimited, Alaska Wilderness

League, Artemis Sportswomen, and the Mennen Environmental Foundation. She also leads fly-fishing trips in Alaska through Sierra Club Outings. Born and raised in the Washington, DC, area, Chris earned a BA in broadcast communications and electronic media from Appalachian State University in Boone, North Carolina, and a JD from Vermont Law School. In 2019, Chris partnered with the Outbound Collective to tell her story on the water. The film *Where I Belong* won 2021 Best Short Film at the Conservation Film Festival. She currently splits her time between Washington, DC, and Haines, Alaska.

LEAH: I believe that we protect what we love and that we can only love what we know intimately. The research of David Sobel and others supports this idea, showing that children who have the opportunity to bond with nature make pro-ecological decisions as adults, whereas children who are only exposed to the horror stories of environmental destruction are more likely to dissociate.[16] Ayana, do you have a childhood love story with the ocean?

DR. AYANA ELIZABETH JOHNSON: The ocean is impossible not to love. My family took me to Key West Florida when I was five years old, and we went on a glass-bottom boat ride where I got to see a coral reef for the first time. It felt like my own personal window into another fascinating universe. There is some crazy shit going on beneath the surface. I mean, octopuses are a thing that exist! I developed this love for the sea and wanted to learn more, so much so that I decided to become a marine biologist on the spot and started a shell collection. At the nearby aquarium, I was able to hold a sea urchin and a starfish. The sea urchin was using its hundreds of tube feet to crawl across my palm. As humans, we have two legs and two arms, and walk around, but there are so many other ways to be a creature on this planet and to make your way through the world. You can have eight legs and siphon jets to get around, or fins. All of these locomotive options captured my imagination. I was stubborn, lucky, and diligent enough to make the childhood dream of becoming a marine biologist a reality. My deep concern for the future of coastal communities, love of the ocean, and desire to contribute solutions to our climate crisis are what keep me in the work so many years later.

LEAH: Chris, you also have a very special relationship with water, namely the Chilkat River in Haines, Alaska, and the vast forest that protects that river. Can you share what is special about this river ecosystem?

CHRIS HILL: Chilkat means "salmon storehouse" in Tlingit and is one of southeast Alaska's top wild coho salmon runs. I love being on the water fly-fishing. Of course I love catching fish, but even more so, I love just being there hearing the water rushing through my waders and observing the wildlife. This river hosts the world's largest congregation of bald eagles in the fall, and I relish watching the eagles come and gather salmon off of the banks. Being in the water brings me into the present moment and makes me feel as if nothing else is happening. Surrounded by the life of the river, I also feel alive and at home. My mind and spirit are calm.

The Tongass National Forest is adjacent to this special river and is one of the last intact temperate rainforests in the world. During a backpacking trip through the Tongass, I walked a bit off the path alone and took off my shoes to sink my feet into the moss. Surrounded by the sounds of water and birds chirping, it was one of my peak moments of feeling alive, connected, and belonging.

LEAH: Ayana, listening to your amazing podcast and getting to know you as a friend and colleague these past years has opened my eyes to the role of the ocean in stabilizing the climate and balancing the atmosphere. As a farmer, I am very focused on the role of soils and plants in the carbon cycle, but don't think nearly enough about the entire planetary system. When we disregard the ocean, what are we missing and why does it matter?

DR. AYANA ELIZABETH JOHNSON: The ocean is the planet's climate stabilizer, but it does that work at its own expense. The ocean has absorbed 90 percent of the excess heat created by burning fossil fuels. As a result, the warmer seawater evaporates more easily, leading to more devastating torrential rains during hurricanes. Many species of fish and other marine animals are making a one-way migration toward the poles to stay cool. Corals can't move, so they are frying in place. The ocean has also absorbed around 30 percent of the excess carbon from the atmosphere. This has changed the very chemistry of seawater, a phenomenon called ocean acidification. It is mind boggling to realize that humans have changed the pH of the entire ocean. The acidity makes it harder for corals to form their skeletons and for shellfish to make their shells. Lost with coral reefs will be food and income for around five hundred million people, many of whom are in the Caribbean and Africa.

It is not an overstatement to say that oceans are the lungs of the earth. Phytoplankton, the base of the marine food web, produces over half the oxygen in the air. Prochlorococcus is both the smallest and most abundant photosynthetic organism on Earth. We don't give enough credence to photosynthesis. People act like solar panels represent the first time anything has made energy out of photons. Even these small beings have fallen victim to human actions; phytoplankton is declining by about 1 percent every year due to warming waters and depleted nutrient content. To continue respiring, we must address the climate crisis and protect the ocean.

LEAH: Arctic scientists agree that climate change is the greatest threat to Arctic biodiversity and exacerbates all other threats. The public has seen images in the media of hungry polar bears (*Ursus maritimus*) struggling to hunt because of prematurely melting sea ice, but of course there is more to the story than the plight of charismatic megafauna. What are the particular threats facing Arctic ecosystems, and why do we need to tune into the messages of this icy world?[17,18]

CHRIS HILL: Climate change is impacting lands, animals, and communities all across the world, and most certainly the Arctic; the current rate of sea-ice loss is unprecedented in the geological history of the last fifteen-hundred-plus years. This means less habitat for polar bears, walruses, and caribou, and increased mortality for their young who are crowded into smaller breeding grounds. Less ice means a darker planetary surface, which leads to more warming in a threatening positive feedback loop. This also means more devastating impacts on the communities that rely on the land and animals for basic living and subsistence. Time is ticking to prevent massive amounts of methane from being released from the Arctic tundra and marine sediments as the ice melts. Methane is a potent greenhouse gas, with thirty times the heat trapping capacity as carbon dioxide.[19]

Extraction processes such as mining, logging, and oil and gas drilling are only adding to the devastating results of climate change. A very personal concern for me is that thirty-five miles upstream from my home in Haines, Constantine Metal Resources is exploring for silver, zinc, copper, and gold deposits in an area of high rainfall and seismic activity. The proposed Constantine-Palmer mine carries the risk of contaminating the Chilkat River watershed and threatening the health of the communities and wildlife that rely on it. The river provides critical spawning habitat for Pacific salmon, eulachon, and trout. The watershed is home to bald eagles, mountain goats, wolves, brown and black bears, moose, coyotes, lynx, otters, and shore birds. It is one of the most biologically diverse regions in Alaska. The acid waste produced by the mining operation would be exacerbated by the geology and climate of the river valley, increasing the likelihood and impact of leaching acidic wastewater into the watershed. Development like this is part of the "polar paradox," where a warming climate makes it easier to build new industry in the Arctic, which in turn fuels more climate change.

LEAH: Ayana and Chris, something I appreciate about both of your work is the emphasis on the sociocultural dimensions of our relationship to aquatic ecosystems. You stand for Indigenous and local people to have access to their fisheries, and critique western industrial exploitation of marine life. Ayana, you wrote, "There are not, in fact, many fish in the sea . . . Technologies developed for war—radar, sonar, helicopters, spotter planes—are used to seek and destroy the remaining fish."[20] This technology-mediated overfishing and pollution devastates marine life and the communities that depend on fisheries. Can you share more about these community impacts?

DR. AYANA ELIZABETH JOHNSON: It is important to understand that fishing is also a social and racial justice issue. We need to look at who has access to the coastline and the fisheries, whose waters are getting polluted, and who bears the disproportionate burden of sea level rise and hurricanes. Communities of color and poor communities are impacted first and worst. I've spent most of my professional career in predominantly Black fishing communities in the Caribbean. During my dissertation research in Curaçao and Bonaire, I learned that ocean preservation was a matter of cultural survival. I loaded up my car with folding chairs, snacks, and beer to share, and hit the road to talk to hundreds of fishermen about their lives on the water. The fishermen reported that the ecosystem had declined dramatically due to industrial fishing from foreign nations, the noise of jet skis and cruise ships, and tourists polluting the water with sunscreen and chemicals. They didn't want their children to go into fishing because they saw no future in it. In contrast, the young white scuba instructors from the Netherlands, who had no historical baseline, thought the ecosystem was pristine and that its primary threat was the local fishermen. They wanted a total ban on fishing. The local folks felt they were being scapegoated and overregulated. Hearing the stories of the fishermen solidified for me the importance of seeing ocean conservation through a justice lens, and needing to ask who is benefiting, who is getting listened to, and whose cultural use of natural resources is being valued.

CHRIS HILL: I agree that it's important to consider the cultural aspects of fishing alongside the environmental considerations. Of course the Tlingit, Haida, and Tsimshian Indigenous people have been in relationship with these fish since time immemorial. I have only been connected since my first fly-fishing lesson on the Brooks River in Katmai National Park, Alaska, in 2012. When I haul in the catch of coho, chum, sockeye, and pink salmon, I feel connected to something much greater than myself. I like catching fish, but more so I love fly-fishing for the healing effects it and nature have on my body. Being outside—recreating outside—has not only helped my physical health, but also my mental health. Recognizing these psychospiritual benefits in myself reinforces my resolve to stand for the rights of Native communities to sovereignty over their own lands, waters, and fisheries.

LEAH: There is a beautiful overlap in both of your work in terms of strategy, as you both are using policy advocacy as a tool for systems change. Ayana, I don't think it's a stretch to say that there would be no Blue New Deal without you. I love how you talk about "stacking papers on papers on papers" in reference to policy memos, op-eds, and the power of the written word as a catalyst for legislative change.[21] Chris, your legislative work has helped stop oil and gas drilling in the Arctic National Wildlife Refuge, and it has opened the path for offshore wind. How did you get into policy, and what are you working on now?

CHRIS HILL: My first job out of law school was community organizing across Appalachia to stop mountaintop removal coal mining and move toward a just transition. I was witnessing these industries blowing up mountains, and meanwhile the communities beneath the mountains were suffering. There were cracked foundations in people's homes, acid drainage into the waterways, lung problems, and cancer. From there, I decided to get into policy to stop extractive industries and move to clean energy. I worked with the Sierra Club on a bill to incentivize offshore wind technology off the coast of Ocean City, Maryland. It took three years to get it passed through the state legislature, and I got to work with HBCUs and communities of color to ensure they would benefit from the green jobs created.

Recently, I have been working on a global campaign to protect half of Earth's lands and waters. Leading scientists have reported that in order to combat the climate crisis, we need to protect 50 percent of the world's lands and waters by 2050, which means 30 percent must be protected in the US by 2030. Only 12 percent is currently protected, so we need more lands and waters protected through legislation on the local, state, and federal levels, and we need to stop extractive practices, like oil and gas drilling, or logging, on lands that are already protected. One of the packages of bills we are working on is PAW+, or the Protecting America's Wilderness and Public Lands Act, which would protect millions of acres of land and hundreds of miles of rivers across the west.[22] Our 2030 deadline is right around the corner. We should have been acting yesterday. If we don't start now, we will be in serious trouble. Protecting half the earth is my wildest dream, and I think it's achievable.

LEAH: Ayana, can you share a bit about your recent policy work on the Green New Deal? You identified a "big blue gap in the Green New Deal." What did you mean by that?[23,24,25]

DR. AYANA ELIZABETH JOHNSON: The Green New Deal Resolution makes only a single passing reference to the world's oceans despite its significance for Americans' lives. The resolution overlooks the fact that 40 percent of Americans live in coastal communities and millions of Americans depend on the ocean for their jobs. As much as the ocean has already contributed to stabilizing the climate by absorbing carbon dioxide and excess heat, it still has more to give in terms of solutions. Together with some close colleagues, I helped to elevate the need to address this "big blue gap" in the Green New Deal. This included advising Senator Elizabeth Warren's presidential campaign on developing a Blue New Deal plan that proposes to both end offshore drilling and streamline permitting processes for offshore wind, while ensuring that wind energy develops in a way that benefits local communities. It focuses on protecting and restoring coastal ecosystems to both sequester carbon and buffer the impacts of sea level rise and storms. The ways it seeks to achieve this include fully funding NOAA's Coastal and Estuarine Land Conservation Program, creating a domestic blue carbon program to value marine carbon sequestration, and expanding protected marine areas. It would also support the scaling of regenerative ocean farming of seaweed and shellfish that would absorb atmospheric carbon and provide nutritious food. Some of the ideas in that plan have been carried forward by the Biden administration, appearing in executive orders and policies. And Urban Ocean Lab, the policy think tank I cofounded, is continuing this work at the city government level.

LEAH: These are incredible accomplishments, and it's not lost on me that you are both moving in spaces that have historically excluded Black people. We are familiar with the stereotype that Black people don't swim, yet Ayana, you are a marine biologist. Environmentalism itself is often misframed as a "white thing." Can you speak on being Black in these spaces?

DR. AYANA ELIZABETH JOHNSON: My dad was Jamaican, and grew up fishing and swimming in Kingston. In 1985, that same summer when I fell in love with coral reefs in Key West, my dad went swimming in the pool where we were staying. All the white folks promptly left the pool, believing it was polluted with his Blackness. I had no idea at the time that the reason I could do all the cannonballs I wanted in the empty pool was the result of insidious racism. Because of segregation and institutional racism, so many Black children don't have access to pools and don't learn to swim. There are kids in LA who have never been to the beach. Even though we were working class and only took a couple of trips in my childhood, my parents made sure I knew how to swim, and I am grateful for that because it opened the door for my career in marine biology and ocean conservation, which enables me to integrate all the things I care most about: civil rights, law, policy, science, people, justice, culture. Plus octopuses are really cool! I respect the intelligence of other species and their right to exist.

LEAH: As you acknowledged, what you experienced personally is experienced systematically by whole communities. You and Dr. Katharine Wilkinson wrote, "The same patriarchal power structure that oppresses and exploits girls, women, and nonbinary people (and constricts and contorts boys and men) also wreaks destruction on the natural world. Dominance, supremacy, violence, extraction, egotism, greed, ruthless competition—these hallmarks of patriarchy fuel the climate crisis just as surely as they do inequality, colluding with racism along the way. Patriarchy silences, breeds contempt, fuels destructive capitalism, and plays a zero-sum game. Its harms are chronic, cumulative, and fundamentally planetary."[26] Snaps! Say more about why racial justice is inexorably linked to environmental concerns.

DR. AYANA ELIZABETH JOHNSON: The daily burdens of racism further inhibit people of color's full participation in environmental advocacy. People of color are significantly more concerned about climate change than white people are—49 percent of white people are concerned, compared to 57 percent of Black people, and 69 percent of Latine people.[27] That's tens of millions of people of color in the US who could be a major part of the solutions we need if unburdened by white supremacy. Even at its most benign, racism is incredibly time consuming and draining, diverting Black genius that could otherwise be focused on environmental solutions.

Although climate change is coming for us all, and even exorbitant wealth ultimately won't save you, it is essential to allocate the most energy to protecting the people who are most vulnerable now. Intense storms, like Hurricane Katrina, and exposure to toxic air pollutants cause much greater harm to communities of color. If we're thinking about how to become more resilient to the impacts of climate change, we must focus on the people who are actually the most impacted. And we must understand that local people are best equipped to lead in their own communities.

If climate organizations fail to prioritize the inclusion of people of color, the movement will never grow large enough to succeed. I simply don't see how we win at addressing the climate crisis without elevating Black, Indigenous, Latine, and Asian leaders. It is not merely a technical challenge we are facing; it's not just about solar panels and electric cars. This is about how we implement solutions, how we replicate and scale them. It's about communities and governments and corporations changing the way they do things. Solving the climate crisis necessitates shifts in just about everything. So we need to find ways that everyone can be a part of this transformation.

LEAH: Chris, I welcome you to also speak to being Black in environmental spaces. We are familiar with the stereotype that Black people don't do winter backpacking and fishing, and yet you are an Arctic angler. What assumptions have you confronted, and how do you see racial justice's import to the environmental movement?

CHRIS HILL: Growing up, I was told by outsiders that Black people don't camp, we don't hike, and we don't swim. Attending wilderness camp as a child, I was the only Black person for a very long time. I didn't see people who looked like me in outdoor spaces or even in the outdoors magazines. That weighed on me a little bit. Because I absolutely loved rock-climbing, backpacking, and snowboarding, I kept pursuing it, but people always tried to tell me what I was or wasn't, or what I should and shouldn't be doing based on the color of my skin. I remember hearing, "Oh, Chris isn't really Black, she loves all white people things." Or folks would assume that I have a white parent who taught me to love nature, when in fact, both of my parents are Black. My grandfather loved fishing; that was essentially all he did. His buddies had a boat and they would go out on the water together. This love of nature was passed down through the generations to me. My grandparents' generation understood how to be in union with nature.

One of the cool things I have noticed over the last couple of years is Black and POC folks visibly taking up space in the outdoors and building community around that. Groups like Brown Girls Climb support folks in feeling more comfortable in the outdoors by leading rock-climbing outings for the BIPOC community. Social media has served as a platform to spread the love of nature, and it allows younger kids to see others who look like them enjoying nature. Even my young niece is catching on; she called me up recently to say, "Chrissy, when you come back do you think you can take me on a hike?" Representation matters.

The environmental conservation movement has protected places over people. It has stolen land from people. It has perpetuated genocide and racism toward people of color. These patterns are deeply rooted in the environmental movement, and people are finally starting to acknowledge that. We can't have a successful conservation movement without centering the well-being and leadership of Black, Indigenous, and people of color, who are most impacted by pollution, devastating storms, and climate change, and who carry ancestral legacies of environment stewardship. We need to work in partnership on issues beyond conservation, like health care and racial justice, all of which are intrinsically intertwined. Ultimately what we are working toward is collective liberation, and it will take all of us working in our interconnected struggles to get there. Like Lilla Watson said, "If you have come here to help me, you are wasting your time, but if you have come because your liberation is bound up with mine, then let us work together."[28]

LEAH: The earth speaks in many languages—the pH of the ocean, the mean water temperature, the thickness of sea ice, the number of salmon in the Chilkat River—as well as the voice that we access through our own stillness and direct engagement with nature. What messages are you hearing from the earth?

CHRIS HILL: I think the earth is saying, "I have given you a lot of grace in the past to do the things you humans imagine you need to do, but time is up. I won't continue to exist in the state of abundance you have come to expect and depend upon if you don't slow your roll and protect my ecosystems. Come to me for strength. Come to me and I will blanket you, I will provide for you, I will heal you, I will hold you. But there needs to be reciprocity in this. You must also protect me." I think there is also an invitation to allow ourselves to be more like elements of the earth. I resonate with how Maya Angelou described a woman in harmony with her spirit as a river flowing, who goes where she will without pretense and arrives at her destination prepared to be herself. We would do well to be taught by the rivers about how to flow gently in harmony with our true nature.

DR. AYANA ELIZABETH JOHNSON: I witness the younger generation listening to the earth in powerful ways. They are bringing a brutal moral clarity to the work. There is a clear right and wrong. Fossil fuel companies are wrong, they need to f—off, and we don't care about the money. As I have aged, I have become more inured to compromise and to taking the wins we can get. At the Global Climate Strike in New York, three hundred thousand activists in New York, who were mostly teens, and millions of people worldwide demanded "systems change not climate change." They are seeing that it's all so broken, and are not willing to back down.

For me personally, a lot of what I hear from the earth is about interdependence. I feel the same way at the shore of the ocean as I do at the top of the mountain. My ego is checked and I feel small in a good way, reminded of my place within the wondrous and intricate whole. I spent most of my marine science research career in coral reefs, and over hundreds of dives, I saw how life there is so intricately intertwined—how each species has a role, how water flows and connects, and how it's all so resilient and tenuous at the same time. I appreciate how the ocean reminds me that I am one individual of one species, and I share this planet with eight million or so other species. The world will go on without me.

RISING WATERS

A Conversation with Queen Quet and
Colette Pichon Battle, Esq.

We have an amazing tolerance for Black pain.

—REV. JESSE JACKSON, AFTER HURRICANE KATRINA

I n 2012, *Hurricane Sandy*, the largest Atlantic hurricane on record, swept across the Caribbean and the entire eastern seaboard of the US. We were alerted to Sandy's arrival on our farm in the middle of the night, when we heard a deafening and perplexing roar from the forest. My spouse and I sat straight up in bed, looked at each other wordlessly, and headed outside. The powerful sound was coming from a newly formed "river" cascading from the forest and headed right toward our crop fields. It was dark, windy, and cold, yet we knew that if we did not act, we might lose our fall harvest. We woke up our young children, ages seven and nine, put shovels in their hands, and got to work digging a trench to divert the waters from the crops. After several muddy hours, we retired to our beds and hoped that our mounded soil would absorb the floodwaters. In the morning, news of devastation began trickling in. Both of the roads, Routes 2 and 22, that serve our town of Grafton were completely washed out, and residents were trapped. Neighboring farms had lost between 50 and 100 percent of their topsoil in the heavy rains. New

York City was without electricity, with elders and people of color dis-proportionately adversely impacted.[1] Our friends in Cuba, Haiti, Puerto Rico, and the Bahamas were facing homelessness and food shortages. Our youngest child wore a life jacket around the farm for days, terrified of being swept away by waters that were slow to recede.

For millennia, the oceans have held just the right amount of heat to support a balanced atmospheric system and stabilized shorelines. Anthro-pogenic climate change is shifting that balance. When seawater warms, it expands, increasing the overall volume of the ocean and causing sea levels to rise.[2] When seawater warms, it also provides the heat energy for stronger tropical cyclones to develop and rapidly intensify.[3] While indus-trialized nations are responsible for 79 percent of the world's greenhouse gas emissions, the impacts of rising sea levels, intensified hurricanes, and other climate disruption disproportionately lands on nations and people who are Black, Indigenous, and poor.[4] Some of the communities at great-est risk of devastation due to a warming climate live in Nigeria, Haiti, Yemen, the Philippines, and Kiribati, with certain areas threatened to be wiped off the map completely as the waters advance.[5]

In the US, as globally, flooding also disproportionately impacts com-munities of color. These disparate burdens were glaring and poignant when Hurricane Katrina hit southeast Louisiana in 2005, claiming 1,800 human lives and causing at least $125 billion in property damage.[6] The damage was most extensive in African American neighborhoods like the Lower Ninth Ward that continue to be left behind in the recovery pro-cess. As a result of people being unable to return home post-hurricane, the Black population of New Orleans plunged by one hundred thousand people—seven percentage points. During this period, the racial income gap also widened. Social networks were disrupted, livelihoods and busi-nesses destroyed, and Black land gobbled up by disaster gentrification. Similarly, when Hurricane Harvey ravaged Texas in 2016, the neighbor-hood most impacted by flooding was 49 percent people of color. A history of systemic racism and redlining has relegated Black and Brown people to marginal properties, including lowlands and floodplains, where they are more susceptible to storm damage and less likely to be eligible for flood insurance. Inland flooding also disproportionately impacts African American populations, notably in cities like Chicago and Detroit, where city sewer systems are neglected and unable to handle storm surges.[7,8,9]

To better understand how rising waters are impacting our folks, we talk with two incredible Black women leaders who are taking a stand for their coastal communities in the face of climate disruption.

QUEEN QUET MARQUETTA L. GOODWINE (she/her) is chieftess of the Gullah/Geechee Nation and a published author, computer scientist, lecturer, mathematician, historian, columnist, preservationist, environmental justice advocate, environmentalist, film consultant, and "The Art-ivist." She is the founder of the premiere advocacy organization for the continuation of Gullah/Geechee culture, the Gullah/Geechee Sea Island Coalition. Queen Quet was one of the first of seven inductees in the Gullah/Geechee Nation Hall of Fame. Queen Quet's accolades include the US Jefferson Award for community service, the Jean Laney Harris Folk Heritage Award for Gullah Advocacy from the state of South Carolina, the Living Legacy Award from the Association for the Study of African American Life and History (ASALH), and the MaVynee Betsch Conservation Award, among others.

COLETTE PICHON BATTLE, ESQ. (she/her), is a generational native of Bayou Liberty, Louisiana. As founder and executive director of the Gulf Coast Center for Law and Policy (GCCLP), she develops programming focused on equitable disaster recovery, global migration, community economic development, climate justice, and energy democracy. Colette worked with local communities, national funders, and elected officials in the post-Katrina and post–Deepwater Horizon disaster recovery. She was a lead coordinator for Gulf South Rising 2015, a regional initiative around climate justice and just transition in the South. In 2015, Colette was selected as an Echoing Green Climate Fellow; in 2016, she was named a White House Champion of Change for Climate Equity; and in 2018, Kenyon College awarded her an Honorary Doctorate. In 2019, Colette was named an Obama Fellow for her work with Black and Native communities on the front line of climate change, and she gave a TED talk, "Climate Change Will Displace Millions. Here's How We Prepare."

LEAH: Ancestor Wangari Maathai wrote, "These experiences of childhood are what mold us and make us who we are. How you translate the life you see, feel, smell, and touch as you grow up—the water you drink, the air you breathe, and the food you eat—shapes what you become. When what you remember disappears, you miss it, and search for it, and so it was for me."[10] How did your homeplace mold you?

COLETTE PICHON BATTLE: Folks place me in New Orleans, but I am from the deep swamps, the green, muddy, fertile intersection of three bayous north of Lake Pontchartrain. We are a big Creole Louisiana Catholic family. Think tribe. Think thirty-two first cousins swimming and playing in the ditch, catching turtles, eels, snakes, frogs, and bugs. I grew up helping my grandmother, who was in a wheelchair, tend to her flower garden. I grew up delighting in the blue herons, cranes, owls, and geese that stopped by on their north-south migration. We hunted and fished for shrimp, crustaceans, and crabs, and came back with a bounty to cook and put on the table with everyone. Folks sometimes forget that Black people are rural, too, and that we are deeply in relationship with the natural world.

QUEEN QUET: I am a Gullah/Geechee native of St. Helena Island, but my family stems from Polawana and Dataw Islands. There are one million Gullah/Geechee living on the Sea Islands and coastal areas between Jacksonville, North Carolina, and Jacksonville, Florida. Every native Gullah/Geechee grew up breathing in the smell of pluff mud as we ventured to the water to gather the family meals of fish, shrimp, oysters, clams, and blue crabs. In the soil, we grow staples of the Gullah/Geechee diet, including rice and vegetables. As a child, they start you with the easy stuff, like putting one seed per hill or scattering certain seeds in a trench. As you get older, you learn what each seed looks like, which weeds to pull, and how to harvest. We grew up with a village of people raising us, and the salt marsh was part of our family, too. The waterways were sacred to us and provided our food. One of our proverbs is, *De wata da bring we an de wata gwine tek we bak* (the water brings us, and the water is going to take us back), so we have to live in balance with the land and waters to keep them healthy for future generations.

LEAH: The farmers in rural Ghana, with whom I lived and worked for six months in my early twenties, had a practice of monitoring climate change. Each year, Chief Zogli and other agriculturalists would notch the start and end dates of the rainy season into their doorpost. They are completely dependent on rainfall as their only source of agricultural water and explained to me that the rainy season has been arriving later each year and ending sooner—and that the thirsty crops struggled to mature. On our farm in upstate New York, we are already experiencing the impacts of anthropogenic climate change, which is causing record rainfall, flooding, and the proliferation of insect pests. Climate change is not an abstract potential future concern for frontline communities; it's a present-day threat to survival. In what ways have you seen climate change impact your home?

COLETTE PICHON BATTLE: We noticed the little things at first—different bugs, tree diseases, and invasive species blown in on the hurricane winds from the Caribbean. I can still remember seeing my first West Nile mosquito. Next, we noticed the persistent waters, and nobody's backyards dried out anymore. The ground became too saturated to sit outside or to mow the grass. And then came the land loss, which has been the hardest to cope with. During deer hunting season, it's a big deal to be able to learn to take down a deer and feed your whole family. Those hunting grounds of my childhood are now open water. Everyone has sad stories of where they used to hunt, trap, and play, and that land has literally disappeared. You can get on a boat and the GPS will show you that you are on land, but you are on open water. I've seen that with my own eyes. The storms now are like nothing that we have ever seen, developing faster, hitting the land stronger, and persisting over land much longer than they are supposed to. Hurricane Ida was a Category 4 when it hit the coast, but there were Category 5 winds in some areas. Because of the devastation of the marsh and wetlands, we have no protection, and the flood waters rise fast. In the middle of the night, I could see things flying, and hear the wind sounding like a train and the trees and electric poles snapping. We spent days after on the boat going to check on the old folks to make sure they had food and water. Then the heat came, 113-degree temperatures and no power, no A/C, and misery.

Growing up I was taught to respect the trees, and I reveled in their strength as a model for how we were going to make it despite what we were up against. Every morning those trees hugged me and said, "Get back out there!" To see them completely uprooted, my heart just broke, and I cried as I was walking. Who cries over trees? Not city folks.

QUEEN QUET: We've seen rapid erosion from sea level rise, and more intense and prevalent tropical storms and hurricanes in the past ten years especially. We went from one extreme about fifteen years ago, with massive drought, to this overabundance of water—the sea level rise, the rains, the floods, the "king tides," all coming in at once. Farmers and the fishing families have suffered financially whether they're involved commercially or practicing our natural tradition of subsistence farming and fishing. We've seen agricultural land inundated because of ocean and creek flooding, and now there is ocean acidification and single-use plastics pollution. People are not catching the same amount of crabs, they're not picking the same amount of oysters, they're not getting the same harvest from the sea. So our food security is something that's been taxed the most. These changes are like stakes being hammered into the heart of those of us from this coastline, because *de land da we famlee and de wata da we bloodline* (the land is our family and the water is our bloodline). Initially, the rapid erosion we saw appeared to be connected to flash floods and hurricanes, but over time, we had to learn terms that do not exist in the Gullah language, such as "sea level rise."

This year in the South, we had hundred-plus-degree weather for weeks, and as a result, our people are suffering because most don't have health care. Am I having heatstroke? I can't go to a doctor; I don't have that kind of money. So of course more people of color, more people of African descent, are dying in heat waves. Additionally, mold and mildew are major issues on the Sea Islands. Who can afford to remediate a home if it gets flooded? Two or three generations of people living there may develop lung problems without realizing why. So people then die of other conditions that develop due to long-term mold exposure.

LEAH: Queen Quet, you were selected, elected, and enstooled by your people to be the first Queen Mother, "head pun de bodee" (head upon the body), and official spokesperson for the Gullah/Geechee Nation. Among your myriad works on behalf of your nation, you convinced Congress to pass the Gullah/Geechee Cultural Heritage Act that established a heritage corridor and protection for sacred and historic sites. You also advocate for the Gullah/Geechee people internationally, including before the United Nations. What is your current work at the local and global level to protect your lands and waters?

QUEEN QUET: I am one of few Gullah/Geechee who cannot stand oysters for eating, even though I am the biggest advocate for oysters. If you harvest thirty bushels of oysters, you can keep them all! My advocacy is for replanting the oyster shells to replenish the beds. The larvae float around, and they need something to connect to and take hold. Every oyster can cleanse fifty gallons of water per day, so imagine what a healthy bed can do for the health of the water. The oysters also provide food for the birds, blue crab, fiddler crab, gulls, and the human population. My mother's father used to replant the oysters, though he didn't call it that back in the day. He would go out every year on a huge boat and shovel off the shells, and he passed down this love of the ecosystem to me. We have also started replanting the spartina grass, which is the main vegetation found in our salt marsh. These efforts protect the maritime forest from erosion and mitigate some of the impacts of sea level rise. The Gullah/Geechee Sea Island Coalition and the Gullah/Geechee Fishing Association have been a part of this work for decades. More recently, we launched the South Atlantic Salt Marsh Initiative to bring together federal, state, and local governments, military officials, and community leaders who recognize the habitat's ability to help protect shorelines against flooding and storm surge. Our nation has survived 150 hurricanes, and we are hoping to continue that legacy of resiliency by conserving about a million acres of marsh in our homelands. The water is also our bloodline, so for us, it's very important to engage in processes to protect the land ahead of time, not wait until the storm comes and then try to rebuild.

We are also working to stop the rampant development, gentrification, and land grabbing of our homelands. Water for us is not about recreation. It's about spirituality. We don't see it as a place to play; we regard it as a sacred ground. You don't see us building a house right on the water, unless that's the last piece of land a family has. These resort developments are disrupting holy ground.

At this point, I have spoken at the United Nations on numerous occasions, but I will never forget the first time. It was 1999 at the hearing of the Commission on Human Rights in Geneva, Switzerland. When it was finally my turn to get up to the mic and speak about the Gullah/Geechee, I told them, "I have to do what God and my ancestors are telling me to do right now," and I switched from English to my native Gullah language. Now, all day the room had been full of chatter, and as the day wore on and folks got restless, it got noisier and noisier. But when I started speaking my language, which no one had ever heard before, it got perfectly quiet. Even the interpreters had to be quiet. The only sound in the room was me speaking Gullah. The applause lasted for so long when I finished, and people swarmed me for copies of my speech. From there, the work has been growing. I recorded the human rights history of the Gullah/Geechee people at the UNESCO head-quarters in Paris, became a directorate member of the International Human Rights Association for American Minorities, and represented our nation at several global climate summits.

LEAH: Colette, we met through your work advocating for the Red, Black, and Green New Deal, the national climate initiative for the Movement for Black Lives, and I soon learned that you are a force of nature, doing so much in defense of our people and the earth. Your organization co-chairs the national Water Equity and Climate Resilience Caucus with PolicyLink, serves on the steering committee of the Ocean Justice Fo-rum, and anchors the five-state, multi-issue initiative Gulf South for a Green New Deal. What is your organization currently doing to build southern Black leadership in the climate space?

COLETTE PICHON BATTLE: Gulf Coast Center for Law and Policy provides legal services and strategy around the climate crisis in the Gulf South. After disasters, we hold pop-up legal clinics and support folks in access-ing recovery resources. Free legal services offer an opening to politicize folks as to the implications of the moment. We ask, "Do you know what you got hit by? Do you understand that this is more than a hurricane? Do you want to get involved?" We want our communities to pay attention to the fact that these disasters are happening more and more to us Black and poor people in the region. We highlight and build upon the already powerful leadership of women in Louisiana, Mississippi, and Alabama. Women are on the front line; people don't talk about them as leaders be-cause they often don't have credentials, but they are the staples of rural communities, holding it down and advocating for climate justice. We are kicking down doors and letting folks in, facilitating the engagement of frontline communities in critical debates on climate. We need southern and Black voices in global conversations. The Gulf South is a critical region when it comes to understanding climate impacts. When I was recently at COP26 (United Nations Climate Change Conference), several presenters talked about the Gulf—how quickly the storms are developing with the warming waters, and about the BP oil disaster, the offshore gas lines, and the fires on our water. I can feel the rightness of this work to move our folks' voices into the global arena.

LEAH: I remember learning in university that cleaning up an oil spill or recovering from a hurricane can increase a country's GDP (gross domestic product) because it spurs economic activity, and in a capitalist system, economic activity is the measure of success.[11] Disturbingly, the harm to the earth and human health from ecological crises does not show up in the balance sheet. Colette, you further expanded my understanding of how economic valuation works to undermine climate solutions. Can you break this down for us?

COLETTE PICHON BATTLE: We must reframe our understanding of the problem. Climate change is not the problem; climate change is the most horrible symptom of an economic system that has been built for a privileged few to extract every precious resource out of this planet and its people—from our natural resources to the fruits of our human labor. In law school, they taught us how to value human life in the context of a wrongful death suit and the civil penalty for that death. We learned to calculate human potential based on factors like longevity, access to education, economic output, and professional potential. I learned the formulas and passed the course with a high grade. I saw these formulas come up again with 9/11. Somebody had to value human life in order to give out the remedy checks. These formulas were employed again in the BP oil disaster in my neighborhood. They were attempting to value human worth, human potential. So I started investigating this idea of valuation. For example, no value is given to people's potential to feed themselves outside of the market economy. The poverty levels in the rural South are high, but people can sustain themselves on natural resources. We can go into the water and get some shrimp and fish. We don't necessarily need money to eat. But the BP oil drilling disaster shut down the fisheries, and we could no longer eat out of the waters. The commercial fisherfolk could point to dollar amounts of losses on paper, so they were valued and compensated, but the subsistence folks couldn't prove the unprovable—the value of their subsistence catch—and got nothing. We see that Black and Indigenous folks, women and nonbinary folks, rural folks, and poor folks are never valued at the same level as their educated white male counterparts, and neither are their land or their homes. Redlining necessarily depreciated the home values of all the Black people living in Eastern New Orleans, simply because it was a Black area. During storm recovery, white people in Lakeview got more money for the same-size house than Black people received. During the worst storm in our history, Hurricane Audrey, rural poor Indigenous and Black people got nothing, not even meager aid or media reporting, even though the storm was five times worse than Katrina and communities were decimated. Disaster recovery is one place where we see legalized, discriminatory devaluation of Black, poor, rural, and uneducated people.

My critique of the climate movement is that it perpetuates a false solution of capitalistic valuation. At COP26, I was listening to an Indigenous woman from the Amazon talk about what she sees when she walks through the forest—the medicines, the foods, the relatives. The next speaker was European and presented various formulas for determining the market value of that forest. The concept of "priceless" does not occur to them.

LEAH: Maurice Small, a Black farmer in Georgia, told me, "If you listen to the earth, it'll be some of the loudest quiet you will ever hear."[12] What do you hear in the loud quiet of your time with the earth?

QUEEN QUET: One thing that people always hear me say came to me as a vision from my ancestors and became the motto for the Gullah/Geechee

Sea Island Coalition, and it's this: *Hunnuh mus tek cyare de root fa heal de tree.* You must take care of the root to heal the tree. If you want to get to the root of a problem, you need to dig for it, because roots that are really solid are not on the surface. I'm ready to work to make sure that the fruit that's produced from this tree in the future is sustainable and healthy. The earth is speaking to me all the time. The earth says, "Be still and know that I am God." When I walk outside, I listen to the oak trees, the pine trees, and the grasses in the field. When someone drives up in a car with a loud engine or honking, they are disrupting a conversation with God. For some folks the radio comes in clear, while others have white noise, and some have just static. We need to tune into the wavelength of the natural world so we can hear.

COLETTE PICHON BATTLE: The earth wants us to have the courage to admit we have taken too much, and to recognize that the entire world is paying the price for the privilege and comfort of just a few people on the planet. Humans have taken enough. There are some things that simply do not belong to us, and that we don't get to take, even though they exist and we have the means to take them. It's time to understand value beyond capital. Growing up, we didn't have any money, but we had a ditch and we could pull some stuff out of it to eat. When folks have no connection and no relationship with the Earth, false solutions rooted in criminalization and capitalization arise that are divorced from the broader ecosystems that sustain all of our lives. It is arrogant to think that technology will save us. It is egotistical to think that we can continue this unjust extractive approach to living on this planet and survive. We must learn to follow—not tokenize, exotify, or dismiss—the leadership and the traditional knowledge of Indigenous peoples of a particular local place. This will be the way to transform from a disposable, individualistic society to one rooted in equity and collective resilience.

Witness

THE EARTH'S SONG

A Conversation with B. Anderson,
Toshi Reagon, and Yonnette Fleming

Protecting the sacred of all ecology
The interdependence of every species
The right to self-determination we affirm
The right to every living being free of harm

Detoxification of water and of land
Ethical use of our resources we demand
To live in balance with nature our lives depend
It's this relationship with Earth we will defend

—TAÍNA ASILI, "NATURE"

Learners in Soul Fire Farm's immersion program huddled around the campfire on the closing night of a week-long program, eager to enjoy the cypher talent share that would close out their time on the land. Amidst the poetry, song, and dance of human bodies, one participant attached an electromagnetic wave reader to the branch of a red maple, which transformed the plant's impulses into melody and rhythm. When we touched the tree, or drummed a pattern on its trunk, the music changed in response. The tree music inspired us to create a spontaneous improvisation symphony of voice and percussion, with the plant's song as the foundation.

It is understood that every known human culture makes music. Even before language evolved, people created music and used music as a means of communication.[1,2] Bone flutes dated to fifty-three thousand years ago were found in the settlements of Cro-Magnon and Neanderthal ancestors, and some archeologists believe human music-making dates back even earlier to several hundred thousand years ago.[3] Many evolutionary scientists argue that we have as powerful an instinct to sing as we have a predisposition for speaking.[4]

It is postulated that humans have learned music-making from the animals, geology, and plants in our environments. The Inuit, Tlingit, and other seafaring peoples have been hearing the sounds of whales through the hulls of their boats for millennia, and have incorporated those sounds into their musical canon. Despite having a seven-octave range, humpback whales utilize musical intervals that are similar to human music scales, with corollary tones and timbres. Their songs follow the "ABA format," beginning with an initial theme, following with an elaboration on the theme, and finally returning to the original theme. The length of their songs is similar to that of a modern ballad.[5]

Similarities between the songs of nature and human music can also be found in elephants, birds, and volcanoes. The songs of the Hutu and Tutsi peoples of central East Africa incorporate the ultra-low frequency tones of elephants.[6,7] Indigenous people living on Tanna Island in Vanuatu created songs and dances based on the sounds of the active volcano Mount Yasur. Birds use many of the same rhythmic variations, intervals, and combinations of notes that humans do.[8] They follow the same scales, sing in canon, and even transpose their motifs into different keys.[9,10,11] The ruby-crowned kinglet (*Regulus calendula*) sings a full octave interval between the stanzas in their song. The canyon wren (*Catherpes mexicanus*) sings in a chromatic scale, and the hermit thrush (*Catharus guttatus*) sings in a pentatonic scale. The Californian marsh wren (*Cistothorus palustris*) communicates with its neighbors through call-and-response songs, employing a repertoire of over 120 fixed sequence themes.[12]

Nearly two thousand years ago, Taoist philosophers proposed that music is "a potent cosmic force capable of expanding human intelligence and enhancing communion with the nonhuman world."[13,14] Modern science suggests that music-making may be a near-ubiquitous language in the animal kingdom, where songs are passed down across the generations and also taught to peers and community newcomers. The combined songs of a bioregion create a unique sonic fingerprint of place. Just as each creature's food and habitat preferences comprise its ecological niche, so does the voice of each creature—with its distinctive timbre, frequency, duration, and amplitude—constitute its unique niche in the orchestra of musicians.

Similarly to how biophony of animal song promotes a harmony of place, so does human music promote cooperation. Scientists propose that the synchronization of body movement and vocalization among ancient humans promoted a sense of group unity that enabled them to engage in the necessary work of mutual support and reliance. Studies have shown that modern human groups that are interdependent are inclined to make music together as a way of further reinforcing group cohesion.[15]

B. Anderson, Toshi Reagon, and Yonnette Fleming are incredible musicians and earth stewards who use sound as a conduit for connecting with nature, meaning, and community healing. It is a delight to be in conversation with them.

B. ANDERSON (they/them) is a somatic and music therapy practitioner, earth steward, mediation teacher, mediator, ritual leader, and community organizer. B. calls on the traditions, legacies, and medicine of their southern Black American, Jamaican Maroon, and Choctaw ancestry as the basis of their healing arts praxis. Their background in sound healing began at the New England Conservatory as a classical musician, exploring traditional and African American folk songs, improvisation, and various music styles from across the world. Their relationship to plant and herbal medicine is rooted in the teachings of their grandmothers and relatives, and has deepened through continued study as an apprentice of Spiritual Plant Medicine with Karen Rose at the Sacred Vibes Apothecary, and through their practice and certification in Ayurvedic Medicine with Dr. Naina Marballi. B. is the founder and steward of Song of the Spirit, a community-based institute in service of keeping alive the wisdom traditions of the African and Indigenous Diaspora. B. sees their earth stewardship work manifest most through the vision of Black Earth Wisdom (BEW), established in 2019. In their sincere and heartfelt commitment to the liberation of all beings through the reconnection and celebration of our beloved BLACK earth, BEW creates a healing space for people of color to reclaim the lineages of their people and the many ways their dignity and divinity are affirmed by the earth.

TOSHI REAGON (she/her) has been described as "a talented, versatile singer, songwriter, and musician with a profound ear for sonic Americana—from folk to funk, from blues to rock." Critic/blogger Eva Yaa Asantewaa continues, "She masters each of these genres with vocal strategies that easily spiral and swoop from the expressively sinuous to the hard-charging, a combination of warmth and mischief."[16] While Toshi's expansive career has landed her comfortably in residence at Carnegie Hall, the Paris Opera House, and Madison Square Garden, you can just as easily find her turning out at a music festival, intimate venue, or local club. Toshi has had the pleasure of working with Lenny Kravitz, Lizz Wright, Ani DiFranco, Carl Hancock Rux, Nona Hendryx, Pete Seeger, Chocolate Genius, and many other amazing artists. Her favorite collaborator, however, is her mom, Bernice Johnson Reagon. Toshi was the recipient of a New York Foundation for the Arts (NYFA) award for music composition and the Black Lily Music and Film Festival Award for Outstanding Performance. She is a National Women's History Month Honoree and is the 2010 recipient of OutMusic's Heritage Award.

YONNETTE FLEMING (they/them) is an urban farmer and lifelong musician who is dedicated to creating advanced tools and systems of Earth wisdom, which balance the inner landscape and build healthy individuals, families, and communities. They strive to provide community solutions to the issues of oppression, food insecurity, health disparities, and social inequities. Farmer Yon, as they are known, has worked to regenerate urban land in order to grow food and advance community resilience to misogyny and food apartheid in Bedford Stuyvesant, Brooklyn, New York. Farmer Yon's approach reflects the unique needs of the Hattie Carthan Community Garden's aging population and the need to advance bold, holistic leadership in order to address equity, inclusion, and resilience. Farmer Yon serves as project catalyst of the Hattie Carthan community food system, which consists of a historic community garden, two community-based markets, and a healing justice apothecary and farm. They are also a founding farmer of Farm School NYC, where they teach food justice. Yon has recorded three albums—*Primordial Pulse*, *Tribute to Tradition*, and *Piano and Drums*. Yon is also a self-published author of three books—*Follow the Flow Poetry*, *A Thyme for Healing*, and *Determined to Thrive Not Survive*. Yon's work is in response to a calling from Spirit for ecological activism in our urban cities.

LEAH: There is a teaching in the *Odu Ifa*, the sacred literature of the Yoruba people and their Diaspora, that there was once a time when animals and human beings spoke the same language and lived together in societies. Perhaps, this ability to communicate persisted in some individuals, even as western civilization pursued a path of separateness. You have a special, intimate connection with animals rooted in a subtle communication. Can you share how that developed?

B. ANDERSON: I was four or five years old playing outside in the yard near our Williamsville, New York, home. My parents and siblings were away, my great-uncle was busy doing some painting on the house, and my grandparents were inside. I found some poison berries and began to play with them, staining my hands and dress, but somehow knowing not to eat them. I then crawled behind the shed outside of the house to take a nap.

Meanwhile, my grandparents noticed my absence and searched for me in vain, eventually calling the police and fire department to assist. When the authorities came, they found me fast asleep behind the shed, stained with berry juice, and surrounded by several bunnies who had assembled and were sleeping all around me. This was my earliest memory of being very close to my animal siblings. Later on, I developed an intimate relationship with deer. They would greet me daily when I came home from school, and we would stare at one another for long stretches of time. In moments when I am experiencing deep sadness, grief, and loss, the deer moves closer to me. The deer bows, I bow in return, and then it gently walks away.

FARMER YON: I have always been attuned to the languages of nature that other people seem unaware of, and worked to translate them. The deer was also one of the first animals to ever speak to me, and I carry deer antlers to this day for my spiritual work of stealth. The birds also spoke to me a long time ago and taught me how to hold council. For example, during a drumming ceremony I was walking back to my cabin in the middle of the night, and I had the honor of witnessing the birds screeching and talking with one another. I became invisible, peeking through the bushes to observe and learn how they held council. The plants have also taught me about their own origins and inspired me to create an herbal immersion program to share the truth of what I was shown.

The animal teachers give me great stealth in my work and affairs. The turtle is my longtime companion of twenty-five years who teaches me to take a 360 look at every issue, and to remember that we are stewards of Turtle Island. Gators and crocodiles help me remember *Aegypt* and the cities we built there. The black bear comes into my consciousness in the wintertime to remind me about the importance of dreamtime visions. The hawk lives in the tree in my backyard and faces revered ancestor Hattie Carthan's home in Brooklyn. The bright yellow anaconda utters the language of my ancestors in South America, as the snake is that Mother Spirit connection that helps me understand medicine, healing, and everything feminine. And the black panther, who is my family's animal signature, speaks to me and helps me write my books.

My ancestral inheritance is a long memory that traces all the way back to the plants and animals holding council. My body, just like yours, contains the journey of our ancestors. Inscribed on our features, our noses, our skin, our hair, is an inheritance that originates in the first bacteria that lived on earth. I have seen the birth of the elements. The whole community of earth is within us. Every spirit, plant, animal, rock, and tree that we meet along the way is our teacher. Our body is the earth, and the earth is a living body. So all of the principles involved in keeping a body healthy apply to the earth. We use herbs in the form of compost tea to heal and remediate the soil, just as we use herbs to heal our body or to treat disease in our chickens. We treat the animals and the soil with the same level of integrity that we treat ourselves.

Part of my identity is that I am energy exploring matter. My identity is bound up in spirit. Anything in lower, material form is just a lesson. All of the work is earth stewardship. There is no other motivation. All I want to see is this: a healthy community, an economy that includes all of us, and for women to be respected as bringers of life and keepers of the earth. After all, it is our moon cycles that authored the invention of human time.

LEAH: Toshi, you speak so powerfully to the importance of reclaiming our sense of belonging on the earth as an initial step to reawakening communion with the natural world. For so many generations, Black people's marginalization on the land led to an estrangement. In your lineage, there has been a homecoming. Can you describe that journey?

TOSHI REAGON: The destruction of the planet can only be normalized insofar as we forget that we are home. This work is about us constantly trying to find our way back home. The idea that I belong here—that I am home and connected to the whole ecosystem of Earth—comes from my lineage of women. It is the most powerful message I got from my people. As the first born on my mother's side of the family, my birth was celebrated as a victory, a culmination of generations of hard work, innovation, and survival. My first breath was a "we did it" moment. They had to go through so much to get to me. It's moving to think that someone through time, through the worst of circumstances, maintained a lineage so that I could exist and belong. They could have passed on the harm they experienced, but instead they passed on a wisdom of spirit, a gratitude for each beautiful day, and a tangible connection to the spirit of the earth, despite the treachery of their existence on this land. My grandmother Beatrice Wise Johnson was strong and loving, powerful and clear. She had her hands on every child within the breadth of her loving reach until she left the earth. My mother, Bernice Johnson Reagon, is the Queen Mother, with whom I travel the universe of time and space, in and out of life and death, sharing multiple planes of existence. Her purpose on Earth is to remind us to vibrate sound through our bodies so that we can know a home within ourselves. We are descendants of the musicians, priests, innovators, builders, water gatherers, and folks who put their hands in the dirt to grow food and sustain life. We pass on all the information we need through songs.

LEAH: Modern science suggests what many of our peoples have long known, that music may be one of the universal languages connecting people with the rest of nature. B., how have you found music to be a connecting force with the earth?

B. ANDERSON: Sound creates shifts in the molecular structure in the body, be it through singing bowls, tuning forks, or the human voice. I have seen this happen in real time. I was at the International Council of the Thirteen Indigenous Grandmothers gathering. The sound of our voices in harmony welcomed the hawks and owls into our circle. The voice can communicate in a frequency that represents a sense of connection and humility in relationship to the natural world. I was recently singing a prayer to the sky at dusk. There were three dogs far away from me, and as I sang, they all came to sit around my feet and join in the prayer. It felt as though I was communicating with an energy or frequency that they hear much clearer than we do. I had to humble myself enough to hear beyond my human supremacy, and to allow myself to listen. Our song was call and response. I was listening, then responding, acknowledging their existence and our connection. When we speak to animals and other nonhuman kin, there is a subtlety and softness to the frequency of what is being shared, and it can easily be missed. The gentleness of the sway of the leaves in the tree in front of me, or the wind chime that just sounded, defies the forced, hard, colonial, dominating pattern of language. Instead, all beings are invited to tap into something simultaneously, something ever present, a consciousness, an awareness rooted in compassion and empathy. We must be gentle and willing to be with ourselves, and with much more than ourselves. Tapping into the subtle body is the space where mediumship and song intersect. When I activate my listening, I hear clear voices from the earth and the ancient stewards of the earth. I hear the ancient ones weeping, expressing deep grief. They keep saying, "They are not listening. They are not doing prayers and ceremonies." They beg us for selflessness, to think of some beings other than ourselves. They implore us to hold ceremonies.

LEAH: Farmer Yon, can you speak about your musical lineage and the role of music in your earth work?

FARMER YON: I have been playing music since I was three years old. I made vows to the living Earth to use my gifts for healing. The rhythms are not for entertainment, but for deep ecological and healing work. My grandma Janey was the parade marshal for the Emancipation Day parade in Guyana, and she was my shining beacon. When I was young and doing protests and direct action, I used my drum to march. I give Grandma Janey credit for my ability to dance and create with the drum spirit, and for all the realms I have known and seen through that spirit. The drum and dance attune my body to what the earth needs now.

I also credit my spiritual tribe of women drummers from Matanzas, from whom I inherited a sacred drumming lineage through my initiations. They invested thousands of hours sharing their wisdom around women drummers and the constraints of patriarchal control of our Sacred Drums. I also must acknowledge and give homage to Hattie Lorax Carthan—who also has an animal signature energy besides her tree presence—Sojourner Truth, María Sabina and the *curanderos*, Harriet Tubman, Lourde, the run-away slaves that are a part of my feminine power cadre, and the power animals that reveal themselves in our communal journeys and are communicating with us as we work on our land.

When I drum, I can access multiple realms of the energy of the living earth. My agreement with the earth is that I am going to share the medicine of the drum with others for healing and in ceremonies. There is a distinct split off. On one side there is oppression, war, and patriarchy. The other side caters to the earth, healing, and opening to the higher realms. I am in service to that higher realm and use the drums to allow everyone to commune with nature and supernature, and with all the energies of life. The earth needs us to drum, sing, dance, make love, and feed our inner selves. With the drums we can access sacred time, communion, regeneration, and make ourselves whole. The ancient mothers come and hold the container with us. Mami Wata, Oshún, Mother Wind, Nana Buruku, and the Iyami all speak to us. We can hear the earth through the drums.

We teach cooperation and teamwork through musical expression. We engage call-and-response patterning. The drum, exchanging rhythm for rhythm, is an instruction for interdependence and cooperation. On so many levels, we are using and applying the pedagogy and ways of being passed down to us from our ancestors.

LEAH: Toshi, I have witnessed your *Parable of the Sower* opera three times and fully intend to make it an annual ritual for as long as you run the show. In her eco-apocalyptic novel *Parable of the Sower*, Octavia Butler describes a dystopian future impacted by global warming and governmental decline. Shortages of food, water, and basic resources lead to a refugee crisis, drug addiction, and rampant violent crime. The protagonist, Olamina, believes that spiritual dysfunction is at the root of the social and environmental crisis and establishes a religion called Earthseed based on the idea that "God is change." After her neighborhood is destroyed by looters, Olamina leads a group of people on a journey to establish a land-based intentional community in Northern California. With the support of your mother, Bernice Johnson Reagon, you put the novel to song and created a visceral, moving, stunning opera that has broken the hearts of audience members wide open. Tell us about *Parable*, the opera.

TOSHI REAGON: I centered myself for this work by connecting the story to my own people. My grandfather was a Baptist minister, so in some ways I was able to use our family to better understand Olamina's ancestors. Olamina's freedom journey started with her fifteen-year-old declaration to her father, that "my God is not your God." We come to find out that her God is Change. Just as our ancestors had to move and change before they could settle, so Olamina journeys. In her bag when she started moving were the tools of awareness, love, kindness, communication, and care, and the journey helped to grow these skill sets and states of mind. Along the journey, Olamina and her companions make a promise not to be violent with one another, not to steal, not to harm. The journey readied them for settling in place. In the same way, generations of Black people have journeyed for freedom, and we have been able to start buying our own land and insist on building right here, tending our soil, growing our babies, going to church, building a sense of belonging.

As Black people, we use music as part of our sacred survival journey and our relationship to spirit. Even when we can't tangibly envision the things we seek, and perhaps not even grasp the notion of freedom, we still have that song in our hearts: "O Freedom over me. Before I'd be a slave, I'd be buried in my grave."[17] We keep insisting on a relationship with freedom. The opera incorporates two hundred years of Black musical tradition to express this relationship.

The book is named after the parable of the sower in the Bible. The parable opens with the sower planting a seed, but it is sown on ground where it will not grow. There are myriad reasons why the seed will not germinate—so many obstacles. But through persistent resowing of the seed, the sower at last places the seed on good ground, and it bears fruit "one hundred fold."[18] My mom composed the sower song that concludes the opera. It is written as a canon, where the voices repeat and layer, and then all the voices come together, just like the path of the sower. Bernice Johnson Reagon is a sonic storyteller. It is one of my favorite songs in the universe. We started getting emails from teachers asking for a version that they could teach to their students. So I created a score and a recording of an accessible version. We arrived at a workshop in St. Paul, Minnesota, and they had already taught four hundred people how to sing the song. We got on stage and started singing "Sower," and this small child way in the back sang the echo. Everyone on stage started crying.

Octavia wrote *Parable* in 1993 forecasting a dystopian 2024. When I first read the book, I thought, "no way can this ever happen," and now you can see that we are living through it. The rise of white supremacy calls in destruction and violence inflicted on marginalized bodies and the earth. We are hurting, and I feel an amplified imperative to focus on our relationship with our living earth. We are fighting to retain human dignity, to be collaborative in our living, and to not once again be assaulted and stolen from by the already powerful, white, and wealthy. As we journey, we have no worries because we are doing what is right to do. Our hearts are at peace as we follow in the footsteps of our ancestors, who lived and loved through the worst of what humans have to offer each other, and who passed down this song medicine despite it all. But this struggle was not their ultimate vision for liberated living, and this is not how we want to live now. There is so much more we could do if we didn't have to fight so hard to breathe.

LEAH: Each of you has cultivated the art of listening to and hearing the voice of the earth. Farmer Yon, was there a particular moment in your adulthood when you were called home to the earth and able to rekindle the listening skills of your childhood?

FARMER YON: I grew up in a society where agricultural science and nature study were a priority, but when I got to the US, I bought into the American Dream. I went into financial management and administration, landing my first job at seventeen years old with a financial institution. There, I learned corporate culture, how to embody professionalism, white logic, and how to excel and put money above every other interest. I was horrendously unhealthy in my body and was working mandatory overtime for twelve to fourteen hours daily. I had so much money and no time to spend it. I did that until September 11, 2001. I worked near the Chamber Street subway stop in New York City. When the catastrophe happened, I was in my suit trying to get to work on time. As the towers fell, everything inside of me fell with them. I realized just how lost I was in the money structure and false measures of success. I walked all the way home with dust on my suit, in my high heel patent leather shoes, from Manhattan to Brooklyn. I made that long walk with thousands of people over a bridge where humans don't usually walk. It felt like a pilgrimage to Mecca. It was then that I understood the volatility of life. I had to deconstruct my false life and build one based on integrity and ancestral wisdom.

There was a planetary call that I answered to bring the Sacred Work into the cities. I answered the call to be in service to the planet. I came to the earth with an open heart and said, "Teach me, mold me, shape me, inform me with a different sort of intelligence." That is what set the template for what we see today in Brooklyn. I steward the Hattie Carthan Herban Farm and Hattie Carthan Community Market, which are both on public land. We went to clear the market plot in 2009, and then in 2012, when the world as we knew it ended, we anchored in a beautiful herb farm. It was previously a petroleum waste lot. Through sweat equity, we transformed it into a home for 170 varieties of medical herbs. We created an apothecary where we transform the herbs into local medicines that neighbors can access for their health and well-being. We see the farm as a health justice project—as a place to begin conversations about the disenfranchisement of healers and herbal wise women like myself, and the economics of the pharmaceutical industry. At this juncture—where our planet is under threat, our foods are nutrient deficit, our children have forgotten the land, and obesity has become a prominent conversation—all of our work as farmers, gardeners, earth stewards, and medicine people becomes even more relevant and important. These processes do not only exist for economic reasons, but also to promote sustainability, to maintain our cultural heritages, to nourish people, and to reconnect our children to the earth.

The earth is calling all of us. It just depends on whether we decide to pick up the baton and carry the responsibility. Waking up happens over and over again in many ways. When we elevate, the earth calls us home again to *overstand* new dimensions.

LEAH: Toshi and B., what does the earth say to you when your ears are open?

TOSHI REAGON: The earth says that we humans are moving faster than anything alive on this planet. We are moving too fast, and ever accelerating. This cancels the humanness of our practices and turns our lives over to machines. This pace enables the normalization of Earth's destruction. We are losing the ease of connecting with one another, and our ability to fall in love with our potential as beings on a planet full of other miraculous and incredible beings who know how to live in ways that are not destructive to the whole. The earth says that we belong here and can stop running away. If we allow ourselves to think of this place as our home and to really learn it, to get close to the elements of air, water, and earth, then we will have what we need to sustain ourselves. She would like us to sit our ass down for just five minutes, stop messing with things, and be brave.

B. ANDERSON: The earth is telling us that the stripping of her stewards from their lands is an atrocity, and it must stop. I was just reading about the displaced women in Afghanistan today and felt it so deep in my body. Over and over and over again, imperialist forces are pillaging the land, the ancestors in the soil, and the people of the soil. The vastness of the devastation is so horribly familiar. This body, my body, my being, was also ancestrally kidnapped. Entire nations, communities, stories, and traditions have been ripped from their place. We need to protect people whose reverent relationships to land are in great danger. The beekeepers in Rwanda are protectors of their forest, and they were extricated from their forest. They took our Congo Basin pygmy family out of the forest, too, where they once tended to this environment, and now the bees are dying and so are the people.

The degradation of the earth is a manifestation of self-hatred. What if we could see us the way the divine body of the earth sees us? As humanity, we feel collective shame and know that things have gone too far. There is no place on earth where we can escape feeling the impact of the floods, fires, and earthquakes. There is no place on earth where the deeper intelligence does not acknowledge what is happening. The subtle body connection to the earth is an extension of our own soma. We ask, "Where in my life have the levees broken?" We are all the fires burning, the anger and suppressed rage. The ancestors buried in the land under Wall Street are pissed off for not being honored and acknowledged, and for the city above them moving further and further from their traditional values. Of course that area will flood, and that flood will be the tears of those countless ancestors. The shame humans carry is knowing that we may have fucked this up, not just for ourselves, but for our babies. There

has been so much self-righteousness, anger, emotional immaturity, ignorance, and justification, and ultimately the slow realization that we are
hurting a loved one. We've arrived at the acknowledgment that we did
something wrong and that we caused harm.

There is only one thing big enough to shift this dangerous entrenched
mindset. It is the sacred Black Earth.

CLIMATE GRIOTS

*A Conversation with Kendra Pierre-Louis
and Steve Curwood*

Rasheed Lockheart, a formerly incarcerated African American fire-fighter, was one of thousands of inmates who compose up to 30 percent of California's wildland firefighting crews. While serving a sentence for armed robbery in San Quentin State Prison, Rasheed repeatedly risked his life to put out raging wildfires. Since the Thirteenth Amendment contains an exclusionary clause permitting slavery as punishment for a crime, Rasheed and his fellow inmates were compensated at just fifty-three cents per hour for their labor.[1] The number of large fires in the western US has doubled between 1984 and 2015, and climate scientists blame the warmer, drier conditions resulting from anthropogenic climate change.[2] In 2020 alone, 4.2 million acres of California's wild forests burned, and incarcerated firefighters, predominantly Black and Latine, were on the front lines.[3] Anthropogenic climate change is a scientifically undeniable reality, and people of color across the globe are bearing the brunt of the impacts, from wildfire smoke to coastal flooding. As Black climate activist Andrea Manning states, "If you're not affected by climate change today, that itself is a privilege."[4]

The ice cores have spoken. As land and sea ice has accumulated over hundreds of thousands of years, it has trapped atmospheric gases in varying concentrations across time. For millennia, the concentration of carbon dioxide (CO_2) in the atmosphere fluctuated, but it never exceeded 300 parts per million (ppm). Starting around the industrial revolution, the burning of fossil fuels, rampant deforestation, and soil tillage have driven atmospheric CO_2 exponentially up to its current level of 419 ppm. The blanket of heat-trapping CO_2 and other greenhouse gases has driven a mean global surface temperature rise of 1 degree Celsius (2.12 degrees Fahrenheit) since the late nineteenth century. The glaciers are retreating, and the permafrost is melting. The rates of sea level rise are accelerating, and the ocean is acidifying. Extreme weather events like heat waves, floods, droughts, hurricanes, and tornadoes are increasing in intensity and frequency.[5]

Within the US, the most severe adverse climate impacts, including flooding, heat waves, poor air quality, and workers' exposure to intense weather, disproportionately fall on racialized and poor communities. A comprehensive peer-reviewed investigation by the Environmental Protection Agency (EPA) released in 2021 found that Black American individuals are projected to face higher repercussions of climate change by every measurable index, as compared to all other demographic groups. From asthma rates to temperature-related death to flooding threats to damaged property and lost lives, Black communities are on the front lines.

These disparate and inequitable climate impacts are felt at a global scale. Twenty-three rich developed countries comprising 12 percent of the global population, including the US, Canada, and much of Western Europe, are responsible for half of greenhouse gas emissions over the past 170 years.[6] By contrast, the countries least responsible for greenhouse gas emissions are hardest hit by climate impacts such as sea level rise, tsunamis, drought, and irregular weather patterns.[7]

Climate change is arguably the most important challenge facing the global community, and yet media coverage of the issue has not caught up with its urgency. Anthropogenic climate change was confirmed in the

1950s,[8] but in the three decades to follow, media coverage on climate science remained sparse. Starting in the 1980s, coverage picked up, but it often reflected an attitude of denial and skepticism about scientific claims in light of entrenched cultural preoccupations with economic growth predicated on natural resource exploitation. The journalistic norm of "balanced reporting" has led to climate skeptics enjoying ample space and attention in the media even though their views represent only a tiny minority of the scientific community.[9] News reporting on climate change also tends to lack the fundamental facts that enable media consumers to be properly informed. For example, the fact that CO_2 released by the burning of fossil fuels creates a greenhouse effect that warms the planet was mentioned in only 0.1 percent of *New York Times* articles on the subject. As a result, a large percentage of the public doesn't fully realize that global warming is happening now, that it's caused by record levels of atmospheric CO_2 from fossil fuel burning, that 99 percent of climate scientists agree on this, and that the changes are effectively irreversible. The public's profound lack of understanding of basic climate facts leads to widespread skepticism and inaction. Media reporting on the disparate racialized impacts of climate change has been even more scant than reporting on the scientific facts.

Even the media's paltry and inexact coverage is under assault. Opponents of international climate policy have worked to recruit scientists who share the fossil fuel industry's climate denial, and to train them in public relations so they could help convince journalists, politicians, and the public that the risk of global warming is too uncertain to justify regulation of greenhouse gas emissions. They measured the success of their project by counting the number of new articles and radio talk shows that raised questions about the validity of climate science.[10]

In West Africa, a griot is a storyteller who learns and shares the community's history, and who advises leaders on crucial matters. Courageous media makers and artists play a corollary role in the US today, and two among them are Kendra Pierre-Louis and Steve Curwood.

KENDRA PIERRE-LOUIS (she/her) is a climate reporter with the Gimlet/ Spotify podcast *How to Save a Planet*, and the author of the book *Green Washed: Why We Can't Buy Our Way to a Green Planet*. As a climate reporter, Kendra focuses on the impacts of a warming world on people. Kendra has an SM (MS) in science writing from the Massachusetts Institute of Technology, an MA in sustainable development with a focus on policy analysis and advocacy from the School for International Training (SIT) Graduate Institute, and a BA in economics from Cornell University.

STEVE CURWOOD (he/him) is executive producer and host of the podcast *Living on Earth*. Steve created the first pilot of *Living on Earth* in the spring of 1990, and the show has run continuously since April 1991. Today, *Living on Earth* with Steve Curwood is aired on more than 250 public radio stations in the US. Steve's relationship with public radio goes back to 1979 when he began as a reporter and host of *Weekend All Things Considered*. He also hosted NPR's *World of Opera*. Steve has been a journalist for more than thirty years with experience at NPR, CBS News, the *Boston Globe*, WBUR-FM/Boston, and WGBH-TV/Boston. He shared the 1975 Pulitzer Prize for Public Service as part of the *Boston Globe*'s education team. Steve Curwood is also the recipient of the 2003 Global Green Award for Media Design, the 2003 David R. Brower Award from the Sierra Club for excellence in environmental reporting, and the 1992 New England Environmental Leadership Award from Tufts University for his work on promoting environmental awareness. He is president of the World Media Foundation, Inc.; a faculty associate of the Harvard University Center for the Environment; and a professor of practice at UMass Boston. Steve lives in Southern New Hampshire on a small woodlot with his wife and family.

LEAH: Kendra, your climate reporting is rich and diversified, touching on everything from wildfires to climate impacts on bumble bees. But let's start with the personal. How have you noticed climate change in the spaces you inhabit?

KENDRA PIERRE-LOUIS: My parents are from a rice farming community in Haiti, but I grew up in the eastern part of Queens, New York. They are paved over now, but I still remember the tall trees and cicadas, coming out en masse in their seventeen-year cycle, buzzing and molting their shells everywhere. I remember distinctly that summers were much cooler then than they are now. As children, we carried jackets in the summer, but we don't do that anymore. As New York City is a transient city, many people do not have forty years of embodied memories of the ecology of the city, but I have viscerally felt the climate change throughout my life.

I am in love with the Arctic; the climate impacts I have observed in Alaska are additional examples. In 2014, I visited a friend's whaling village that I will not name in order to protect them. It took over twenty-four hours to get there, from New York to Seattle to Anchorage, and then way up on the northern slope. This community still brings up the whales in the traditional way, where they strip the carcass and leave the remains on the sea ice to melt back into the ocean. We had a thrilling close encounter with a polar bear during that trip. More recently, in 2019, I went to McNeil Bear Sanctuary in Alaska with that same friend.[11] We took a sea plane and were able to watch the brown bears feast on the river salmon. At points, the bears were so close to me that I could smell them. That ecosystem is so beautiful. It's a strong reminder of my own humanity and that we don't have control over the earth. The Arctic is a humbling space, and one that commands respect.

That year, Alaska was on fire, and there was also an unprecedented heat wave, with 90-degree temperatures each day. The heat was so intense that I returned home with a raging chest infection and a sunburn. Average temperatures in the Arctic that year were at their second highest since the year 1900, which has had massive impacts on sea ice, fisheries, ecosystems, and Indigenous communities.

LEAH: Steve, when you started the regular weekly broadcast of *Living on Earth* in 1991, I was ten years old. I still remember listening to your show on public radio on trips with my dad in our old station wagon. I remember your early coverage of topics from wetlands to lead poisoning to the perceived tension between social and environmental justice. At the time, you were a rare voice focused on the environment amidst the cacophony of other journalistic priorities. How and why did you decide to create an environmental program, and how do you see it impacting people?

STEVE CURWOOD: In the research process for a book on climate disruption, I went to Woods Hole, Massachusetts, to interview Dr. George Woodwell, a biologist who was the lead author on a paper documenting climate change for President Jimmy Carter in the 1970s. George told me about the process of biotic feedback, how a warming planet would lead to more carbon and methane being released from high latitudes, which would generate a runaway positive feedback loop with even more warming. He scared the pants off of me. I thought, "Oh shit, this is huge!" The Roper Organization had conducted a survey at the time showing that 85 percent of the public did not even register the notion of global warming. Since no one was talking about this on public radio, I decided to do that rather than write a book about it.

I went to the Corporation for Public Broadcasting, and they were not interested in supporting it. They told me I would run out of stories in six months, and joked that the show would be about "dying on earth." I persisted. One of the reasons I persisted was because of my mother, who was a feminist woman of color who earned her doctorate and struggled to get tenure. As a person of color myself, I related to the environment. The white global north discounts people of color, and the white global north also discounts the environment. The natural environment is treated like property in the way many of my ancestors were treated like property. Both the earth and people of color are treated as discardable.

My mentor right out of college was Tom Winship, editor of the *Boston Globe*. I was a kid intern with him during the time of the Pentagon Papers. He laid it out for me, explaining that you can't have an operating democracy unless people have the right information. We can see the devastating impacts today, when what I call "antisocial media" distributes inaccurate information. I was also impacted by the reporting of Tristram Coffin, who founded the *Washington Spectator* and was highly critical of the lack of equity in DC. I knew that climate change was the most important thing going on. If we didn't get the climate issue addressed, then nothing else would matter—not war and peace, not racial justice. I understood that it was my duty as a journalist to tell the best story, and dammit if I didn't have a zillion listeners, couldn't convince people to care, or didn't get much support. I could have been wrong and misjudged the magnitude of the threat of climate change, but I needed to get this stuff on the record—and it turns out I wasn't wrong.

I think that *Living on Earth* has made an important contribution in its three decades. We reported on the international climate meetings when no one was reporting on them, and that advanced the conversation. We also got to ask important questions of people in power. I will never forget the day I walked into Senator John Kerry's office and asked why he signed the 1997 Byrd-Hagel Resolution, which effectively prohibited the US from ratifying the Kyoto Protocol because of its stipulation that we could not sign any treaty that would put the US at an economic disadvantage or let developing countries off the hook for emissions reduction. I asked him to consider that the climate negotiations had institutional racism and economic colonialism baked right in, preferencing the Annex 1 countries, which were majority white (with the exception of Japan, which was designated "honorary white" under apartheid South Africa). He was startled by these questions, but they got him thinking and made him consider a new framework.

Overall, I feel both great and horrible. I have done a tremendous service telling the story of climate change and other aspects of environmental degradation, like endocrine disruptors, species extinction, the chemical industry, and so on. At the same time, telling the story is not sufficient, because we are still headed over the cliff like a bunch of lemmings.

LEAH: Kendra, you seem to share Steve's sentiments about the impending cliff edge. In *Green Washed,* you wrote,

> *We are the environmental equivalent of the US moments from dropping the bomb on Hiroshima. We are Guttenberg before he unveiled his printing press, the ancient residents of Easter Island poised to cut down the last tree, the Bolsheviks just before launching the October revolution. In short, we are human society on the edge of either environmental collapse or social evolution—and how and what we consume is a critical piece of that picture.*[12]

You have done a lot of really important reporting on the climate over the past decade. You wrote about the purple sea urchins in the waters of Northern California that are driven by warming waters to completely mow down the kelp forests and other essential vegetation.[13] You developed a harrowing series that envisions a US without the Environmental Protection Agency.[14] Perhaps my favorite is your article on what air pollution, COVID-19, and police violence have in common in terms of their disproportionate impact on communities of color.[15] Have you experienced barriers to reporting on the stories that matter?

KENDRA PIERRE-LOUIS: Among the values I learned from my Catholic upbringing and my immigrant parents was "blessed are the meek, blessed are the poor." I was taught that there is such a thing as right and wrong, and that my job was to punch up and not punch down, defending what is right. I had to quit working at the *New York Times* because I felt like I was constantly in trouble for doing the right things. It's not in me to "go along to get along." If I stayed, I would have had to compromise values that I just couldn't compromise. They wanted to edit out of my stories anything that contextualized climate impacts on people of color and marginalized groups. I was advocating for those most impacted by climate change, the Indigenous community and Black community, to be covered in the content we produced. I could not get them to greenlight a single ecojustice story until 2018. It was not until after George Floyd's murder that the climate desk started covering US communities of color. I got tired of them cutting out my content and tired of having these fights. In an environment where I had to constantly defend myself and the things I knew were right, I did not have the space to be wrong. As a journalist, I need a safe space to be privately wrong so I can learn and grow, and so I do not have to be publicly wrong. Always being on the defensive did not allow me to be wrong.

Another thing that concerns me is the public's growing apathy with large-scale devastation. With COVID-19, the first ten thousand deaths were horrifying to the public, but when we reached five hundred thousand, it didn't resonate. The year 2020 was the most active Atlantic hurricane season on record, causing over four hundred deaths and $50 billion in damages, and yet there was almost no media coverage or conversation. Our society has already become accustomed to mass death in a way that is horrifying for me. I worry that we are also becoming accustomed to the horrors of climate disaster and that we will accept devastation as the new baseline.

LEAH: Steve, you have not shied away from pointing out the culpability of the oil industry and the federal government in the climate disaster. Can you speak to the entrenched powers of the fossil fuel economy and any clapback you have received for your truth telling?

STEVE CURWOOD: Peter Dykstra unearthed this story for us on a vaccine riot that took place on September 28, 1885, in Montreal, Canada. An angry

mob, mostly French speaking, stoned the health administration building and set fire to the public health official's house to protest a smallpox
vaccine mandate. The BS they were being sold was that the inoculations
were political, a way for the British to oppress the French population.
The BS being sold to us today by the fossil fuel industry—and other
extractive industries—is that they are entitled to make a profit. As we
speak, natural gas in Europe is ten times last year's price. Gasoline and
diesel prices are up in the US by at least one-third. This is because of
market manipulation by the biggest exporters of hydrocarbons—the US,
Saudi Arabia, and Russia. For Putin, climate deals represent an existen-
tial threat to his dictatorship. The entire GDP of Russia is under two
trillion per year, and the EXXON deal that Obama threw out alone was
worth a half billion. Russia sells hydrocarbons and that's it. If the world
comes together and stops using hydrocarbons, then that's it for them. We
are in the thrall of industry. It has captured the government of the US,
of Australia, and increasingly of other countries. The industry is very
powerful, and they are taking us down.

People from the fossil fuel industry have threatened me and have gone
after our funding. This is so tragic because the same people making money
on this are not seeing that their actions will seriously harm the lives of their
children and their children's children. There has been this trope that the
poorest among us will be hit first and worst, and that it's noble to help the
poor and least advantaged around climate disruption. While this is true,
we need to stop kidding ourselves that this is not an emergency for all humanity. Money will not buy people out of this predicament. If you talk to
Michael Mann, a climatologist at Penn State, he will show you a straight-
line extrapolation that results in a sea level rise of a dozen feet or more
by the end of the century. Since every guess has undershot the real data,
perhaps we are looking at twenty feet or more. My two-year-old grand-
daughter will experience that. Can you imagine Boston, New York City, or
Houston with that much sea level rise? Fossil fuels are killing us. In the US
alone, three hundred thousand people die each year from breathing in the

fine particulates that hydrocarbon burning puts out. Globally, that's eight million deaths. Just for our health, we need to get rid of this stuff, not to mention its disruption of planetary climatic balance. We have not figured out how to free ourselves from the grip.

LEAH: Studying environmental science in college, I was taught that environmental problems were caused by human overpopulation, and that the burden of blame and responsibility fell to African families who needed to have fewer children. This overtly racist assumption also happens to be scientifically wrong. In the famous IPAT equation (Impact = Population x Affluence x Technology), the *A* for Affluence has an outsized influence on the overall environmental impact of a society. For example, one study estimates that it would take five Earths to support the human population if everyone's consumption patterns were similar to the average US resident, whereas global humanity would only require 0.7 Earths if everyone consumed resources like the average resident of India.[16] Kendra, you address the problem of overconsumption in *Green Washed*, and I wonder if you could summarize some of your findings that expand on this point.

KENDRA PIERRE-LOUIS: Yes, absolutely. In researching *Green Washed*, I landed on one simple truth: purchasing green can be good, but buying less is better. This simple truism is key to unlocking the door to our future sustainability. For example, researchers at the Aalto University in Finland showed that an individual's climate impact via CO_2 emissions is determined by how many goods they consume. Whether we're talking about energy, clothes, food, or shelter, the sheer volume and pace of our consumption is the root problem.

Ironically, the most significant reductions in US carbon emissions have come as a result of global economic recessions. According to the US Energy Information Administration (EIA), carbon dioxide emissions declined by 2.8 percent in 2008 and by a whopping 7 percent in 2009, the largest absolute and percentage decrease since the EIA started recording annual carbon data in 1949. As a result of the COVID-19 pandemic, carbon emissions dropped around 6 percent in 2020.[17] Even though societal consumption is clearly the root cause of our climate woes, we don't act because of one unsettling truth. If we were to reduce our consumption to a level that was ecologically sustainable, our entire global economic system would collapse. This isn't hyperbole. Our economic system is based on the need for perpetual growth; we either grow our economy or it dies. As measured by the GDP, each year the economy must be bigger than the last.

Our economic system does not recognize that Earth is a finite planet with limited resources, nor that perpetual economic growth is not possible. As a whole, Earth is a closed system. Almost all of the resources at our disposal are located within the planet. Our only external input is energy from the sun in the form of solar radiation. A society built to depend heavily on nonrenewable resources is a society built on quicksand. We are already running out of resources—from depleted fish stocks to mineral resources to water itself.

Herman Daly, emeritus professor at the University of Maryland and chief economist for the World Bank, suggests three rules for an ecologically sustainable economic system. One: Renewable resources must be used no faster than the rate at which they regenerate. Two: Nonrenewable resources such as minerals and fossil fuels must be used no faster than renewable substitutes for them can be put into place. Three: Pollution and wastes must be emitted no faster than natural systems can absorb them, recycle them, or render them harmless.[18]

Until we rethink our entire economic system and replace GDP as our measurement of success, we will not be able to act in accordance with these natural limits.

LEAH: Steve, talk to us about endurance. You have been in the work of climate reporting and environmental storytelling for decades, outlasting many of your colleagues. Do you have a practice of nature immersion and earth-listening that shores you up?

STEVE CURWOOD: Stephen Kellert and E. O. Wilson collaborated on a book called *The Biophilia Hypothesis* that explained how our evolution alongside wild creatures led to instinctual responses to these creatures, such as our innate fear of snakes or spiders. The book summarized several studies, including one by Gordon Orians that had groups of scientists struggling with a problem to do one of two things: take a walk in nature or have another cup of coffee. Those who took a walk in nature could solve problems better. Other studies showed that hospitalized patients who had a view out the window recovered more quickly than those who could see an abstract painting or a blank wall. People in hospitals with natural views also needed less pain medication.[19] In summary, the biophilia hypothesis proposes that human beings have a genetic predisposition to love nature and to seek affiliation with other life forms.

After I talked to Wilson for the podcast series, I changed my whole plan for what I would do. I was living in Cambridge raising my children and was busy in the city with work, soccer games, and urban life. I grew up on thirty-three acres of land in New Hampshire that my mother had purchased to get us out of our Roxbury ghetto. I was two when we moved to the farmhouse, which had no heat or plumbing inside, just an old burner in one room and a wood stove, which she converted to coal. My grandmother had a garden there where she grew vegetables. My mother, who was on junior faculty at Harvard at the time, was also a birder. If she wanted to go birding on a Saturday morning, I would get dragged out of bed and taken along. I hated it back then. As an adult, I knew that I would eventually retire back to our family land that I had been renting out to friends and visiting some weekends, but I realized I needed to live there. I knew I needed the trees and the wildlife, the moose walking through our yard, and the bald eagles. I needed to be forest bathing every day and taking long walks with the occasional company of the dog.

Over thirty years of *Living on Earth*, I have had three major producers with me. They each last about a decade. When they fully understand what is happening with the climate emergency, it becomes overwhelming, and they decide to go. One reason I think I can stick with it is because I get my daily dose of green and the company of other creatures. With my Quaker Friends background, I am happy to meditate, and I especially enjoy walking meditation. Having time in nature and listening to the earth, uninterrupted by people, is what makes it possible for me to do this work.

LEAH: What about you, Kendra? What is the earth communicating to you?

KENDRA PIERRE-LOUIS: I think the Earth's message to all humans is the same, but only one party is listening. She says, "I will outlast you. You are bacteria in my gut, here at my mercy and pleasure." Until the Earth goes careening into the sun, she will be just fine. She will find her own equilibrium whether or not that includes us.

While the Earth will adapt to life without humans, we cannot live without her. Affluent, capitalistic, white men dominate the conversations about moving to another planet. Their proposal comes from a place of not believing in limits and their deep discomfort with the idea that the planet can control them. Just as adolescents rage against their parents, not wanting to live by their rules and threatening to leave, the juvenile impulse is to escape the limits of the planet. But the rules on other planets are much harsher, such as having no atmosphere or magnetosphere. We can't run away from limits.

A WITNESS PEOPLE

A Conversation with Alice Walker and Dr. Joshua Bennett

'Tis like the loss of Paradise
Or Eden's garden left in gloom
Where grief affords us no device
Such is thy lot, my native home . . .
How can I from my seat remove
And leave my ever devoted home
And the dear garden which I love,
The beauty of my native home?

—GEORGE MOSES HORTON, "THE SOUTHERN REFUGEE" (1865)

t was July 2015, and twenty sweaty, soiled, and jubilant aspiring farmers were pulling carts and carrying muddy tools out from the field at Soul Fire Farm. We had just finished a hands-on orcharding class during the Black and Latine Farmers Immersion and were eager for the lunch gong to sound. To fill the moments of restless anticipation, Ross Gay—a guest facilitator and, unbeknownst to us, a *New York Times* bestselling poet—offered an impromptu reading. "You guys want to hear a poem?" he asked buoyantly, with his characteristic wide, generous smile. We huddled gratefully under the shade of a nearby maple, and listened. Ross read from the *Catalog of Unabashed Gratitude*, an excerpt from which follows:

. . . with hundreds and hundreds of other people,
We dreamt an orchard this way,
Furrowing our brows,
And hauling our wheelbarrows,
And less than a year later there was a party
At which trees were sunk into well-fed earth,
One of which, a liberty apple, after being watered in
Was trampled by a baby barefoot
With a bow hanging in her hair
Biting her lip in joyous work
And friends this is the realest place I know,
It makes me squirm like a worm I am so grateful,
You could ride your bike there
Or roller skate or catch the bus
There is a fence and a gate twisted by hand,
There is a fig tree taller than you in Indiana,
It will make you gasp.
It might even make you want to stay alive even, thank you . . .[1]

Something broke open for the listeners. We had just been down in the orchard, installing rodent cages and learning how to create guilds of symbiotic plant assemblages at the base of trees. We were in the orchard, but we were not fully seeing the orchard until Ross elucidated it for us. It was the realest place we knew. It made us want to stay alive. It was worthy of a whole-hearted "thank you." There were gasps and also tears.

Ross was not the first African American literary artist to write about nature—far from it. The African American eco-literary tradition stretches back at least into the late 1700s and serves as a reservoir of insights into the relationship between Black people and environmental belonging. Black eco-literature is not confined to treatises of ecological awe, but rather explores the complex interplay of ecological burden and ecological beauty. Black eco-literature does not set pristine wilderness apart from human beings, but instead defines humans as natural and part of the ecological family. Early African American writers who talked about the environmental burdens borne by Black people include Harriet Jacobs (b. 1813), Frederick Douglass (b. 1818), W. E. B. Du Bois (b. 1868), and Jayne Cortez (b. 1936). Black writers who explored nature as a source of teaching, inspiration, and belonging include Phillis Wheatley (b. 1753), Albery Whitman (b. 1851), and Henry Dumas (b. 1934). Ecowomanist Black writers include Zora Neale Hurston (b. 1891), Toni Morrison (b. 1931), and Octavia Butler (b. 1947). Lucille Clifton (b. 1936) blew open the world of Black eco-poetics, establishing with utter clarity the "bond of live things everywhere" in her work "being property once myself" when she wrote, "being property once myself / i have a feeling for it / that's why i can talk / about environment . . ."[2]

Eco-literature is fundamentally about being a witness. The eco-author is like the "witness tree," an ancient tulip poplar rooted in Dorchester County, Maryland, that watched Harriet Tubman make thirteen freedom missions to bring seventy people out of bondage. The witness names what is, records history in its growth rings, and reminds us to look carefully enough so as to see what is true. The witness people are the rememberers and the awakeners.

Two giants in eco-literature are Alice Walker and Dr. Joshua Bennett. Our conversation explores the role of literature and art in fomenting an ecological ethic, the connection between Black people and nonhuman nature, and the role of the Black eco-literary witness in remembering and awakening.

ALICE WALKER (she/her) is an internationally celebrated writer, poet, and activist whose books include seven novels, four collections of short stories, four children's books, and volumes of essays and poetry. She won the Pulitzer Prize in Fiction in 1983 and two National Book Awards (1974 and 1983), and was one of the inaugural inductees into the California Hall of Fame. Walker's selected works include *The Temple of My Familiar, Possessing the Secret of Joy, We Are the Ones We Have Been Waiting*

For: Inner Light in a Time of Darkness, and *The Color Purple*. Her work has been translated into more than two dozen languages, and her books have sold more than fifteen million copies. Walker has been an activist for all of her adult life and believes that learning to extend the range of our compassion is available to all. She is a staunch defender not only of human rights, but of the rights of all living beings.

JOSHUA BENNETT, PHD (he/him), is the Mellon Assistant Professor of English and Creative Writing at Dartmouth. He is the author of four books of poetry and criticism: *The Sobbing School* (Penguin, 2016), winner of the National Poetry Series and a finalist for an NAACP Image Award; *Being Property Once Myself* (Harvard University Press, 2020); *Owed* (Penguin, 2020); and *The Study of Human Life* (Penguin, 2022). Bennett earned his PhD in English from Princeton University, and an MA in theater and performance studies from the University of Warwick, where he was a Marshall Scholar.

LEAH: Joshua, until hearing your story, I had assumed that every adult who takes a stand for the earth had a delightful early childhood experience in nature that made them fall in love with the environment. You had a very different entry point into your feelings of care and connection with the earth. Can you talk about the role of literature as a portal when direct experiences with nature are lacking at best and terrifying at worst?

DR. JOSHUA BENNETT: My earliest experience of nature was getting chased home from school by the neighborhood dog. I grew up in an area of Yonkers where dogfighting was prominent. People would feed their dogs gunpowder—it was terrible. That fear of dogs that I felt in my youth was part of an intergenerational inheritance. My father integrated his high school in Birmingham, Alabama, and had canine squads marshaled by Bull Connor sicced on him as a little boy, as he was part of the general insurgencies we have come to call the Civil Rights Movement.

As a child, I was rarely outside. I knew about lynching as a young person, but not about trees. I first encountered the natural world through literature. In the Book of Genesis, I was fascinated by the concept of *nefesh*, the idea that spirit falls on all creatures. Lions and tigers have *nefesh*—it is not something anthropocentric. The idea that there was a measure of spirit and, therefore, a larger moral and ethical relationship between plants, water, animals, and human beings, was always part of my imagination. While quite suppressed in the church settings I found myself in, I learned to listen to the earth while sitting in the quiet of my bedroom, meditating on the text I was given, and that helped me to understand who I was. I had a children's book about Dr. George Washington Carver, who learned how to cultivate peanuts by listening to peanuts. Carver became one of my first heroes. The more I read, the more I gained a sense that I was living in a beautiful, mystically infused Black world that had something to do with plants and animals. I understood that my tradition was in relation to other beings who were said to have no interior life, much like Black people were said to have no interior life.

LEAH: Alice, you wrote, "I explore my awareness, beginning in childhood, of the limitations of the patriarchal Christianity into which I was born, as well as my realization, over time, that my most cherished instinctual, natural self, the pagan self, was in danger of dying from its oppression by an ideology that had been forced on my ancestors, under the threat of punishment or death, and was, for the most part, alien to me."[3] What literature and experiences of your childhood informed this understanding of spirituality and nature?

ALICE WALKER: My spirituality is completely earth-based. I was an early evacuee from the church in my teens. I could not fathom why a people from a place none of us had ever visited or knew anything about should take precedence over the people who I knew in my community, especially my parents, and most especially my mother. It seemed to me that if there was to be a goddess anywhere, it would be my mother. I say that honestly, because she seemed able to create things out of nothing. We had very little and yet we never felt poor. We dreaded our shacks, but she transformed them. If we were hungry, she managed to grow food enough to feed us from her garden, which we could always see from our front porch or the window. She grew everything: corn, carrots, potatoes, beans, squash, okra, different kinds of peas, of course collards, kale, and even cauliflower, though it didn't grow well in the heat. It was impossible not to recognize the magic in that. We helped her as much as we could, but the primal force was my mother's spirit. Her spirit was connected to her faith in the earth, and it enabled her to provide for her needs and for the needs of her children.

I am a real lover of the spirit of Jesus. He was a revolutionary and he pledged allegiance to the earth. At the same time, the Bible has many parts that are destructive to us and that have taught us shame about our very being. Being Black in the Bible is always negative. The tradition of enslavement is preached and practiced in the Bible. By the time the preacher finishes telling you the story of Joseph's enslavement in Egypt, you think slavery is normal. It isn't. There are many places in the Bible meant to make us settle for our position as a subjugated people. I had a difficult time with that. They all seemed to be stories about people I didn't know, who did not live in my community, and who I could not see or communicate with.

On the other hand, we were told wonderful nature stories in our family and community, like those about Brer Rabbit and Mr. Fox. Nature had given us characters with which to make our own stories, and we did so. The stories I grew up with were earth stories given to us by African American, Cherokee, Choctaw, and other people in the community. One such story is "Tar Baby," where Brer Rabbit gets in a fight with the tar baby when he gets no response to his polite greetings. Brer Rabbit argues with the tar baby, and of course the tar baby stays silent because he is not real. Brer Rabbit hits the tar baby and still does not get a response, so he hits him again and again until he is trapped and stuck in the tar. Tar baby is a mirage, and his whole purpose is to capture you. This is an illustration of how we need not keep fighting with the lifeless things that suck up all of our energy and attention. Many humans are literally stuck to ideas and objects, thinking that they are in conversation with a real being that can answer them in some helpful way when it actually cannot. They are addicted to something that is not alive.

I felt interested in the Bible stories. But as I grew more perceptive, I could see the subtle way they further enslaved us in a belief system that took us a greater distance from earthbound wisdom. As I wrote, "It is fatal to love a God who does not love you—a God specifically created to comfort, lead, advise, strengthen, and enlarge the tribal borders of someone else. We have been beggars at the table of a religion that sanctioned our destruction—our own religions denied, forgotten; our own ancestral connection to All Creation, something of which we are ashamed. I maintain that we are empty, lonely, without our pagan-heathen ancestors; that we must lively them up within ourselves, and begin to see them as whole and necessary and correct: their earth-centered, female-reverencing religions, like their architecture, agriculture, and music, suited perfectly to the lives they led. And lead, those who are left, today. All people deserve to worship a God who also worships them. A God that made them, and likes them. That is why Nature, Mother Earth, is such a good choice."[4]

LEAH: The history of ecological thought in the US is widely said to have begun with Ralph Waldo Emerson and Henry David Thoreau, and been advanced by the contributions of Aldo Leopold, John Muir, and Rachel Carson. The conventional history encapsulates the predominant western understanding of nature as an entity separate from humanity and the belief that it was not until the mid-twentieth century that theorists began exploring human life as part of nonhuman nature.[5] Black people are mentioned nowhere as environmental thinkers or stewards. From reading your work, Josh, I imagine that you would beg to differ with these mainstream myopic conclusions.

DR. JOSHUA BENNETT: I'm hoping we can finally set down the nonsensical notion that Black writers, artists, and activists have not been historically committed to environmental justice, the flourishing of nonhuman life, and any number of larger philosophical questions pertaining to the natural world.

For one, it is impossible to extricate Black liberatory struggle from its relationship to nature. Consider Nat Turner and the ecological revelation he has when he looks in the sky and sees war in the clouds. From the earth he is given a vision of Black insurrection as the way forward, and it becomes part of how he imagines Black well-being. Consider Harriet Tubman navigating the swamps, the hills, and the woods in the dark. Consider *petit marronage*, which involved people hiding in trunks of trees to see their lovers and build families, and to negotiate labor conditions. I don't know how one could say that the Black radical tradition or the Black aesthetic tradition is in any way separated from nature. It's clear that our ancestors had rich, complex ways of thinking about the earth in all of its bounty, which informed their journeys to liberation and continue to be fundamental to our vision for how we might maintain our freedom today. We stay free by meditating on our relationship to dirt, air, birds, and water, because we are part of them.

All of our Black classical texts are ecological. Frederick Douglass, Harriet Jacobs, Henry Bibb, Phillis Wheatley, June Jordan, Lorraine Hansberry, Alice Walker, and Toni Morrison are environmental thinkers. Think about the way Lucille Clifton talks about the greenness of Jesus or her poem on cutting greens, where the cutting board turns black, then the greens turn black, then the whole kitchen turns black. She puts it all on the table—the connection of *live things* everywhere. She is not just making the connection between human and nonhuman life, between Black people and plants, but even to the objects around us. I am captivated by moments like that in Black writing that push against the grain of traditional humanism and demand our attention. It's across the canon, not just a niche concern. *Song of Solomon*, *Native Son*, *Their Eyes Were Watching God*, and *Salvage the Bones* are ecological texts. Black people care deeply about this stuff, and we have always cared about it.

This complex, nuanced, fraught relationship to nonhuman life, and animal life in particular, is part of our intellectual inheritance. We remember the fields, and we remember what it was like to live and die outside. For people who were once legally considered living commodities, how could we not have developed these robust ways of thinking about other forms of life likewise denied interiority, spirit, and imagination?

LEAH: Let's dig a little deeper into this idea of the connection between Black people and nonhuman animal life. In your book, *Being Property Once Myself: Blackness and the End of Man*, you write,

> It is Du Bois's theorization of Black persons as tertium quid, "somewhere between men and cattle, . . . a clownish, simple creature, at times even lovable within its limitations, not straitly foreordained to walk within the veil," that motivates much of my ongoing interests in thinking of Black lives as those that are often positioned as outside the human-animal divide altogether and placed elsewhere in a zone of nonbeing where the kinds of extravagant violence so often deployed against, and solely reserved for, animals is made allowable, deemed necessary in order for white society to function at peak performance. The nature of this dual bind—that is, the historical experience of being configured as a not-quite human form of life, indeed, as a human nonperson—as well as the body of literature that emerges from within that confinement, is this study's primary concern.[6]

How does your book attempt to illuminate Blackness in the animal kingdom?

DR. JOSHUA BENNETT: The book is interested in how animals appear in the Black literary imagination, specifically in the work of five Black novelists and poets: Richard Wright, Toni Morrison, Zora Neale Hurston, Jesmyn Ward, and Robert Hayden. Traditionally, in my experience, people have tended to avoid this question of the animal as it pertains to Black people, precisely because of this lived, fraught, actual proximity between Black people and nonhuman animals in chattel slavery. I don't think it's just about racist caricatures. I think there are actual felt memories of living on the plantation, living outdoors alongside animals, being whipped because the oxen got away from you, etc. Part of what I'm fascinated by is the counterintuitive move that Black authors make, where they don't repudiate the animal, but instead embrace it. It's incredible to me that they can take something historically used against our people to readily deride us, to denigrate us, to say, "You are nothing," and that they would nonetheless still cast their lot with the animals. It's powerful, and it testifies to the strength of the Black moral and ethical imagination.

Part of what it means to be Black in America is to have a certain relationship to those forms of life and nonlife that are not human. To be Black has historically meant to be considered as a sociolegal nonperson. Frederick Douglass, in his *Narrative of the Life of an American Slave*, gives us so many powerful examples of this. At one point, the oxen drag Douglass through the forest, and while he is eventually able to bring them back, he—rather than the oxen—is punished because the oxen have been given a higher value than him. In another scene, after the master dies, the sheep, cattle, oxen, and humans are lined up and sold side by side. The relationship to nonhuman life is a fundamental aspect of Black experience that we have to take seriously and that our ancestors certainly took seriously. We cannot think the literature pops ex nihilo into the present outside of the context of that experience that people actually lived through. To be Black is to be reduced from the outside, but nonetheless to have something bountiful and powerful on the inside.

To be part of this tradition is to cast your lot with the animals, to understand that human life is not the only form of life worthy of mourning or ethical engagement. The animals are my kin, my truest kin, since we all belong to the earth. The lie of whiteness is that we can separate ourselves from the earth. In considering animals as co-laborers, friends, and partners in the field, Black people resisted a social order predicated on confinement, and opened to a more radical sociality grounded in the desire for a world without cages or chains. It follows that prison and police abolition has environmentalist roots, viewing human life as part of all life on earth. Black children are six times more likely than white children to be killed by police, and police killing is among the leading causes of death for Black men. There is the irreducible fact of Mike Brown's body in the street and the assertion by community residents that he was left there *like an animal*. Black people are life on earth. To constantly wage asymmetric warfare on the planet in the name of private profit, with minerals mined from the earth to build tanks, guns, bullets, and cages, is antilife. Abolition is necessary to save the earth.

LEAH: Alice, what do you see as the role of the writer specifically, and the artist generally, in inspiring an ecological ethic? You wrote, ". . . I can't stand the abuse of the planet and the rampant lack of compassion for the Earth. If you want a world where people are concerned about life on the planet, then you have to be concerned and work for change. But everyone is responsible for the whole creation and the artist has his or her own part to do."[7] Can you expand on this idea?

ALICE WALKER: It's hard to defend something you don't know. It's very challenging to defend something that you have no resonance or experience with. Many people think of the earth as dirt. It is dirt, but it's golden dirt, and it contains everything.

Artists and poets are essential because they connect us to what we cannot see. They open our eyes to what we are blind to, and help us feel the Mother speaking. Poets who love the earth and express it in a way that you can feel it make you more likely to experience that connection yourself. Many people would not notice the earth except through a poem or a painting.

I have lived a long time and read a lot of poets who transmit this resonance. The ancient Japanese poets Matsuo Bashō and Kobayashi Issa wrote haikus that were all about being present in nature. When you read them, you have a sense of the poet understanding the absolute essential gift that is each thing in nature, whether rock or cloud. *Leaves of Grass*, by Walt Whitman, means so much to so many generations. There is a book contained in each phrase of the poems. The grass becomes the poem, becomes the book, becomes the gift to you in understanding the connection to all things. Nature evokes our humanity and our creativity. When the city is one's whole world, it's as if one of the senses is lost, and people can no longer relate to or glorify nature. Cities kill more poets and painters than we'll ever know about.

LEAH: Alice, many of the characters in your novels have an intimate relationship with nature and, as you say, inspire us to resonate with what we may have been previously unable to touch. One of these characters is Shug Avery in *The Color Purple*, who says of the trees, "My first step from the old white man was trees. Then air. Then birds. Then other people. But one day when I was sitting quiet and feeling like a motherless child, which I was, it come to me: that feeling of being part of everything, not separate at all. I knew that if I cut a tree, my arm would bleed. And I laughed and I cried and I run all round the house. I knew just what it was."[8]

Meridian Hill in your 1976 novel *Meridian* is another such character. She comes to understand the interconnectedness and sacredness of all things in relation to the Indigenous Sacred Serpent Mound and the ancient Sojourner magnolia tree at her school. You wrote, "This tree filled her with the same sense of minuteness and hugeness, of past and present, of sorrow and ecstasy that she had known at the Sacred Serpent. It gave her a profound sense of peace (which was only possible when she could feel invisible) to know slaves had found shelter in its branches. When her spirits were low, as they were often enough that first year, she would sit underneath the Sojourner and draw comfort from her age, her endurance, the stories the years told of her, and her enormous size. When she sat beneath the Sojourner, she knew she was not alone."[9]

Can you talk about how these Black women characters understood their connection to the earth?

ALICE WALKER: In the case of Shug, she was able to see through the phoniness of the church that her father preached in. Her father was an unforgiving man and could not honor the flower that she herself was as a young woman, so she gave her allegiance to nature itself instead. She understood that her own father, even though he wore purple as a religious decoration in his stole, was incapable of affirming the divinity in nature. Shug was a powerful and fine teacher, and this is what caused Celie to fall in love with her. From Shug, Celie learned something that the preachers in church could never see: that nature is remarkable and that one element can teach you the whole of creation, but you have to learn how to see it.

In *Meridian*, the Sacred Serpent is an Indigenous burial mound. I have sat with one in Ohio, and there you feel and understand that humans on this planet, in this part of the world, have created burial mounds in such a way that they imitated actual life on earth rather than heaven. Ceremonial structures can be built like a giant eagle, as is the one in my hometown, or like a sacred serpent that grounds you in your place in the cosmos, not trying to get in a spaceship and fly off to some other world. At the Sacred Serpent, Meridian "saw the faces of her family, the branches of trees, the wings of birds, the corners of houses, blades of grass, and petals of flowers rush toward a central point high above her, and she was drawn with them, as whirling, as bright, as free as they."

The Sojourner was a sacred tree, the largest magnolia in the country, and one that had witnessed the atrocities of plantation life before a college was constructed around her. Meridian understood Sojourner to be sustaining, as she had lived through a couple of centuries at least, and could bring peace and endurance to those who sat beneath. The Tree said, "Life didn't start yesterday, you can lean on me, and we won't quit."[10] That is why it's tragic that the Saxon College students destroyed Sojourner. In their pain and confusion, they removed the tree. This is something we often do with our own pain. It was a Black man who assassinated Malcolm X, and we later learned that this fact was covered up by other Black people in the community. It reminds us that we as a people are often cutting down the wrong tree. I understand the frustration, but if we were far more connected to nature, we would stop doing that.

LEAH: As artists who witness and remember, I would love to hear from you both what you think the earth is trying to tell humanity at this moment.

DR. JOSHUA BENNETT: My first impulse is a vernacular one. She says, "Y'all trippin'." The earth would also say the impulse is there to live in harmony with all life, because there clearly are communities all across the planet that live in more robust communion with the planet. We have to honor those realities as actual. I worry that when we talk discursively about ecological catastrophe, we make it seem more universally dispersed than it is. Carbon footprint, as an example, is not a generalized problem—we know in fact which nations, industries, and extractive practices are most to blame for the destruction of the planet. What that also means is that there are people who remember how to tend to the earth, and they are everywhere, though they are not the ones who wield state power. So I think the earth would say, "Rise all people of conscience!" To be frank, this change will require revolutionary action. When we separate Black political struggle from environmental thinking we do real damage to ourselves. Prison, police terror, and incarceration are also ecological problems. The minerals mined to make those weapons also destroy the earth. We have not been able to have those conversations because people are divided into these hierarchical factions that fundamentally miss the point.

Black earth wisdom is rooted in love. It's present in all of our forms of literature, orature, songs, folks tales, and vernacular stylings. Black people know we belong to the earth. It has something to do with our relationship to premature death, but also our relationship to life, persistence, and a serious commitment to human survival. There is an ancient wisdom shared by Black people and the earth. And I will cite the great genius, singular living thinker, Sylvia Wynter, who says, "Black people are a *witness people*."[11] We are called to witness that the earth is alive, the earth remembers, and we have a responsibility to steward the earth.

LEAH: Alice, you wrote, "Our thoughts must be on how to restore to the Earth its dignity as a living being; how to stop raping and plundering it as a matter of course. We must begin to develop the consciousness that everything has equal rights because existence itself is equal. In other words, we are all here: trees, people, snakes, alike. We must realize that even tiny insects in the South American jungle know how to make plastic, for instance, they have simply chosen not to cover the Earth with it."[12] Can you share what you are hearing from the earth?

ALICE WALKER: The earth is flooding people out, snowing them in, tumbling their mountains, and breaking up their glaciers. She is storming and making it clear that she is pretty sick of us as humanity. I don't blame her, as I think that humans have been disrespectful in so many ways. Not all of us of course. The ones who somehow gain control of all of us, they have been so disrespectful that the earth is answering in rage. I wrote a poem about an insight I had, a visitation, where a new political party was formed called the Mother Defend Yourself Party. Self-defense is her work, and our job is to start a new tradition honoring her right to that destructive rage. When a huge flood wipes out vast areas, we are to go with our offerings and make peace, sharing that we understand why she felt the need to riot.

The only thing that gives me hope now is people awakening and understanding how we have been misled and lied to, how we have been abused. We have been led to disregard nature, to poison and abuse nature, to hoard and to sell nature. The most challenging thing I have had to witness in my lifetime is the callousness of how people treat this beautiful Mother. Even though I am not Monsanto, nor the person who put the poison in the drinking water, I am human. The earth feels as though everyone is now complicit, which is a great sorrow. She does not differentiate; she is universally fed up with all of us.

My mother was a very poor woman living in Georgia with all of her children on a hard-scrabble corner of a farm. Did she ever stop making things beautiful? No. That is where we are now, if we can open to this consciousness. Even though Earth is fed up with humanity—and who can blame her—we are still part of this world. We can create beauty in her honor. We can create beauty while she rages. Her wind is magical even as it blows us away. The storm brings fear, but it is also beautiful. We are no different than the vegetation, composting ourselves endlessly. In our short time here, we must make beauty in honor of this magical planet and universe.

Closing

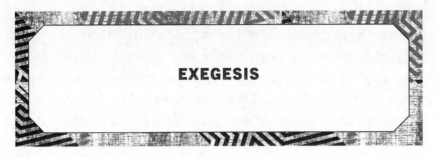

EXEGESIS

A Conversation between the Author and the Earth

There is a dangerous magic to an upstate New York ice storm. Even as power lines strain and sag under the weight of fallen trees and roads become minacious black ice rinks, the earth offers up a singular and dramatic tableau. Each tree—trunk, branch, and twig—is coated with a crystalline encasement that catches the sunlight in a dazzling display. Branches laden with verglas bend and weave into one another as frozen basketry. The forest transforms herself into a maze of bent-over hemlock caves, rainbow prism icicle jewels, and tinkling arboreal wind chimes. It was during a walk in this icy landscape, jaw open in awe, that the land instructed me on how to conclude *Black Earth Wisdom*.

As a daughter of two preachers and a devout student of several world religions—Judaism, Ifa, Vodun, Christianity, and Buddhism—I know what it means to read sacred texts with painstakingly exhaustive reverence. I have spent long hours dedicated to biblical exegesis, sometimes focused on a single line or word in the text, peeling back the layers of meaning to reveal divine intention. As devotees, we study sacred texts not to attempt to dominate God, but to learn how to honor the gift of our existence and to elucidate the spiritual instructions for living well. On this lucent day, the land invited me to apply this same detailed, careful, and deferential study to the earth herself. The message was that the earth is a sacred text to be explored with a comparable attentiveness to the ways we humans study our Quran, Tripitaka, Bible, Vedas, Torah, or *Odu Ifa*. After all, these sacred texts are just human approximations of the original, primary source—nature's earth and her universe.

I was invited to undertake an exegesis of the earth. I wondered then, what would be the first chapter, or more precisely, the first verse of my exegetical exploration. As if to answer my pondering, a rotting log promptly tripped me and I tumbled into the snow. "So, it's you," I acknowledged, smiling silently. I dusted off and rose to my knees, leaning in to read the decomposing trunk.

In Islam, Christianity, and Judaism, there are four levels of exegetical analysis. Caliph Ja'far al-Sadiq taught that the Quran has four levels of interpretation, writing, "The Book of God has four things: literal expression (*'ibāra*), allusion (*ishāra*), subtleties (*laṭā'if*), and deepest realities (*ḥaqā'iq*). The literal expression is for the common folk (*'awāmm*), the allusion is for the elite (*khawāṣṣ*), the subtleties are for the friends of God (*awliyā'*), and the deepest realities are for the prophets (*anbiyā'*)."[1] In Christianity, the four senses that inform exegesis are literal, allegorical, tropological, and anagogical.[2] In Judaism, the process of exegesis is known as PaRDeS, an acronym for the four deepening levels of interpretation: Peshat, Remez, Derash, and Sod. The PaRDeS system is often regarded as mystically linked to the word *pardes* (Hebrew פַּרְדֵּס), meaning orchard.[3] As the PaRDeS system is most familiar to me, and also symbolically connects to trees, I decided to travel its four rungs in studying the rotting log before me.

Peshat (רְמֵז): The literal, direct, and surface meaning

Brushing back the dusting of snow, it becomes apparent that the log is decomposing from the outside in. The heartwood is robust, the sapwood is punky, and the bark has already returned to the forest floor. An ambitious adolescent sweet birch (*Betula lenta*) plunges its stilted roots into the ground on either side of the rotting log. A thick blanket of hair-cap moss (*Polytrichum commune*) clings to the rich humus layer atop of the log, alongside kidney lichens and brown rot fungi. The pattern of decomposition and the tree's service as a nurse log to the birch make it most certainly an eastern white pine (*Pinus strobus*) that died over thirty years ago. The remnants of its root ball point to the west, and a broad depression remains in the ground where the roots once held firm. A thunderstorm microburst likely sent those winds from the west decades ago, toppling this shallow-rooted pine and setting the wheel of decomposition in motion.[4] I lean my face closer to the ancestor pine, and despite the frosty conditions, I can still smell the richness of the organic matter made of her surrendered growth rings.

Remez (רֶמֶז): The allegorical, hidden, or symbolic meaning

The giving over of her body to the moss and the birch are this pine's final acts of generosity. I ponder the innumerable benignities that preceded the moment of our meeting. Grandmother pine's seeds, bark, and foliage were food for gophers, beavers, snowshoe hares, porcupines, gray squirrels, red squirrels, white-footed mice, eastern chipmunks, eastern cottontails, black-capped chickadees, evening grosbeaks, pine siskins, and dozens of others. She provided emergency nutriment to white-tailed deer who averted starvation, and offered safe haven to black bear cubs hiding from predators. Her branches provided breeding and nesting sites for sharp-shinned hawks, great horned owls, golden-crowned kinglets, hairy woodpeckers, yellow-bellied flycatchers, black-burnian warblers, orchard orioles, and twenty more winged species. Her children provided the sturdy, workable timbers of my hand-built farmhouse and the nutrient-rich needles that I use to make my winter teas.

Teasing apart the decomposing layers, I pull up a generous web of mycelial fibers. These are mycorrhizal fungi, the networkers of the "wood wide web" who shunt carbon, minerals, and messages between the roots of forest trees. Given her age and girth, grandmother pine was likely a mother or hub tree, whose access to the canopy gave her the ability to pass surplus photosynthate to those who were shaded below. In the process of feeding sugar water to her neighbors, this pine also sequestered about fifty pounds of carbon every year and produced enough oxygen to supply my family of four with all of our inhalations.[5] She wasn't resentful about the increasing acidity of the rain, graciously tolerating the ever-lowering soil pH without showing any ill effects. Nor did she violently retaliate when 99 percent of her old growth forests were decimated across the region; she simply continued to grow, share, and generate.

With the white pine tree's capacity for generosity and grace, it is no wonder that the *Dekanawide*, the Peacemaker, chose her as the Great Tree of Peace. The white pine became a symbol of unity of the nations of the Haudenosaunee Confederacy. The tree had four symbolic roots, the Great White Roots of Peace, spreading north, east, south, and west. If any other nation ever wished to join the league, it would have to follow the White Roots of Peace to the source and take shelter beneath the tree. The white pine had broad branches that provided shelter for the chiefs and the Peacemaker to join together in deliberations. The needles clustered in groups of five, symbolized the uniting of the five nations: the Mohawk, Oneida, Onondaga, Cayuga, and Seneca.[6] The Tree of Peace promised an era beyond enmity and conflict, and toward health, justice, righteousness, and peace.

Derash (דְּרַשׁ): The comparative, temporal,
and interpretative meaning

This majestic, peaceful grandmother is just one of 111 species in the genera *Pinus*, one of the 629 living species in the division Pinophyta (conifers), one of the more than 260,000 seed-bearing plants, and one of 320,000 species in the vast kingdom Plantae.[7] She may have descended from the earliest known tree on earth, *Wattieza*, which was identified from 385-million-year-old fossils in Haudenosaunee territory, so-called Upstate New York. The decomposing tree body now before me lies in the very place where *Wattieza* once stood at a modest twenty-six feet, capturing sunlight with its frond-like branches and reproducing by spores.[8]

Tracing her story further back to just over one billion years ago, an endosymbiosis between a single-celled protist and a photosynthesizing cyanobacteria gave rise to the chloroplast. Grandmother pine is the descendant of this union, retaining hundreds of chloroplasts in every needle whose chlorophyll receive gases via the stomata, mix them with sunlight, and make carbohydrates. The conversion of solar energy into chemical energy was invented by cyanobacteria about 2.4 billion years ago, leading to the oxygenation of the earth's atmosphere.[9] Without photosynthesis, there would be no protective ozone layer, as ozone is the molecular combination of three oxygen atoms. All life would be deep in the ocean safe from the harm ultraviolet light inflicts on DNA. Terrestrial life is possible because of chlorophyll.[10]

Reaching more deeply, we see that most of grandmother pine's body is elegantly composed of the six elements essential for life: carbon, hydrogen, nitrogen, oxygen, phosphorus, and sulfur. Approximately fifteen billion years ago, the universe began as an extremely hot and dense region of radiant energy that rapidly expanded in an event known as the Big Bang. As the universe swelled and began to cool, the first atoms of hydrogen and helium were born. The remainder of the heavier elements formed in the nuclear reactions of stars. The first star formed about 400 million years after the Big Bang, and it was the death of these early stars that generated all of the carbon, oxygen, and other elements that comprise living beings.[11] Grandmother tree is made of extant stardust.

Sod (סוֹד): The esoteric and mystical meaning,
as given through revelation

Through grandmother pine's decomposing form I travel to the stars and witness the inception of time and space. I see that all of the universe is contained in this singular rotting log. I see that God is contained within, is the Place that contains, and is the Spirit that permeates this ancestor tree, just as God permeates all beings. My heart breaks open with awe and love. I am kneeling before this log and now my kneeling becomes worship, and I listen to what instruction she will impart.

It is this: For all of her life and death, through all reincarnations back to the dawn of time, she has been an author of intricate beauty, an artist of generosity.

As younger siblings of creation, our sacred duty is to emulate our elders—the trees, the mountains, the hawks, and the stars. Just as they model, we too are here to make beautiful and intricate gifts. When we allow our hearts to open in love, and when we dedicate ourselves to the singular purpose of creating beauty, there is no space left for harm, greed, or violence. When we see the divine presence in each being and allow ourselves to enter into kincentric interdependence, then we finally arrive at healing and liberation for ourselves and all the earth.

MAMA NATURE TOLD ME

By Naima Penniman

Mama Nature told me

I am part of you
You are part of me

When we forgot
she re-membered us

When we were lost
she found us

     Mama Nature told me

     We have more than enough to go around

          She showed me
          a glowing paper birch
          at the edge of the forest
          on a south facing slope

          endowed to grow twice as big
          with all the sunlight it could ever drink

it could tower over
shade out the rest

it disperses its surplus sugars
to boost the other trees instead

    Could we be like that?

    Let go of excess
    practice fair distribution of sustenance
    regardless of what slope we were born on

Mama Nature told me

We are stronger together

    She showed me
    the interspecies marriage
    of algae and fungi

    who fell in love across kingdoms
    birthed a new lifeform
    capable of making home on stone
    adept at staying alive
    in the harshest conditions

    Could we be like that?

    Join forces across difference
    weave our powers
    individual but undividable
    in the midst of unthinkable circumstances
    learn how to flourish together

Mama Nature told me

Blackness is precious

and must be respected
and must be protected from artificial light
and must be tended

She showed me
the indigo night
the miracle of starlight
the deep dark ocean
the rich black soils
brimming with life

Mama Nature told me

Nothing and no one is disposable
It all goes back to the cycle

She showed me
There is no such thing as "away"

not for our waste
heaped high in landfills
or amassing in the Pacific

not for our people
deemed throwaway
warehoused in cages
and open air prisons

There is no escaping

the totality of this single beating Earth
the inseparable web
of our perpetual relations

There is no mistaking

All of us belong

Mama Nature told me

You
are made of
the same matter
as stardust

Remember your connection to everything

She showed me
the animate force of existence pulsing all around us
doing everything in its power to regenerate life

Even in death

She showed me
a hollowed out tree
still standing
long dead

a hatchery for starlings
a porcupine den
a perch for owls
a hideout for bats
a food cache for chipmunks
a nuthatches nest

Could we feel our ancestors' love like that?

Tangible and present all around us
sheltering and nourishing us
supporting our flourishing

Could we be eternal?

Mama Nature told me

Death energizes life
Life necessitates death

She showed me
cypress seeds enclosed in cones
sealed shut with resin

the hardened shell
the trapped potential

the awakening flame
the wild inferno

the melting walls
the bursting open

the smoky wind
the scattered soaring

the fertile ashes
the blaze warmed soil

the open sky
the space to grow

and grow

and grow

Could we be like that?

Rising from devastation

preparing the way
for the next stage of thriving

Mama Nature told me

Transformation is inevitable

Adaptation is essential

Change creates openings

She showed me
how dolphins evolved dorsal fins across generations
to withstand the wild movement of the ocean

how plants befriended fungi
who helped them migrate out of water
who taught them how to grow roots
who showed them how to survive on scorched land

to do what had never been done before
until together they transformed the atmosphere
built soil over stone
and patiently
unmistakably
changed
the entire
world

Could we be like that?

Work together to do the unthinkable
and shift the course of destiny

Mama Nature asked me

What will be your contribution?

How will you partner with renewal
to nurture evolution?

What are you willing to let go of?
How are you willing to grow?

Will you remember
you are intrinsic to something bigger?

What will you give rise to
with the life force you've been given?

Mama Nature asked me

Can you hear me?

and
are
you
listening?

ACKNOWLEDGMENTS

B *lack Earth Wisdom* is a tapestry of voices and would not have been born without the generosity and trust of the interviewees and contributors. I offer my thanks to Awise Agbaye Wande Abimbola, Yeye Luisah Teish, Awo Enroue Onigbonna Sangofemi Halfkenny, Ibrahim Abdul-Matin, Chris Bolden-Newsome, adrienne maree brown, Toi Scott, Audrey Peterman, Rue Mapp, Dr. Lauret Edith Savoy, Teresa Baker, T. Morgan Dixon, James Edward Mills, Angelou Ezeilo, Dr. J. Drew Lanham, Dillon Bernard, Latria Graham, Savi Horne, Dr. Carolyn Finney, Pandora Thomas, Greg Watson, Dr. Leni Sorensen, Dr. Claudia J. Ford, Ira Wallace, Aleya Fraser, Sharon Lavigne, Dr. Dorceta Taylor, Dr. Ayana Elizabeth Johnson, Chris Hill, Colette Pichon Battle, Queen Quet, B. Anderson, Toshi Reagon, Yonnette Fleming, Kendra Pierre-Louis, Steve Curwood, Ross Gay, Naima Penniman, Maurice Small, Alsie Parks, Whitney Jaye, Germaine Jenkins, Ayo Ngozi, Dr. Joshua Bennett, and Alice Walker for sharing your time and brilliance. May this book honor and amplify your wisdom.

The entire manuscript came together in just four winter months of disciplined focus. This feat was made possible by the tireless support of research assistant Clara AgborTabi, content editor and data organizer

Neshima Vitale-Penniman, and copyeditor Elizabeth Henderson. I offer my thanks to the Soul Fire Farm team and family—Jonah, Naima, Neshima, Emet, Brooke, Kai, Ria, Ife, Cheryl, Azuré, Shay, Danielle, Hillary, Briana—for holding down our sacred collective work and encouraging me during the writing process.

I offer humble gratitude to the Mohican Nation for their stewardship over millennia of these lands upon which I live and work. The animals, plants, fungi, waterways, and minerals of this land are the beings who spoke this book into existence. To my spiritual teachers, Awise Abimbola, Awo Agboola, Manye Maku, Awo Onigbonna, Iya Ajisebo Abimbola, Jun San, and Rev. Adele Smith-Penniman, I salute you and say *"Modem-yoo! Aboru Aboye Abosise!"*

I give thanks to all those who believed in the seed of the idea and nourished it with fertile compost. Thank you to sibling B. Anderson for founding the Black Earth Wisdom archive and sharing the name with this book. Thank you to Jennifer Baker and the Amistad team for launching this volume into the world. Thank you to the Kalliopeia Foundation for funding the interview and writing process.

Mother Earth, I offer gratitude for your generous patience with me and all of humanity as we remember how to listen. May the words and songs of our mouths, the meditations of our hearts, and the work of our hands be acceptable to you.

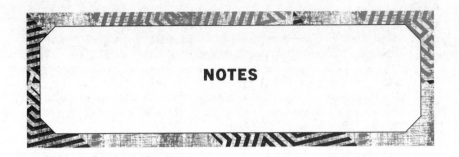

NOTES

Introduction: A Watatic Childhood

1   JoAnn M. Valenti and Tavana Gaugau, "Report: Continuing Science Education for Environmental Journalists and Science Writers (In Situ with the Experts), *Science Communication* 27, no. 2 (2005): 300–10.

2   Nayyirah Waheed, *Salt* (n.p.: CreateSpace, 2013).

3   Thomas Hart Benton, "Manifest Destiny," *Congressional Globe* 29, no. 1 (1846): 917–18.

4   Klaus W. Flach, Thomas O. Barnwell, and Pierre Crosson, "Impacts of Agriculture on Atmospheric Carbon Dioxide," in *Soil Organic Matter in Temperate Agroecosystems: Long-Term Experiments in North America*, eds. E. A. Paul et al. (Boca Raton, FL: CRC Press, 1997).

5   Mary Annaise Heglar, "The Fight for Climate Justice Requires a New Narrative," *Inverse*, August 20, 2019, https://www.inverse.com/culture/58632-mary-annaise -heglar.

6   Wendell Berry, *The Hidden Wound* (San Francisco: North Point Press, 1989).

7   Glenn Clark, *The Man Who Talks with the Flowers: The Intimate Life Story of Dr. George Washington Carver* (1939; repr., Mansfield Center, CT: Martino Fine Books, 2011).

These Roots Run Deep: A Prayer of Homage to Our Earth-Listening Black Elders

1   Penny S. Bernard, "Ecological Implications of Water Spirit Beliefs in Southern Africa: The Need to Protect Knowledge, Nature, and Resource Rights" (2003), https:// www.academia.edu/63070727/Ecological_Implications_of_Water_Spirit_Beliefs _in_Southern_Africa_The_Need_to_Protect_Knowledge_Nature_and_Resource _Rights.

2   Gérard Chouin, "Sacred Groves in History: Pathways to the Social Shaping of Forest Landscapes in Coastal Ghana," IDS Bulletin 33, no. 1 (2002): 39–46, https://core.ac.uk/download/pdf/43539751.pdf.

3   Yaa Ntiamoa-Baidu, "Indigenous Beliefs and Biodiversity Conservation: The Effectiveness of Sacred Groves, Taboos and Totems in Ghana for Habitat and Species Conservation," *Journal for the Study of Religion, Nature and Culture* 2, no. 3 (January 2008): 309–26, https://doi.org/10.1558/jsrnc.v2i3.309.

4   E. C. Alohou et al., "Fragmentation of Forest Ecosystems and Connectivity between Sacred Groves and Forest Reserves in Southeastern Benin, West Africa," *Tropical Conservation Science* 10 (2017): https://doi.org/10.1177/1940082917731730.

5   T. B. Nganso et al., "Review of Biodiversity in Sacred Groves in Ghana and Implications on Conservation," *Current Trends in Ecology*, vol. 3, 2012.

6   John H. Atherton, review of *Origins of African Plant Domestication*, by Jack R. Harlan, Jan M. J. de Wet, and Ann B. L. Stamler, *ASA Review of Books* 5 (1979): 120–23, https://doi.org/10.2307/532430.

7   Pablo B. Eyzaguirre, "The Ecology of Swidden Agriculture and Agrarian History in São Tomé," *Cahiers d'Études Africaines* 26, no. 101/102 (1986): 113–29, https://www.jstor.org/stable/4392026.

8   Stephen Leahy, "National Geographic: Traditional Slash and Burn Agriculture Sustainable Solution to Climate Change," Rights + Resources, March 13, 2012, https://rightsandresources.org/blog/national-geographic-traditional-slash-and-burn-agriculture-sustainable-solution-to-climate-change/.

9   Akinola A. Agboola, "Crop Mixtures in Traditional Systems," in *Agro-Forestry in the African Humid Tropics*, ed. L. H. MacDonald (Tokyo: United Nations Univ. Press, 1982), accessed October 12, 2021, https://archive.unu.edu/unupress/unupbooks/80364e/80364E08.htm.

10   Amanda Stone et al., *Africa's Indigenous Crops* (Worldwatch Institute), https://www.doc-developpement-durable.org/file/Culture/Fertilisation-des-Terres-et-des-Sols/agroforestrie/principes/Africa-s-Indigenous-Crops.pdf.

11   Paul Yeboah, email communication to author's research assistant, August 4, 2017.

12   Emmanuel Kreike, "Architects of Nature: Environmental Infrastructure and the Nature Culture Dichotomy," Wageningen Univ., Wageningen, The Netherlands, September 19, 2006, 226–32.

13   Julianna White, "Terracing Practice Increases Food Security and Mitigates Climate Change in East Africa," Research Program on Climate Change, Agriculture, and Food Security, May 11, 2016, https://ccafs.cgiar.org/news/terracing-practice-increases-food-security-and-mitigates-climate-change-east-africa.

14   Mark Hertsgaard, "The Great Green Wall: African Farmers Beat Back Drought and Climate Change with Trees," *Scientific American*, January 28, 2011, https://www.scientificamerican.com/article/farmers-in-sahel-beat-back-drought-and-climate-change-with-trees/.

15   Muhammad Nuraddeen Danjuma and Salisu Mohammad, "A Catalyst for Restoration in the Dry Lands," *IOSR Journal of Agriculture and Veterinary Science* 8, no. 2 (March 2015): 1–4, https://iosrjournals.org/iosr-javs/papers/vol8-issue2/Version-1/A08210104.pdf.

16   James Fairhead et al., "Indigenous African Soil Enrichment as a Climate-Smart Sustainable Agriculture Alternative," *Frontiers in Ecology and the Environment* 14, no. 2 (March 2016): 71–76, https://doi.org/10.1002/fee.1226.

17   Shweta Yadav and Munir Ahmad, "A Review on Molecular Markers as Tools to Study Earthworm Diversity," *International Journal of Pure and Applied Zoology* 5, no. 1 (January 2017): 62–69, https://www.researchgate.net/profile/Shweta-Yadav-9/publication/331629920_A_REVIEW_ON_MOLECULAR_MARKERS_AS_TOOLS_TO_STUDY_EARTHWORM_DIVERSITY/links/6069f15d45851561

4d35eb6b/A-REVIEW-ON-MOLECULAR-MARKERS-AS-TOOLS-TO-STUDY
-EARTHWORM-DIVERSITY.pdf.

18   Judith A. Carney, "'With Grains in Her Hair': Rice in Colonial Brazil," Univ. of
      California, Los Angeles, *Slavery & Abolition* 25, no. 1 (2004), 1–27, https://doi.org
      /10.1080/0144039042000220900.

19   Kimberly K. Smith, *African American Environmental Thought: Foundations*
      (Lawrence: Univ. Press of Kansas, 2007), 28.

20   Sarah Mitchell, "Bodies of Knowledge: The Influence of Slaves on the Antebellum
      Medical Community," VTechWorks Home, Virginia Tech, July 12, 1998, https://
      vtechworks.lib.vt.edu/handle/10919/36885.

21   Stephanie M. H. Camp, *Closer to Freedom: Enslaved Women and Everyday Resistance
      in the Plantation South* (Chapel Hill: Univ. of North Carolina Press, 2004).

22   Smith, *African American Environmental Thought.*

23   Caleigh Dwyer, "The Construction of the African Slave Identity: Defying Hegemony
      through Syncretic Religious Practices," *Denison Journal of Religion* 16 (2017): 7,
      https://digitalcommons.denison.edu/religion/vol16/iss1/7.

24   Henry William Ravenel, *Recollections of Southern Plantation Life* (1936). Natalie P.
      Adams, "The 'Cymbee' Water Spirits of St. John's Berkeley," *African Diaspora
      Archaeology Newsletter* 10, no. 2 (June 2007): 3, https://scholarworks.umass.edu
      /cgi/viewcontent.cgi?article=1252&context=adan.

25   Neil Tickner, "Archaeologists Find Hidden African Side to Noted 1780s Maryland
      Building," EurekAlert, University of Maryland, February 14, 2011, https://www
      .eurekalert.org/news-releases/793623.

26   Federal Writers' Project: Slave Narrative Project, vol. 1: Alabama, Aarons-Young to
      1937, 1936, https://www.loc.gov/resource/mesn.010/?sp=115&r=-0.851,0,2.701,1
      .415,0.

27   Richard Grant, "Deep in the Swamps, Archaeologists Are Finding How Fugitive
      Slaves Kept Their Freedom," *Smithsonian Magazine*, September 2016, https://www
      .smithsonianmag.com/history/deep-swamps-archaeologists-fugitive-slaves-kept
      -freedom-180960122/.

28   Marcus P. Nevius, *City of Refuge: Slavery and Petit Marronage in the Great Dismal
      Swamp, 1763–1856* (Athens: Univ. of Georgia Press, 2020).

29   "Brister's Hill," The Walden Woods Project, accessed October 12, 2021, https://
      www.walden.org/property/bristers-hill/.

30   Elise Virginia Lemire, *Black Walden: Slavery and Its Aftermath in Concord, Massa-
      chusetts* (Philadelphia: Univ. of Pennsylvania Press, 2009).

31   Sondra A. O'Neale, "Phillis Wheatley," Poetry Foundation, accessed October 12,
      2022, https://www.poetryfoundation.org/poets/phillis-wheatley.

32   Catherine L. Albanese, *Nature Religion in America: From the Algonkian Indians to the
      New Age* (Chicago: Univ. of Chicago Press, 1990).

33   Robert B. Betts and James J. Holmberg, *In Search of York: The Slave Who Went
      to the Pacific with Lewis and Clark*, revised ed. (Boulder: Univ. Press of Colorado,
      2000).

34   "Edmonstone, John: Enslaved Man to (Free as a) Bird-Stuffer," National Records
      of Scotland, accessed October 12, 2021, https://www.nrscotland.gov.uk/research
      /learning/features/john-edmonstone-enslaved-man-to-free-as-a-bird-stuffer.

35 Addie Clay, "'When Nature Resumes Her Loveliness': The Slave Narratives as Ecoliterature" (undergraduate research thesis, Ohio State Univ., 2019), https://kb.osu.edu/bitstream/handle/1811/87467/Addie_Clay_Undergraduate_Thesis.pdf.

36 Allison Keyes, "Harriet Tubman, an Unsung Naturalist, Used Owl Calls as a Signal on the Underground Railroad," *Audubon*, February 25, 2020, https://www.audubon.org/news/harriet-tubman-unsung-naturalist-used-owl-calls-signal-underground-railroad.

37 Dann J. Broyld, personal communication with author, July 11, 2017.

38 Julie Doyle Durway, "Beyond the Railroad," *Appleseeds*, March 2004, 30.

39 Roland Richardson, "From Sea to Shining Sea," *Parks & Recreation*, April 2017, 30–31, https://www.nrpa.org/parks-recreation-magazine/2017/april/from-sea-to-shining-sea-improving-equitable-access-to-public-lands-for-all/.

40 Frank C. Drake, "The Moses of Her People," *New York Herald*, September 2, 1907.

41 "Solomon Brown: First African American Employee at the Smithsonian Institution," Smithsonian Institution, accessed October 12, 2021, https://siarchives.si.edu/history/featured-topics/stories/solomon-brown-first-african-american-employee-smithsonian-institution.

42 Lance Newman, "Free Soil and the Abolitionist Forests of Frederick Douglass's 'The Heroic Slave,'" *American Literature* 81, no. 1 (March 2009): 127–52, https://doi.org/10.1215/00029831-2008-053.

43 Smith, *African American Environmental Thought*.

44 James Finley, "'The Land of Liberty': Henry Bibb's Free Soil Geographies," *ESQ: A Journal of the American Renaissance* 59, no. 2 (2013): 231–61, https://doi.org/10.1353/esq.2013.0021.

45 Lewis Garrard Clarke and Carver Gayton, *Narrative of the Sufferings of Lewis Clarke, during a Captivity of More Than Twenty-Five Years, among the Algerines of Kentucky, One of the So Called Christian States of North America* (Seattle: Univ. of Washington Press, 2012).

46 Martin Robinson Delany, "Official Report of the Niger Valley Exploring Party" (1861; Project Gutenberg, 2007), https://www.gutenberg.org/cache/epub/22118/pg22118.txt.

47 Albery A. Whitman, "Rape of Florida," American Verse Project, accessed October 12, 2021, stanza 14, lines 172–180, https://quod.lib.umich.edu/a/amverse/BAE7427.0001.001/1:5?rgn=div1;view=fulltext.

48 "General Farm Notes: Controlling Insects," *The Negro Farmer*, April 1914, quoted in Dianne D. Glave, *Rooted in the Earth: Reclaiming the African American Environmental Heritage* (Chicago: Lawrence Hill Books, 2010).

49 Booker T. Washington, *Working with the Hands: Being a Sequel to "Up from Slavery," Covering the Author's Experiences in Industrial Training at Tuskegee* (New York: Doubleday, Page, 1904).

50 Mark D. Hersey, *My Work Is That of Conservation: An Environmental Biography of George Washington Carver* (Athens: Univ. of Georgia Press, 2011).

51 Shelton Johnson, "Buffalo Soldiers," National Parks Service, US Department of the Interior, May 10, 2021, https://www.nps.gov/yose/learn/historyculture/buffalo-soldiers.htm.

52   Charles Henry Turner, "The Homing of Ants: An Experimental Study of Ant Behavior," (PhD diss., Univ. of Chicago, 1907).

53   W. E. B. Du Bois, *Darkwater: Voices from within the Veil* (New York: Harcourt, Brace, 1920; Project Gutenberg, 2008), https://www.gutenberg.org/ebooks/15210.

54   W. E. B. Du Bois, *The Souls of Black Folk; Essays and Sketches* (Chicago: A. G. McClurg, 1903; New York: Johnson Reprint Corp., 1968).

55   Smith, *African American Environmental Thought.*

56   Sarah Anne Pfitzer, "Unnatural Disasters: Environmental Trauma and Ecofeminist/Ecowomanist Resistance in Zora Neale Hurston's *Their Eyes Were Watching God* and Jesmyn Ward's *Salvage the Bones*," (honors thesis, Belmont Univ., 2020), https://repository.belmont.edu/honors_theses/9.

57   John Claborn, "Sawmills and Swamps: Ecological Collectives in Zora Neale Hurston's *Mules and Men* and *Their Eyes Were Watching God*," in *Civil Rights and the Environment in African-American Literature, 1895–1941* (London: Bloomsbury Academic, 2017), 111–32, http://dx.doi.org/10.5040/9781350009455.ch-004.

58   Pfitzer, "Unnatural Disasters."

59   Dianne D. Glave, "'A Garden So Brilliant with Colors, So Original in Its Design': Rural African American Women, Gardening, Progressive Reform, and the Foundation of an African American Environmental Perspective," *Environmental History* 8, no. 3 (July 2003): 395–411, https://doi.org/10.2307/3986201.

60   Barbara J. Heath, Eleanor E. Breen, and Lori A. Lee, *Material Worlds: Archaeology, Consumption, and the Road to Modernity* (Oxfordshire, UK: Routledge, 2019).

61   Brenda Lanzendorf, "The Joneses of Porgy Key: Arthur and Lancelot," National Parks Service, US Department of the Interior, June 18, 2020, https://www.nps.gov/bisc/learn/historyculture/the-joneses-of-porgy-key-page-3.htm.

62   Tammy Parece and James Campbell, "A Survey of Urban Community Gardeners in the USA," https://www.researchgate.net/publication/321668363_A_survey_of_urban_community_gardeners_in_the_USA.

63   Fred Ferretti, "Urban Conservation: A One-Woman Effort," *New York Times*, July 8, 1982, https://www.nytimes.com/1982/07/08/garden/urban-conservation-a-one-woman-effort.html.

64   Jason E. Wambsgans and William Lee, "'Ready to Explode': How a Black Teen's Drifting Raft Triggered a Deadly Week of Riots 100 Years Ago in Chicago," *Chicago Tribune*, July 21, 2019, https://www.chicagotribune.com/history/ct-1919-chicago-riots-100th-anniversary-20190719-k4dexppvd5c6bkqbfwhgxfiacy-story.html.

65   Glave, *Rooted in the Earth*, 98–103.

66   Effie Lee Newsome, *Gladiola Garden: Poems of Outdoors and Indoors for Second Grade Readers* (Washington, DC: Associated Publishers, 1940), digital copy available from the Schomburg Center for Research in Black Culture, Jean Blackwell Hutson Research and Reference Division, New York Public Library Digital Collections, https://digitalcollections.nypl.org/items/fe1f0f30-9955-0134-b54d-00505686a51c.

67   Booker T. Whatley and George DeVault, *Booker T. Whatley's Handbook on How to Make $100,000 Farming 25 Acres: With Special Plans for Prospering on 10 to 200 Acres* (Emmaus, PA: Regenerative Agriculture Association, 1987).

68   Monica M. White, *Freedom Farmers: Agricultural Resistance and the Black Freedom Movement* (Chapel Hill: Univ. of North Carolina Press, 2018).

69   "Oldest National Park Ranger Shares 'What Gets Remembered,'" *Tell Me More*, NPR, May 15, 2014, https://www.npr.org/2014/05/15/312707926/oldest-national -park-ranger-shares-what-gets-remembered.

70   Toni Morrison, *Sula* (New York: Alfred A. Knopf, 2019 [1973]), 174.

71   Henry Dumas and Eugene B. Redmond, *Echo Tree: The Collected Short Fiction of Henry Dumas* (Minneapolis: Coffee House Press, 2003).

72   Maniklal Bhanja and Stella Thomas, "Ecocritical Perspectives in Select Novels of Toni Morrison," *PostScriptum: An Interdisciplinary Journal of Literary Studies* 3, no. 2 (July 2018): 162–69, https://doi.org/10.5281/zenodo.1318961.

73   Maud Cuney-Hare and William Stanley Braithwaite, *The Message of the Trees: An Anthology of Leaves and Branches* (Boston: Cornhill, 1918).

74   Ashley McNeil, "Moving Forward Initiative: The African American Experience in the Civilian Conservation Corps," The Corps Network, August 17, 2017, https:// corpsnetwork.org/moving-forward-initiative-the-african-american-experience-in -the-civilian-conservation-corps/.

75   David N. Pellow, *Garbage Wars: The Struggle for Environmental Justice in Chicago* (Cambridge, MA: MIT Press, 2004).

76   "Mavynee 'Beach Lady' Betsch's Biography," The HistoryMakers, accessed October 21, 2021, https://www.thehistorymakers.org/biography/mavynee-beach -lady-betsch-39.

77   Mohsen Ibrahim Abdel, "Grief for What Is Human, Grief for What Is Not: An Ecofeminist Insight into the Poetry of Lucille Clifton," *International Journal of English and Literature* 5, no. 8 (October 2014): 182–93, https://doi.org/10.5897 /IJEL2014.0634.

78   Lucille Clifton, "Blessing the Boats," in *The Collected Poems of Lucille Clifton, 1965–2010*, eds. Kevin Young and Michael S. Glaser (Rochester, NY: BOA Editions, 2012).

79   Kimberly N. Ruffin, "'I Got the Blues' Epistemology: Jayne Cortez's Poetry for Eco-Crisis," *MELUS* 34, no. 2 (2009): 63–80, https://www.jstor.org/stable/20532679.

80   Wangari Maathai, *Unbowed: A Memoir* (New York: Alfred A. Knopf, 2008).

81   Abdul Rasheed Na'allah, *Ogonis Agonies: Ken Saro-Wiwa and the Crisis in Nigeria* (Trenton, South Africa: Africa World Press, 1998).

82   Laura Hurst, "Shell Loses Nigeria Oil License to State Company in Court Ruling," *Bloomberg*, August 20, 2021, https://www.bloomberg.com/news/articles/2021 -08-20/shell-loses-nigeria-oil-license-to-state-company-in-court-ruling.

83   Dinizulu Gene Tinnie, "1945 'Wade-In' Yields Colored Beach," *South Florida Times*, http://www.sfltimes.com/news/local/1945-wade-in-yields-colored-beach.

84   "Why Black Americans Are More Likely to Be Vegan," BBC News, September 11, 2020, https://www.bbc.com/news/world-us-canada-53787329.

85   John Francis, *Planetwalker: How to Change Your World One Step at a Time* (Point Reyes Station, CA: Elephant Mountain Press, 2005).

86   Stephanie LeMenager, Teresa Shewry, and Ken Hiltner, *Environmental Criticism for the Twenty-First Century* (New York: Routledge, 2012).

87   Melissa Vargas, *Confronting Environmental and Social Crises: Octavia E. Butler's Critique of the Spiritual Roots of Environmental Injustice in Her Parable Novels* (Boise, ID: Boise State Univ. Press, 2009).

88   Shirley Sherrod, "The Struggle for the Land: A Story from America's Black Belt,"
        NonProfit Quarterly, https://nonprofitquarterly.org/the-struggle-for-the
        -land-a-story-from-americas-black-belt/.

89   *Freedom: A Documentary History of Emancipation, 1861–1867*, series 3, vol. 1, *Land
        and Labor, 1865*, eds. Steven Hahn et al. (Chapel Hill, NC: Univ. of North Carolina
        Press, 2008), 699–700.

90   Dorceta E. Taylor, *Toxic Communities: Environmental Racism, Industrial Pollution, and
        Residential Mobility* (New York: New York Univ. Press, 2014).

91   Brooks Berndt, "A Case for the Mother of the Environmental Justice Movement:
        Dollie Burwell," *The Pollinator* (blog), United Church of Christ, September 20, 2017,
        https://www.ucc.org/pollinator_a_case_for_the_mother_of_the_environmental
        _justice_movement/.

92   Lauren Stanforth, "Youth Leader Yusuf Burgess, 64," *Times Union* (Albany, NY),
        December 10, 2014, https://www.timesunion.com/local/article/Yusuf-Burgess-dies
        -was-nature-lover-child-5943210.php.

93   *Proceedings, First National People of Color Environmental Leadership Summit*, ed.
        Charles Lee (New York: United Church of Christ Commission for Racial Justice,
        1992), http://rescarta.ucc.org/jsp/RcWebImageViewer.jsp?doc_id=32092eb9
        -294e-4f6e-a880-17b8bbe02d88/OhClUCC0/00000001/00000070.

It Is Time for a New Covenant

1   Wande Abimbola, *Sixteen Great Poems of Ifá* ([Paris]: UNESCO, 1975).

2   Eduardo Brondizio et al., "IPBES, 2019. Summary for Policymakers of the Global
        Assessment Report on Biodiversity and Ecosystem Services of the Intergovernmen-
        tal Science-Policy Platform on Biodiversity and Ecosystem Services," *Population
        and Development Review* 45, no. 3 (2019): 680–81.

3   World Wildlife Fund, *Living Planet Report 2020: Bending the Curve of Biodiversity
        Loss*, eds. R. E. A. Almond, M. Grooten, and T. Petersen (Gland, Switzerland:
        WWF, 2020).

4   "Species Directory," World Wildlife Fund, accessed February 18, 2022, https://
        www.worldwildlife.org/species/directory?direction=desc&sort=extinction
        _status.

5   National Geographic Society, *Exploring Your World: The Adventure of Geography*
        (Washington, DC: National Geographic Society, 1993).

6   Edward O. Wilson, *Half Earth: Our Planet's Fight for Life* (New York: Liveright,
        2016).

7   Luisah Teish, *Jambalaya: The Natural Woman's Book of Personal Charms and Practi-
        cal Rituals* (New York: HarperOne, 2021).

8   The "roads" of an Orisa refer to different facets and manifestations of the energy of
        that Orisa.

9   Wande Abimbola and Ivor L. Miller, *Ifá Will Mend Our Broken World: Thoughts
        on Yoruba Religion and Culture in Africa and the Diaspora* (Roxbury, Nigeria: AIM
        Books, 2003), 19–20.

10   Wande Abimbola, *Ifa Divination Poetry* (New York: NOK Publishers, 1977).

All That Breathes Gives Praise

1   Lynn White, "The Historical Roots of Our Ecological Crisis," *Science* 155 (1967): 1203–7.

2   John M. Clements, Aaron M. McCright, and Chenyang Xiao, "Green Christians? An Empirical Examination of Environmental Concern within the US General Public," *Organization & Environment* 27, no. 1 (2013): 85–102.

3   Aimie L. B. Hope and Christopher R. Jones, "The Impact of Religious Faith on Attitudes to Environmental Issues and Carbon Capture and Storage (CCS) Technologies: A Mixed Methods Study," *Technology in Society* 38 (2014): 48–59.

4   John Michael Talbot, "Here I Am Lord," on *Table of Plenty*, Troubador for the Lord, 1997.

5   Ibrahim Abdul-Matin, "Exclusive: Ground Zero Mosque Goes Green," *The Daily Beast*, July 14, 2017, https://www.thedailybeast.com/exclusive-ground-zero-mosque -goes-green.

6   "National Black Church Initiative Environmental Initiative," National Black Church Initiative, accessed February 18, 2022, https://www.naltblackchurch.com /environment/index.html.

7   James Bruggers, "These Clergy Are Bridging the Gap between Religion and Climate," Inside Climate News, June 27, 2022, https://insideclimatenews.org /news/27062022/religion-climate-change/.

8   *George Washington Carver in His Own Words*, ed. Gary R. Kremer (Columbia: Univ. of Missouri Press, 1987).

9   Muhammad ibn Isa ibn Surah At-Tirmidhi, *Sunan al-Tirmidhi*, Hadith 317.

10   Pope Francis, "Encyclical Letter Laudato Si' of the Holy Father Francis on Care for Our Common Home," *Libreria Editrice Vaticana*, May 24, 2015, https://www.vatican .va/content/francesco/en/encyclicals/documents/papa-francesco_20150524_enciclica -laudato-si.html.

11   Jephté Guillaume, "Ibo Lele," Spiritual Life Music, 2019.

12   Jonah 4:9–11 (King James Version).

13   "Drinking-Water," World Health Organization, accessed June 14, 2019, https:// www.who.int/news-room/fact-sheets/detail/drinking-water.

14   Brian Clark Howard and Alejandra Borunda, "Eight Mighty Rivers Run Dry from Overuse around the World, from Colorado to the Aral Sea," *National Geographic*, accessed May 3, 2021, https://www.nationalgeographic.com/environment /article/rivers-run-dry.

15   Linda Villarosa, "Pollution Is Killing Black Americans. This Community Fought Back," *New York Times*, July 28, 2020.

16   W. E. B. Du Bois, *The Souls of Black Folk* (New York: Signet Classics, 2012).

17   Mathew 25:40 (King James Version).

18   John W. Martens et al., "Is the Ethiopian Eunuch the First Gentile Convert in Acts?," *America Magazine*, September 23, 2015.

19   Psalm 96:12 (King James Version).

20   Seyyed Hossein Nasr, *Man and Nature: The Spiritual Crisis in Modern Man* (Dunstable, England: ABC International Group, 1997).

Queer Earth Biomimicry

1   Sherry Ritter, "Underground Network Distributes Resources—Mycorrhizal Fungi," *AskNature*, November 3, 2020, https://asknature.org/strategy/fungal-network-distributes-resources/.

2   Ferris Jabr, "The Social Life of Forests," *New York Times*, December 3, 2020.

3   Li-Li Li et al., "Cooperating Elephants Mitigate Competition until the Stakes Get Too High," *PLOS Biology* 19, no. 9 (2021): e3001391.

4   C. Cutts and J. Speakman, "Energy Savings in Formation Flight of Pink-Footed Geese," *Journal of Experimental Biology* 189, no. 1 (1994): 251–61.

5   "Why Is Pollination Important?" US Forest Service, accessed February 21, 2022, https://www.fs.fed.us/wildflowers/pollinators/importance.shtml.

6   Zhi Y. Kho and Sunil K. Lal, "The Human Gut Microbiome—A Potential Controller of Wellness and Disease," *Frontiers in Microbiology* 9 (2018): 1835.

7   G. G. Dimijian, "Evolving Together: The Biology of Symbiosis, Part 1," *Baylor University Medical Center Proceedings* 13, no. 3 (2000): 217–26.

8   Bruce Bagemihl, *Biological Exuberance: Animal Homosexuality and Natural Diversity* (New York: St. Martin's Press, 2000).

9   Philip M. Peek, "The Sounds of Silence: Cross-World Communication and the Auditory Arts in African Societies," *American Ethnologist* 21, no. 3 (1994): 474–94.

10   Oyinkan Medubi, "A Cross-Cultural Study of Silence in Nigeria—An Ethnolinguistic Approach," *Journal of Multicultural Discourses* 5, no. 1 (2010): 27–44.

11   Colin M. Turnbull, *The Forest People* (New York: Simon and Schuster, 1962).

12   adrienne maree brown, *Emergent Strategy: Shaping Change, Changing Worlds* (Chico, CA: AK Press, 2017).

13   adrienne maree brown, "Love Is an Emergent Process," adrienne maree brown, April 11, 2011, https://adriennemareebrown.net/tag/emergence/

14   Regina Bailey, "Seven Fascinating Facts about Fungi," ThoughtCo., September 9, 2018, https://www.thoughtco.com/interesting-facts-about-fungi-373407.

15   Amy Maxmen, "Poverty Plus a Poisonous Plant Blamed for Paralysis in Rural Africa," Salt, NPR, February 23, 2017, https://www.npr.org/sections/thesalt/2017/02/23/515819034/poverty-plus-a-poisonous-plant-blamed-for-paralysis-in-rural-africa.

16   Maxmen, "Poverty Plus a Poisonous Plant," Salt.

Reading the Sky

1   "Martin Luther King Denied 1960 Vacation to New Brunswick," CBC News, January 16, 2015, https://www.cbc.ca/news/canada/new-brunswick/martin-luther-king-denied-1960-vacation-to-new-brunswick-1.2901514.

2   Leah Asmelash, "Outdoor Recreation Has Historically Excluded People of Color. That's Beginning to Change," CNN, December 14, 2021, https://www.cnn.com/2021/12/14/us/national-parks-history-racism-wellness-cec/index.html.

3   Mark David Spence, *Dispossessing the Wilderness: Indian Removal and the Making of the National Parks* (Oxford: Oxford Univ. Press, 2000).

4   Gleb Raygorodetsky, "Indigenous Peoples Defend Earth's Biodiversity—But They're in Danger," *National Geographic*, November 16, 2018, https://www.nationalgeographic.com/environment/article/can-indigenous-land-stewardship-protect-biodiversity-.

5   Jedediah Purdy, "Environmentalism's Racist History," *New Yorker*, August 13, 2015.

6   "John James Audubon," Audubon, accessed April 29, 2021, https://www.audubon.org/content/john-james-audubon.

7   Brentin Mock, "The U.S. National Park Service Grapples with Its Racist Origins," *Bloomberg*, August 26, 2016, https://www.bloomberg.com/news/articles/2016-08-26/at-its-centennial-anniversary-the-u-s-national-park-service-tries-to-diversify-its-visitors-and-workforce.

8   David Scott and Kang Jae Jerry Lee, "People of Color and Their Constraints to National Parks Visitation," *George Wright Forum* 35, no. 1 (2018): 73–82.

9   Gianluca Mezzofiore, "A White Woman Called Police on Black People Barbecuing. This Is How the Community Responded," CNN, May 22, 2018, https://www.cnn.com/2018/05/22/us/white-woman-black-people-oakland-bbq-trnd/index.html.

10   Elizabeth Joseph and Eric Levenson, "Black Birdwatcher in Central Park 911 Call Doesn't Want to Be Involved in Prosecution of Amy Cooper, NYT Reports," CNN, July 8, 2020, https://www.cnn.com/2020/07/08/us/christian-cooper-central-park/index.html.

11   Peter Nabokov and Lawrence L. Loendorf, *American Indians and Yellowstone National Park: A Documentary Overview* (Yellowstone National Park, WY: National Park Service, Yellowstone Center for Resources, 2002).

12   Livia Gershon, "Wounded Knee and the Myth of the Vanished Indian," JSTOR Daily, February 17, 2020, https://daily.jstor.org/wounded-knee-and-the-myth-of-the-vanished-indian/.

13   Spence, *Dispossessing the Wilderness*.

14   Catherine Silva, "Racial Restrictive Covenants History: Enforcing Neighborhood Segregation in Seattle," Seattle Civil Rights and Labor History Project, 2009, https://depts.washington.edu/civilr/covenants_report.htm.

15   W. E.B. Du Bois, *Darkwater: Voices from Within the Veil* (New York: Harcourt, Brace, 1920).

16   Jamie Carter, "Ten U.S. Dark-Sky Parks You Need to Visit: To Mark International Dark Sky Week, Here Are Some of the Nation's Finest Stargazing Spots, Where Artificial Light Is All but Absent," *Sky and Telescope*, April 16, 2018, https://skyandtelescope.org/astronomy-blogs/astronomy-holidays-stargazing-tour/10-dark-sky-parks-in-the-u-s-you-need-to-visit/.

17   Fabio Falchi et al., "The New World Atlas of Artificial Night Sky Brightness," *Science Advances* 2, no. 6 (2016).

18   "80% of World Population Lives under Skyglow, New Study Finds," International Dark-Sky Association, June 10, 2016, https://www.darksky.org/80-of-world-population-lives-under-skyglow-new-study-finds/.

19   Ron Chepesiuk, "Missing the Dark: Health Effects of Light Pollution," *Environmental Health Perspectives* 117, no. 1 (2009).

20   Joanna Macy, *World as Lover, World as Self: Courage for Global Justice and Ecological Renewal* (Berkeley, CA: Parallax Press, 2007).

21   Edward O. Wilson, *Biophilia*, rev. ed. (Cambridge, MA: Harvard Univ. Press, 1984).

22   Richard Louv, *Last Child in the Woods: Saving Our Children from Nature-Deficit Disorder* (Chapel Hill, NC: Algonquin Books, 2008).

23   "Awardee 2011 Juan D. Martinez," Explorer Directory, National Geographic, accessed August 1, 2022, https://explorer-directory.nationalgeographic.org/juan-d-martinez.

24   *The Color Purple*, directed by Steven Spielberg (Warner Bros. Pictures, 1985).

So We Walk

1   John Francis, *Planetwalker* (Washington, DC: National Geographic, 2008).

2   Sewell Chan, "Did Harriet Tubman Really Say That?," *New York Times*, August 27, 2008.

3   Kristine Engemann et al., "Residential Green Space in Childhood Is Associated with Lower Risk of Psychiatric Disorders from Adolescence into Adulthood," *PNAS* 003, no. 11 (2019): 5188–93.

4   T. Morgan Dixon and Vanessa Garrison, "The Trauma of Systematic Racism Is Killing Black Women. A First Step toward Change . . ." Filmed May 19, 2017, TED Talk, https://www.ted.com/talks/t_morgan_dixon_and_vanessa_garrison_the_trauma_of_systematic_racism_is_killing_black_women_a_first_step_toward_change?language=en.

5   "What Is a Nor'easter?," SciJinks, NOAA, accessed February 24, 2022, https://scijinks.gov/noreaster/.

6   Akiima Price, "Meaningful Nature Engagement in Stressed Communities," lecture, On Belonging in Outdoor Spaces Lecture Series, March 10, 2021, https://www.onbelongingoutdoors.org/speakers.

7   Rob Garner, "Saharan Dust Feeds Amazon's Plants," NASA, February 22, 2015, https://www.nasa.gov/content/goddard/nasa-satellite-reveals-how-much-saharan-dust-feeds-amazon-s-plants.

Each One Teach One

1   Noel King and Walter Ray Watson, "Nina Simone's 'Lovely, Precious Dream' for Black Children," NPR, January 8, 2019, https://www.npr.org/2019/01/08/683021559/nina-simone-to-be-young-gifted-and-black-american-anthem.

2   "Data USA: Environmental Science," Data USA, 2019, https://datausa.io/profile/cip/environmental-science.

3   Leila Gonzales and Christopher Keane, "Diversity in the Geosciences," American Geosciences Institute, October 19, 2020, https://www.americangeosciences.org/geoscience-currents/diversity-geosciences.

4   Laura A. McClure et al., "Green Collar Workers: An Emerging Workforce in the Environmental Sector," *Journal of Occupational and Environmental Medicine* 59, no. 5 (2017) 445–45.

5   Dorceta E. Taylor, *The State of Diversity in Environmental Organizations* (Ann Arbor, MI: Green 2.0, July 2014).

6   Kristine Engemann at al., "Residential Green Space in Childhood Is Associated with Lower Risk of Psychiatric Disorders from Adolescence into Adulthood," *PNAS* 116, no. 11 (2019): 5188–93.

7   Jenny Rowland-Shea at al., "The Nature Gap," Center for American Progress, July 21, 2021, https://www.americanprogress.org/article/the-nature-gap/.

8   Majora Carter, "Transforming Urban Injustice into Beauty and Empowerment" in *Dream of a Nation: Inspiring Ideas for a Better America*, ed. Tyson Miller (Asheville, NC: SE Innovation, 2011).

9   "Each One, Teach One Virtual Gallery," Green City Force, accessed June 3, 2021, https://greencityforce.org/2021/02/22/each-one-teach-one-virtual-gallery/.

10   J. Drew Lanham, *The Home Place: Memoirs of a Colored Man's Love Affair with Nature* (Minneapolis, MN: Milkweed Editions, 2017).

11   The Audubon Christmas Bird Count is a long-standing wildlife census event; "Audubon Christmas Bird Count," Audubon, accessed June 3, 2021, https://ny.audubon.org/get-outside/audubon-christmas-bird-count.

12   Peter Dykstra, "Mercy, Mercy Me: Marvin Gaye," *Environmental Health News*, January 10, 2021, https://www.ehn.org/marvin-gaye-mercy-me-environment--2649790775.html.

13   Lanham, *The Home Place.*

14   Aldo Leopold, *A Sand County Almanac: And Sketches Here and There* (New York: Oxford Univ. Press, 1949).

15   Ken Kimmell, "What Is Earth Day Live? The Largest Online Mass Mobilization in History," The Equation, April 16, 2020, https://blog.ucsusa.org/ken-kimmell/what-is-earth-day-live-the-largest-online-mass-mobilization-in-history/.

16   "Wangari Maathai: Facts," Nobel Prize, accessed August 1, 2022, https://www.nobelprize.org/prizes/peace/2004/maathai/facts/.

17   Lanham, *The Home Place.*

18   Shirley Caesar, "The World Didn't Give It to Me," SonicHits, 1975.

A Home in This Rock

1   Joseph R. Johnson to Gen. O. O. Howard, August 4, 1865, "Northern Teacher to the Freedmen's Bureau Commissioner," Freedmen and Southern Society Project, History Department, University of Maryland, http://www.freedmen.umd.edu/J%20Johnson.htm.

2   Henry Louis Gates Jr., "The Truth behind '40 Acres and a Mule,'" PBS, September 18, 2013, https://www.pbs.org/wnet/african-americans-many-rivers-to-cross/history/the-truth-behind-40-acres-and-a-mule/.

3   Equal Justice Initiative, "Lynching in America: Confronting the Legacy of Racial Terror," 3rd ed., 2017, https://lynchinginamerica.eji.org/report/.

4   Todd Lewan and Delores Barcaly, "Land Taken from Blacks through Trickery, Violence and Murder," Associated Press, January 27, 2017.

5   Carol Estes, "Second Chance for Black Farmers: After Decades of Discrimination, Black Farmers Are Struggling for Justice," *Yes!*, July 1, 2001, https://www.yesmagazine.org/issue/reclaiming-commons/2001/07/01/second-chance-for-black-farmers.

6   Nathan Rosenberg and Bryce Stucki, "The Butz Stops Here: Why the Food Movement Needs to Rethink Agricultural History," *Journal of Food Law and Policy* 13, no. 1 (2017): 12–25.

7   Allison Alkon, "Paradise or Pavement: The Social Constructions of the Environment in Two Urban Farmers' Markets and Their Implications for Environmental Justice and Sustainability," *Local Environment* 13, no. 3 (2008): 271–89.

8   Pete Daniel, "African American Farmers and Civil Rights," *Journal of Southern History* 73, no. 1 (2007): 3–38.

9   National Agriculture Statistics Service, "United States Farms with American Indian or Alaska Native Producers," 2017 Census of Agriculture: Race/Ethnicity/Gender Profile, 2017, https://www.nass.usda.gov/Publications/AgCensus/2017/Online_Resources/Race,_Ethnicity_and_Gender_Profiles/cpd99000.pdf.

10   Thomas Mitchell, "Restoring Hope for Heirs Property Owners: The Uniform Partition of Heirs Property Act.," *State and Local Law News* 40, no 1 (2016): 6–15.

11   Leah Douglas, "African Americans Have Lost Untold Acres of Land over the Last Century: An Obscure Legal Loophole Is Often to Blame," *The Nation*, June 26, 2017.

12   Margaret Walker, "Lineage," in *This Is My Century: New and Collected Poems* (Athens: Univ. of Georgia Press, 2013).

13   Vann R. Newkirk, "The Great Land Robbery," *The Atlantic*, June 16, 2020.

14   Savi Horne, "When You Hold the Land You Have to Keep It," in *To the Best of Our Knowledge*, podcast, August 22, 2020, https://www.ttbook.org/show/growing-justice.

15   *Far and Away*, directed by Ron Howard (Universal City, CA: Universal Pictures, 1992).

16   Shelton Johnson, *Gloryland: A Novel* (San Francisco: Sierra Club Books, 2009).

17   Carolyn Marie Finney, *Black Faces, White Spaces: Reimagining the Relationship of African Americans to the Great Outdoors* (Chapel Hill: Univ. of North Carolina Press, 2014).

18   George Carlin, *Jammin' in New York* (1992, Orland Park, IL: MPI Home Video, 2006), DVD.

19   Iyanla Vanzant, *Acts of Faith: Daily Meditations for People of Color* (New York: Atria Books, 1993).

Rooted in the Earth

1   Chris Bolden-Newsome, personal communication with the author, February 18, 2016.

2   F. H. King, *Farmers of Forty Centuries; Or, Permanent Agriculture in China, Korea, and Japan* (Madison, WI: Mrs. F. H. King, 1911).

3   Judith Ann Carney and Richard Nicholas Rosomoff, *In the Shadow of Slavery: Africa's Botanical Legacy in the Atlantic World* (Berkeley: Univ. of California Press, 2011).

4   Christien H. Ettema, "Indigenous Soil Classifications: What Is Their Structure and Function, and How Do They Compare to Scientific Soil Classifications?" (Athens: Univ. of Georgia, 1994).

5   Shweta Yadav and Muner Mullah, "A Review on Molecular Markers as Tools to Study Earthworm Diversity," *International Journal of Pure and Applied Zoology* 5, no.1 (2017): 62–69.

6   James Fairhead et al., "Indigenous African Soil Enrichment as a Climate-Smart Sustainable Agriculture Alternative," *Frontiers in Ecology and the Environment* 14, no. 2 (2016): 71–76.

7   Akinola Agboola, "Crop Mixtures in Traditional Systems," in *Agro-Forestry in the African Humid Tropics*, ed. L. H. MacDonald (Tokyo: United Nations Univ., 1982).

8   Julianna White, "Terracing Practice Increases Food Security and Mitigates Climate Change in East Africa," Research Program on Climate Change, Agriculture and Food Security, May 11, 2016, https://ccafs.cgiar.org/news/terracing-practice-increases-food-security-and-mitigates-climate-change-east-africa.

9   K. Flach, T. O. Barnwell, and P. Crosson, "Impacts of Agriculture on Atmospheric Carbon Dioxide: Semantic Scholar," in *Soil Organic Matter in Temperate Agroecosystems*, eds. E. A. Paul et al. (Boca Raton, FL: CRC Press, 1997).

10   Gaynor Hall, "Black Farmers Fight Pipeline Plan in Pembroke Township," WGN9, December 16, 2021, https://wgntv.com/news/cover-story/black-farmers-fight-pipeline-plan-in-pembroke-township/.

11   Tony Briscoe and Rashod Taylor, "Conservationists See Rare Nature Sanctuaries. Black Farmers See a Legacy Bought Out from under Them," ProPublica, October 14, 2021, https://www.propublica.org/article/conservationists-see-rare-nature-sanctuaries-black-farmers-see-a-legacy-bought-out-from-under-them.

12   Yrsa Daley-Ward and Kiese Laymon, *Bone* (New York: Penguin Books, 2017).

13   Bob Marley, "Corner Stone," on *Soul Rebels*, Trojan Records, 1970.

14   Alana Semuels, "No, Most Black People Don't Live in Poverty or Inner Cities," *The Atlantic*, October 14, 2016.

15   "Dare to be Naive: Boston Urban Gardeners," 12 Degrees of Freedom, accessed July 18, 2022, http://12degreesoffreedom.org/bostonurbangardeners.html.

16   Germaine Jenkins, email communication with the author, March 2, 2021.

Oldways

1   Cecilia Galbete et al., "Food Consumption, Nutrient Intake, and Dietary Patterns in Ghanaian Migrants in Europe and Their Compatriots in Ghana," *Food & Nutrition Research* 61, no. 1 (2017): 1341809.

2   Stephen J. O'Keefe et al., "Fat, Fibre and Cancer Risk in African Americans and Rural Africans," *Nature Communications* 6, no. 1 (2015).

3   Constance Brown-Riggs, "Ethnic Cuisine—A Bridge to Health Equity," *Today's Dietitian* 21, no. 2 (2019): 24.

4   Lindsey Smith Taillie, "Who's Cooking? Trends in US Home Food Preparation by Gender, Education, and Race/Ethnicity from 2003 to 2016," *Nutrition Journal* 17, no. 1 (2018).

5   Jessie A. Satia, "DIET-Related Disparities: Understanding the Problem and Accelerating Solutions," *Journal of the American Dietetic Association* 109, no. 4 (2009): 610–15.

6   Satia, "DIET-Related Disparities."

7   Molly Glick, "Wild Food for All," Sierra Club, September 29, 2020, https://www.sierraclub.org/sierra/wild-food-for-all.

8   Baylen J. Linnekin, "Food Law Gone Wild: The Law of Foraging," *Fordham Urban Law Journal* 45, no. 4 (2018): 995–1050.

9   Robin Wall Kimmerer, "The Serviceberry: An Economy of Abundance," *Emergence*, December 10, 2020, https://emergencemagazine.org/essay/the-serviceberry/.

10   Paula Gardiner et al. "A Systematic Review of the Prevalence of Herb Usage among Racial/Ethnic Minorities in the United States," *Journal of Immigrant and Minority Health* 15, no. 4 (2012): 817–28.

11   C. J. Ford, "Watering the Gardens of the Grandmother of Plants," *TEA: The Ethnobotanical Assembly* 6 (2020).

12   Claudia Jeanne Ford, "Weed Women, All Night Vigils, and the Secret Life of Plants: Negotiated Epistemologies of Ethnogynecological Plant Knowledge in American History" (diss., Antioch Univ., 2015), https://aura.antioch.edu/etds/221/.

13   Claudia Jeanne Ford, "Pain Pollen: The Story of Cotton," Ecofemme, July 29, 2019, https://ecofemme.wordpress.com/2019/07/29/pain-pollen-the-story-of-cotton/.

14   Ayo Ngozi, email communication with the author, March 4, 2021.

15   Enrique Salmon, "Kincentric Ecology: Indigenous Perceptions of the Human-Nature Relationship," *Ecological Applications* 10, no. 5 (2000): 1327.

16   Kim Severson, "Food Scholar, Folk Singer, Blunt Speaker: The Many Lives of Leni Sorensen," *New York Times*, Sept 21, 2021, https://www.nytimes.com/2021/09/21/dining/leni-sorensen-food-scholar-historian.html.

Hope Is a Seed

1   Beverly Bell, "Haitian Farmers Commit to Burning Monsanto Hybrid Seeds," Huffington Post, May 17, 2010, https://www.huffpost.com/entry/haitian-farmers-commit-to_b_578807.

2   Gloria Kostadinova, "Peasant Farmers Unite to Secure Food Sovereignty," *BORGEN*, March 20, 2017.

3   Jared Metzker, "Haitian Farmers Lauded for Food Sovereignty Work," ReliefWeb, OCHA, August 14, 2013, https://reliefweb.int/report/haiti/haitian-farmers-lauded-food-sovereignty-work.

4   Beverly Bell, "Black Farmers' Lives Matter: Defending African-American Land and Agriculture in the Deep South," La Vía Campesina, October 7, 2015, https://viacampesina.org/en/black-farmers-lives-matter-defending-african-american-land-and-agriculture-in-the-deep-south/.

5   "Who Owns Nature?," ETC Group, November 11, 2008, https://www.etcgroup
     .org/content/who-owns-nature.

6   Jasmine Virdi, "Vandana Shiva Fights Patents on Seeds," Synergetic Press, Febru-
     ary 1, 2021, https://synergeticpress.com/blog/sustainability-ecology/vandana
     -shiva-fights-patents-on-seeds/.

7   "Farmers Trapped in Unsustainable Cycle by Biotechnology, Seed Consolidation,"
     National Sustainable Agriculture Coalition, July 9, 2021, https://sustainableagri
     culture.net/blog/farmers-trapped-in-unsustainable-cycle-by-biotechnology-seed
     -consolidation/.

8   Hilary Clarke, "Crop Biodiversity: Use It or Lose It," Food and Agriculture Organi-
     zation of the United Nations, accessed March 2, 2022, https://www.fao.org/news
     /story/pt/item/46803/icode/.

9   Mark Wilson, "Infographic: In 80 Years, We Lost 93% of Variety in Our Food
     Seeds," Fast Company, accessed July 9, 2018, https://www.fastcompany.
     com/1669753/infographic-in-80-years-we-lost-93-of-variety-in-our-food-seeds.

10   Martin Prechtel, *The Unlikely Peace at Cuchumaquic: The Parallel Lives of People as
     Plants: Keeping the Seeds Alive* (Berkeley, CA: North Atlantic Books, 2012).

11   Black Dirt Farm Collective, "What and Why Afroecology?," Climate Justice Alliance
     Food Sovereignty Working Group, accessed August 1, 2022, https://climatejustice
     alliance.org/workgroup/food-sovereignty/?lang=es.

I Can't Breathe

1   Nexus Media, "Four Black Advocates Who Are Diversifying the Climate Move-
     ment," Peril and Promise: The Challenge of Climate Crisis, PBS, February 20,
     2019, https://www.pbs.org/wnet/peril-and-promise/2019/02/four-black
     -advocates-climate-movement/.

2   Art Harris, "Checks Came in the Mail, But the Poison Is Still in the Catfish," *Wash-
     ington Post*, June 4, 1983, https://www.washingtonpost.com/archive/politics
     /1983/06/04/checks-came-in-the-mail-but-the-poison-is-still-in-the-catfish
     /15d23e49-9a3b-477e-8116-5d8ce5328e44/.

3   Mike Hollis, "Environmental Justice Case Study: DDT Contamination," Triana
     Justice Page, Univ. of Michigan, accessed July 18, 2022, http://websites.umich
     .edu/~snre492/triana.html.

4   Harris, "Checks Came in the Mail."

5   Robert D. Bullard, "Environment and Morality Confronting Environmental Rac-
     ism in the United States," United Nations Digital Library, October 2004, https://
     digitallibrary.un.org/record/537777?ln=en.

6   "Environmental Justice History," Office of Legacy Management, US Department
     of Energy, accessed March 2, 2022, https://www.energy.gov/lm/services
     /environmental-justice/environmental-justice-history.

7   "How Did the Environmental Justice Movement Arise?" EPA, accessed March 2,
     2022, https://www.epa.gov/environmentaljustice/environmental-justice-timeline.

8   Peter Beech, "What Is Environmental Racism and How Can We Fight It?," World
     Economic Forum, July 31, 2020, https://www.weforum.org/agenda/2020/07/what
     -is-environmental-racism-pollution-covid-systemic/.

9   "How Did the Environmental Justice Movement Arise?" EPA.

10   EPA, *Climate Change and Social Vulnerability in the United States: A Focus on Six Impacts* (Washington, DC: US Environmental Protection Agency, EPA 430-R -21–003, 2021), www.epa.gov/cira/social-vulnerability-report.

11   Peter John Fos, Peggy Ann Honore, and Russel L. Honore, "Air Pollution and COVID-19: A Comparison of Europe and the United States," *European Journal of Environment and Public Health* 5, no. 2 (2021).

12   "Fast Facts on Environmental Racism," Sustained Kitchen, June 7, 2020, https:// www.sustained.kitchen/latest/2020/6/6/fast-facts-on-environmental-racism.

13   Nexus Media, "Four Black Advocates Who Are Diversifying the Climate Movement."

14   Charles Lee, ed., *The First National People of Color Environmental Leadership Summit* (New York: United Church of Christ Commission for Racial Justice, 1991), 29.

One Blue Planet

1   "Ocean Life: The Marine Age of Discovery," UNESCO, November 15, 2012, https://www.unesco.org/en/articles/ocean-life-marine-age-discovery.

2   WoRMS: World Register of Marine Species, accessed February 25, 2022, https:// www.marinespecies.org.

3   "How Much Oxygen Comes from the Ocean?" National Ocean Service, NOAA, accessed October 5, 2017, https://oceanservice.noaa.gov/facts/ocean-oxygen .html.

4   Fanglin Sun and Richard T. Carson, "Coastal Wetlands Reduce Property Damage during Tropical Cyclones," *PNAS* 117, no. 11 (2020): 5719–25.

5   Troy Kitch, "Coastal Blue Carbon," December 5, 2019, in *Making* Waves, produced by National Ocean Service, podcast, https://oceanservice.noaa.gov/podcast/may14 /mw124-bluecarbon.html.

6   Francesco Bassetti, "Water Scarcity: Glaciers Sound the Alarm," *Foresight*, August 3, 2021.

7   Wande Abimbola, in conversation with the author, August, 8, 2020.

8   OECD, "Ocean Economy and Developing Countries," *The Ocean*, accessed March 3, 2022, https://www.oecd.org/ocean/topics/developing-countries-and -the-ocean-economy/.

9   David Biello, "Oceanic Dead Zones Continue to Spread," *Scientific American*, August 15, 2008.

10   "Raw Incident Data," *IncidentNews*, NOAA, accessed October 9, 2016, https:// incidentnews.noaa.gov/raw/index.

11   Cyril Villemain, "'Turn the Tide on Plastic' Urges UN, as Microplastics in the Seas Now Outnumber Stars in Our Galaxy," *UN News*, United Nations, February 23, 2017, https://news.un.org/en/story/2017/02/552052-turn-tide-plastic-urges-un -microplastics-seas-now-outnumber-stars-our-galaxy.

12   Robert J. Diaz and Rutger Rosenberg, "Spreading Dead Zones and Consequences for Marine Ecosystems," *Science* 321, no. 5891 (2008): 926–29.

13   "Ocean Acidification," NOAA, April 1, 2020, https://www.noaa.gov/education /resource-collections/ocean-coasts/ocean-acidification.

14   Rebecca Lindsey, "Climate Change: Mountain Glaciers," Climate.gov, accessed August 12, 2021, https://www.climate.gov/news-features/understanding-climate /climate-change-mountain-glaciers.

15   Convention on Wetlands, *Global Wetland Outlook: Special Edition 2021* (Gland, Switzerland: Secretariat of the Convention on Wetlands, 2021).

16   David Sobel, *Beyond Ecophobia: Reclaiming the Heart in Nature Education* (Great Barrington, MA: Orion Society, 1996).

17   "A More Potent Greenhouse Gas than Carbon Dioxide, Methane Emissions Will Leap as Earth Warms," *ScienceDaily*, accessed March 3, 2022, https://www .sciencedaily.com/releases/2014/03/140327111724.htm.

18   Tom Yulsman, "The Shifting Polar Paradox: As the Arctic Meltdown Continues, Will the Arctic Oil Rush Go On?" *Discover Magazine*, November 20, 2019.

19   Christophe Kinnard et al., "Reconstructed Changes in Arctic Sea Ice over the Past 1,450 Years," *Nature News*, November 23, 2011.

20   Ayana Elizabeth Johnson, "What I Know about the Ocean," Sierra Club, December 12, 2020, https://www.sierraclub.org/sierra/future-oceans-environmental-justice -climate-change.

21   Ayana Elizabeth Johnson and Alex Blumberg, "An Origin Story of the Blue New Deal," June 17, 2021, in *How to Save a Planet*, podcast., https://gimletmedia.com /shows/howtosaveaplanet/2ohwd7k.

22   Diana DeGette and Chris Hill, "Protecting America's Wilderness, Taking on the Climate Crisis," Sierra Club, August 12, 2021, https://www.sierraclub.org/articles /2021/08/protecting-america-s-wilderness-taking-climate-crisis.

23   "We Need a Blue New Deal for Our Oceans," Warren Democrats, accessed March 3, 2022, https://elizabethwarren.com/plans/blue-new-deal.

24   Ayana Elizabeth Johnson, "Opinion: Our Oceans Brim with Climate Solutions. We Need a Blue New Deal," *Washington Post*, December 10, 2019.

25   Johnson and Blumberg, "An Origin Story of the Blue New Deal," podcast.

26   Ayana Elizabeth Johnson and Katharine Keeble Wilkinson, *All We Can Save: Truth, Courage, and Solutions for the Climate Crisis* (New York: One World, 2021).

27   Matthew Ballew et al., "Which Racial/Ethnic Groups Care Most about Climate Change?" Yale Program on Climate Change Communication, June 30, 2020, https://climatecommunication.yale.edu/publications/race-and-climate-change/.

28   Lilla Watson, speech, United Nations Decade for Women Conference, Nairobi, 1985.

Rising Waters

1   Jacob William Faber, "Superstorm Sandy and the Demographics of Flood Risk in New York City," *Human Ecology* 43, no. 3 (2015): 363–78.

2   "Sea Level Change: Observations from Space," NASA, accessed September 13, 2021, https://sealevel.nasa.gov/.

3   Jeff Berardelli, "How Climate Change Is Making Hurricanes More Dangerous," Yale Climate Connections, April 5, 2021, https://yaleclimateconnections.org/2019/07 /how-climate-change-is-making-hurricanes-more-dangerous/.

4   "Developed Countries Are Responsible for 79 Percent of Historical Carbon Emis-
    sions," Center for Global Development, accessed August 18, 2015, https://www
    .cgdev.org/media/who-caused-climate-change-historically.
5   Tara Law, "These Six Places Will Face Extreme Climate Change Threats," *TIME*,
    September 30, 2019.
6   "Costliest U.S. Tropical Cyclones Tables Updated," National Hurricane Center,
    January 1, 2001, https://www.nhc.noaa.gov/news/UpdatedCostliest.pdf.
7   National Academies of Sciences, Engineering, and Medicine, *Framing the Challenge
    of Urban Flooding in the United States* (Washington, DC: National Academies Press,
    2019).
8   Thomas Frank, "Flooding Disproportionately Harms Black Neighborhoods,"
    Scientific American, June 2, 2020.
9   EPA, *Climate Change and Social Vulnerability in the United States: A Focus on Six
    Impacts* (Washington, DC: US Environmental Protection Agency, EPA 430-R
    -21–003, 2021), www.epa.gov/cira/social-vulnerability-report.
10 Wangari Maathai, *Unbowed* (Harlow, UK: Penguin, 2012).
11 Junko Mochizuki et al., "Revisiting the 'Disaster and Development' Debate—
    Toward a Broader Understanding of Macroeconomic Risk and Resilience," *Climate
    Risk Management* 3 (2014): 39–54.
12 Maurice Small, email communication with the author, February 6, 2021.

The Earth's Song

1   Elizabeth Tolbert, "Music and Meaning: An Evolutionary Story," *Music and Mean-
    ing* 29, no. 1 (2001): 84–94.
2   John Blacking, *How Musical Is Man?* (Seattle, WA: Univ. of Washington Press, 2000).
3   Patricia M. Gray et al., "The Music of Nature and the Nature of Music," *Science*
    291, no. 5501 (2001), 52–54.
4   N. Bannan, "The Consequences for Singing Teaching of an Adaptationist Approach
    to Vocal Development," in *Music in Human Adaptation*, eds. D. J. Schneck and J. K.
    Schneck (Blacksburg: Virginia Polytechnic Institute and State Univ., 1997).
5   Patricia M. Gray et al., "The Biology of Music—Response," *Science* 292, no. 5526
    (2001): 2432–33.
6   Gray et al., "The Music of Nature and the Nature of Music," 52–54.
7   Gray et al., "The Music of Nature," 52–54.
8   Charles Hartshorne, *Born to Sing: An Interpretation and World Survey of Bird Song*
    (Bloomington, IN: Indiana Univ. Press, 1992).
9   Edward Allworthy Armstrong, *A Study of Bird Song* (New York: Dover Publica-
    tions, 1973).
10 Melissa Evans et al., "Wood Thrush (*Hylocichla mustelina*)," version 1.0, in Birds of
    the World, ed. A. F. Poole, Cornell Lab of Ornithology, Ithaca, NY, accessed March
    4, 2020, https://birdsoftheworld.org/bow/species/woothr/cur/introduction.
11 D. E. Kroodsma, E. H. Miller, and H. Oullet, *Acoustic Communication in Birds:
    Production, Perception and Design Features of Sounds* (New York: Academic Press,
    1982).
12 Gray et al., "The Music of Nature," 52–54.

13   K. De Woskin, "Chinese Philosophy and Aesthetics," in *The Garland Encyclopedia of World Music: East Asia*, eds. Robert C. Provine, Yosihiko Tokumaru, and J. Lawrence Witzleben, vol. 7 (New York: Routledge, 2002).

14   F. S. Lawson, "Being Audient: Similarities between Chinese Taoism and Western Acoustic Ecology," *Interdisciplinary Humanities* 26, no. 2 (2009).

15   W. J. McNiell, *Keeping Together in Time: Dance and Drill in Human History* (Cambridge, MA: Harvard Univ. Press, 1995).

16   Eva Yaa Asantewaa, "Toshi Reagon Brings the Power," Infinite Body, March 2, 2010, https://infinitebody.blogspot.com/2010/03/toshi-reagon-brings-power.html.

17   Joelle Jackson, "Odetta (1930–2008)," BlackPast, accessed May 20, 2021, https://www.blackpast.org/african-american-history/odetta-1930-2008/.

18   Jeffrey E. Burkart and Chris Sharp, *The Seeds That Grew and Grew: Matthew 13:1–9; 18–23* (St. Louis, MI: Concordia Pub. House, 1997).

Climate Griots

1   Justine Calma, "They Were Incarcerated Firefighters, Now They Want to Change How California Fights Fires," *The Verge*, August 28, 2020, https://www.theverge.com/21404720/incarcerated-firefighters-california-wildfires-pandemic-covid-19.

2   M. F. Wehner et al., "Droughts, Floods, and Wildfires," in *Climate Science Special Report: Fourth National Climate Assessment*, eds. D. J. Wuebbles et al., vol. 1 (Washington, DC: US Global Change Report Program), accessed March 9, 2022, https://science2017.globalchange.gov/chapter/8/.

3   "2020 Wildfire Activity Statistics," California Department and Fire Protection, 2020, https://www.fire.ca.gov/media/0fdfj2h1/2020_redbook_final.pdf.

4   Natasha Piñon, "How to Make Sure Racial Justice Is Part of Climate Activism," Mashable, October 29, 2021, https://in.mashable.com/social-good/8009/how-to-make-sure-racial-justice-is-part-of-climate-activism.

5   "Evidence: How Do We Know Climate Change Is Real?" Global Climate Change: Vital Signs of the Planet, NASA, accessed August 1, 2022, https://climate.nasa.gov/evidence/.

6   Nadja Popovich and Brad Plumer, "Who Has the Most Historical Responsibility for Climate Change?" *New York Times*, November 12, 2021.

7   Caroline M. Dunning, Emily C. L. Black, and Richard P. Allan, "The Onset and Cessation of Seasonal Rainfall over Africa," *Journal of Geophysical Research: Atmospheres* 121, no. 9 (2016): 405–11.

8   Spencer R. Weart, *The Discovery of Global Warming* (Cambridge, MA: Harvard Univ. Press, 2008).

9   Maxwell T. Boykoff and S. Ravi Rajan, "Signals and Noise: Mass-Media Coverage of Climate Change in the USA and the UK," *EMBO Reports* 8, no. 3 (2007): 207–11.

10   J. H. Cushman, "Industrial Group Plans to Battle Climate Treaty," *New York Times*, April 26, 1998.

11   "McNeil River—State Game Sanctuary and Refuge Area Overview," McNeil River State Game Sanctuary and Refuge, Alaska Department of Fish and Game, accessed March 9, 2022, https://www.adfg.alaska.gov/index.cfm?adfg=mcneilriver.main.

12   Kendra Pierre-Louis, *Green Washed: Why We Can't Buy Our Way to a Green Planet* (Brooklyn, NY: IG Pub., 2012).

13   Kendra Pierre-Louis, "California's Underwater Forests Are Being Eaten by the 'Cockroaches of the Ocean,'" *New York Times*, October 22, 2018.

14   Kendra Pierre-Louis, "This Is What America Looked Like before the EPA Cleaned It Up," *Popular Science*, February 25, 2017, https://www.popsci.com/america-before-epa-photos/.

15   Kendra Pierre-Louis, "'I Can't Breathe': What Air Pollution and Police Violence Have in Common," Sierra Club, July 15, 2020, https://www.sierraclub.org/sierra/i-can-t-breathe-covid-pollution.

16   Free Public Data Set, Global Footprint Network, accessed March 9, 2022, https://www.footprintnetwork.org/licenses/public-data-package-free/.

17   Carol Rasmussen, "Emission Reductions from Pandemic Had Unexpected Effects on Atmosphere," Global Climate Change, NASA, November 9, 2021, https://climate.nasa.gov/news/3129/emission-reductions-from-pandemic-had-unexpected-effects-on-atmosphere/.

18   Nicholas Georgescu-Roegen, "The Entropy Law and the Economic Process in Retrospect," *Eastern Economic Journal* 12, no. 1 (1986): 3–25.

19   Stephen R. Kellert and Edward O. Wilson, eds., *The Biophilia Hypothesis* (Covelo, CA: Island Press, 1995).

A Witness People

1   Ross Gay, *Catalog of Unabashed Gratitude* (Pittsburgh: Univ. of Pittsburgh Press, 2015).

2   Lucille Clifton, "being property once myself," in *How to Carry Water: Selected Poems* (1972; Rochester, NY: BOA editions, 1987).

3   Alice Walker, *Anything We Love Can Be Saved: A Writer's Activism* (London: Phoenix, 2005).

4   Alice Walker, *Living by the Word: Selected Writings, 1973–1987* (San Diego: Harcourt Brace, 1988).

5   Mark Long, "Environmental Writing," American Literature, Oxford Biographies, November 26, 2019, https://www.oxfordbibliographies.com/view/document/obo-9780199827251/obo-9780199827251-0206.xml.

6   Joshua Bennett, *Being Property Once Myself: Blackness and the End of Man* (Cambridge, MA: Harvard Univ. Press, 2020).

7   Alice Walker, *The World Has Changed: Conversations with Alice Walker*, ed. Rudolph P. Byrd (New York: New Press, 2011).

8   Alice Walker, *The Color Purple* (London: Longman, 2003).

9   Alice Walker, *Meridian* (New York: Pocket Books, 1976).

10   Walker, *Meridian*.

11   Sylvia Wynter, Afro-American Culture and Social Order ("Soundings" interview sponsored by the National Humanities Center), interview by Wayne J. Pond, audio, November 22, 1981.

12   Walker, *Living by the Word*.

Exegesis

1   Farhana Mayer, trans., *Spiritual Gems: The Mystical Qur'an Commentary Ascribed by the Sufis to Imam Ja'far al-Sadiq (d. 148/765)* (Louisville: Fons Vitae, 2011), 1.

2   Pauline A. Viviano, "The Senses of Scripture," Catechetical Sunday, United States Conference of Catholic Bishops, Washington, DC, 2008, https://www.usccb.org /bible/national-bible-week/upload/viviano-senses-scripture.pdf.

3   "PaRDeS," Ask the Rabbi, Ohr Somayach, accessed July 18, 2022, https://ohr.edu /ask_db/ask_main.php/163/Q2/.

4   Tom Wessels, *Reading the Forested Landscape* (Woodstock, VT: Countryman Press, 1997).

5   David J. Nowak, Robert Hoehn, and Daniel E. Crane, "Oxygen Production by Urban Trees in the United States," *Arboriculture & Urban Forestry* 33, no. 3 (2007): 220–26.

6   "Symbols," Haudensosaunee Confederacy, accessed July 18, 2022, https://www .haudenosauneeconfederacy.com/symbols/.

7   "Numbers of Threatened Species by Major Groups of Organisms (1996–2010)," International Union for Conservation of Nature, March 11, 2010.

8   B. Meyer-Berthaud and A. L. Decombeix, "Palaeobotany: A Tree without Leaves," *Nature* 446, no. 7138 (2007): 861–62.

9   Poul Erik Jensen and Dario Leister, "Chloroplast Evolution, Structure and Functions," *F1000 Prime Reports* 6, no. 40 (2014).

10   G. C. Dismukes et al., "The Origin of Atmospheric Oxygen on Earth: The Innovation of Oxygenic Photosynthesis," *PNAS* 95, no.5 (2001): 2170–75.

11   Jennifer A. Johnson, Brian D. Fields, and Todd A. Thompson, "The Origin of the Elements: A Century of Progress," *Philosophical Transactions of the Royal Society A* 378, no. 218018 (2020).

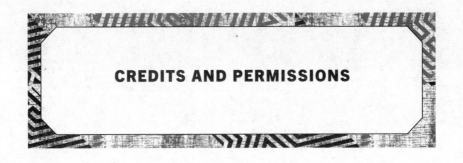

CREDITS AND PERMISSIONS

Cover art by Naima Penniman, original painting entitled *Listening to the Earth*.

ABOUT THE EDITOR

Leah Penniman is a Black Kreyol farmer, mother, soil nerd, author, and food justice activist from Soul Fire Farm in Grafton, New York. She co-founded Soul Fire Farm in 2010 with the mission to end racism in the food system and reclaim our ancestral connection to land. As co-ed and farm director, Leah is part of a team that facilitates powerful food sovereignty programs, including farmer training for Black and Brown people, a subsidized farm food distribution program for communities living under food apartheid, and domestic and international organizing toward equity in the food system. Leah has been farming since 1996, holds an MA in science education and a BA in environmental science and international development from Clark University, and is a member of clergy in both Vodun and Ifa. Leah trained at Many Hands Organic Farm, Farm School MA, and internationally with farmers in Ghana, Haiti, and Mexico. She also served as a high school biology and environmental science teacher for seventeen years. The work of Leah and Soul Fire Farm has been recognized by the Soros Racial Justice Fellowship, Fulbright Program, Pritzker Environmental Genius Award, Grist 50, and James Beard Leadership Award, among others. Her books, *Farming While Black: Soul Fire Farm's Practical Guide to Liberation on the Land* (2018) and *Black Earth Wisdom: Soulful Conversations with Black Environmentalists* (2023), are love songs for the land and her people. Learn more at www.soulfirefarm.org and @soulfirefarm.